Caregivers

The Unsung Heroes
of Our Day

Dr. Tom and Dawn Randall

Table of Contents

Introduction

The term "hero" is a word earned by and reserved for individuals that display courage and determination in settings that put all that they are at risk for others. No one signs up to be a hero. It is sadly earned at the intersection of happenstance and hell. In a moment of time, a hero is born merely by the mixing of "courage" and "determination" to overcome an adversity. His or her actions breathe into the atmosphere as "inspiration."

This can't be better displayed than in the little lady whom I refer to as my wife. Courage and determination mix within her each day, not just to arise and handle her broken, pain-filled body, but to do so in such a way that any who meet her know her Lord is very alive within her. Indeed, she is an inspiration to many.

Yet, another way we sense this quality of inspiration occurs when we witness a blending together of "a strength of human spirit" with a "compassion" for others. Most often, these types come out of the shadows to lend a helping hand and encourage someone to overcome or expand beyond his or her limits. In truth, many inspirational heroes in life occur because of someone "in the shadows," referred to as a caregiver.

Typically unnoticed and unseen, these unheralded messengers of compassion extend themselves with a blend of comfort, encouragement, help and at times well-chosen words of advice that has a way of generating a strength within its recipients. These special individuals I refer to as "Unsung Heroes," for seldom will anyone even notice that they exist, let alone all that they have done in the service of another.

The world understands that pain and suffering are part of our common language. Where the attention in a crisis rightfully focuses on the afflicted person, at the same time there are those uniquely called upon to courageously enter the unknown arenas of service referred to as caregiving. What about these persons whose lives are now totally altered due to the added responsibilities involved in caring for their loved ones? How are they to understand or deal with the anguish that now silently screams from within their souls, when the outcome entails a life-altering disability or terminal diagnosis? How do they calm their own fears, dry their own tears and handle the complexities that flood life as they have known it? Even when they do not yet grasp the full nature of the consequences and challenges facing them, how are they to respond to the questions that imply a seeming ineptness of God's protection for their loved one? What influence and lessons do such occurrences have on the caregivers, their families and the community in which they live? What subtle messages surface when spouses, parents or family members find themselves besieged with the extra load and personal losses that accompany being caregivers? How do these caregivers handle the demands, when the added duties repeat themselves daily and there is no foreseeable end? How do they deal with such adversity, and what can be done for caregivers who, in a matter of time, will feel the full effects brought on by the challenges that continue to morph with the disabled person's condition?

Disabilities and adversities have no boundaries, and their effects extend beyond their immediate victims to those unwantedly conscripted into service. Here stand the unsung heroes of our day. Faced with life-altering losses and crises of their own, these unheralded heroes find themselves summoned into a service that casts them "into the shadows" of another. Courage, determination, strength of human spirit and compassion for others mix to ignite a power and love that fuels the downtrodden caregivers with the necessary strength for their journey.

Neither my wife nor anyone I know willingly entered **"disability World"** thinking it was the greatest place on earth. Neither do I recall hearing of someone waiting in line to get a lifetime membership card to **"caregivers unlimited."** Still, for many of us we awake each day to chronic pain, suffering, disability and the arduous task of **caregiving** for someone who holds a dear part of our hearts. "We become caregivers by choice, by default or by obligation; we assume the role because the alternatives are unacceptable," but for these unsung heroes, as with any hero, it isn't about the medals or heroics they have shown. They do what they do because it just seems like the right thing to do.

Not all displays of courage and determination end well. Their courage erodes, their determination runs out, or their compassion for others becomes consumed by their own plights. Still others find any sense of joy snuffed out by the winds of loss and pain. Certainly, the disheartening stories are more numerable than the tales of inspiration.

Springs of compassion that come with the adrenalin at the first steps of handling a crisis, carries the caregivers in the early stages of crisis. "Let's fix it! We can beat it!" become the mantras. However, as the complexities and demands lengthen into long-term commitments, it becomes apparent that the caregivers themselves need and deserve support, validation and spiritual renewal as they travel along their own caregiver's journey.

Caregivers, the Unsung Heroes of Our Day attempts to do just that by allowing us to see into the homes of those affected by adversity and look through a different set of lenses, namely those who have traversed the path as caregivers. "Give me the caregiver," I have said on a number of occasions, "and I have the major influence upon the direction of that home." The key to helping families adversely affected by evil's ills flows from those who live in the shadows and provide an inside look at being and caring for caregivers. No one book can address every issue that will arise or every scenario that comprises the caregiver's world. Yet for those who care to understand about this world or themselves, entering into the realm of caregiving will reveal priceless treasures when they mingle with seasoned caregivers, especially those whose ultimate hope rests in their relationship to Almighty God.

The dream for this work was born in the crucible of adversity, and the passions were conceived under the guiding hand of Our Lord in compensation for what was patiently endured. *Caregivers, the Unsung Heroes of Our Day*, I pray, entitles the readers to break from their arduous tasks and, for the sake of all, ponder the thoughts that have been formulated in adversity's crucible. It offers a glimpse into the caregiver's world and ultimately addresses the question, "How am I to handle adversity?" Specifically, the work then addresses caregivers and those who care for them, while providing help to the seasoned caregiver and those finding themselves being introduced to this world.

Mahatma Gandhi aptly coined the statement, "a nation's greatness is known by the way it treats its weakest members." It is my desire that the insights expressed in this work can offer a degree of understanding, helpful insights and a friend who helps his readers, the unsung heroes of our day, find strength to fulfill their most meaningful of tasks, namely caring for someone who is weak and who in all probability shares the same home, holidays, traditions and history.

Keeping our country great can be reduced by our media to an economic, political, religious or military issue. However, from God's perspective, a country's moral strength flows from the godly virtues that come to light and makes its greatest impact by the way it extends to those who are weak and in need. Let's begin by acknowledging this as the way of God with all humanity.

Chapter 1
In the Shadows

Everywhere I go among people who know my wife and me, the first questions people will ask me always pertain to the well-being of my wife. "How is Dawn? How is she doing?" Sincerity and concern accompany their questions, and who better to ask, than me. After all, I appear normal and I can talk, smile and answer even the real tough questions pertaining to her latest condition. When our circumstances find us together making new acquaintances, their inquisitiveness to know the story behind her wheelchair often beckons for a retell of her story. Often, it is I who is called upon to act as the narrator to Dawn's story. Yet, if I am not careful, my mind, like those of other caregivers, can be easily misdirected to pondering how my life has been reduced to living "in the shadow" of another. The "How is…" question is rarely asked of me the caregiver. After all, remember I appear normal. I can talk and smile and answer the really tough questions but the truth be known, seldom do people see the hurt that accompanies my every day as I offer the hope of drying one of her tears and place a smile on her face.

Many years have passed since we exchanged those vows that brought us together in 1972 as husband and wife and now after 25 plus years of personally being a caregiver, I have come to realize one very important truth that has only enriched our being best friends, even in the face of adversity. Her story is my story. What she encounters, I encounter. When she goes down, I hurt. When she pulls through and smiles, I smile. Her opportunities to inspire someone find me rejoicing with her. Yet, my story simultaneously is her story.

I can tell her story with clarity and though her story involves more drama, when I tell her story, I find myself unveiling a real part of my own life. My heart's longings as we both know are no less valuable to her and our Lord. Her story, just like mine, is our story that we choose to share with others. What gives us ownership to the story has been that we have had to live it together. We feel every hurt together. Every accomplishment involves us both and as we have learned that, each moment has drawn us closer together as best friends, just as God intended. Yet, of even greater significance, both of us see that collectively our story fits into a greater story that has enabled us to join with many people throughout history. It is the story of Christ at work through all the crises and joys we encountered. He brought us the opportunities of interacting with many people about the truths and principles that have not only restored and refreshed our lives with Our Lord, but also presented the opportunity to restore us to our rightful relationship with God.

There were many times we desired that the disability would not be a focal point in our conversations and that we could just enjoy normal talk. Yet, we learned that our honest acceptance and willingness to speak directly to the issues pertaining to "Our Story," when asked, became a source of encouragement to many.

To set the stage for what this book will address, I begin with how this dream to encourage caregivers and their families was born. It would be 16 years into my caregiving experience and 31 years into my pastor and pastoral counseling role before it would surface. But the uniqueness of how it happened and what it exposed us to have enabled us to overcome many hurdles, any one of which should have shut us down years ago. We know it as part of our story, and we write it, if for no other reason than to tell our children's children how our precious Lord has taken two unlikely sinners committed to Christ, and walked us through a crucible of personal pain and suffering. Yet it was during this long episode in our lives that a passion for families needing comfort and encouragement, like what we had learned along our journey, was ignited.

Years, did you notice that? Years had found us going through personal pain and suffering before our story would even come into existence. Yet the process the Lord used to encourage and comfort us had only been refined in our thoughts by His continuously addressing the foundational question that lingered over us throughout it all and serves as the basis for this book. "How Lord, are we to handle adversity?" which, as you will see, draws us each step of the way into a communion with God Himself that is beyond any earthly value.

A Noble Dream is Born

Seventeen doctoral students sat around the conference tables. One had come from Africa while others had been missionaries around the world. Pastors and professors from Canada and around the United States graced

2

the room, both male and female. For about a week, Dr. Enoch Wan had been guiding the group as, one by one, each student presented his or her anticipated thesis proposal. Because all of the candidates were seasoned professionals in their fields, a certain passion accompanied each person's chosen theme. On this particular day I found myself facing this group for the second time. Only the day before they had shredded my choice of topic, which had honestly left me somewhat frustrated. When I returned home, like a losing pitcher somberly walking into his locker room, I found myself pausing at the front door. As I stepped in, it was only minutes before my wife's interests in my day's activity sounded across the air waves. "How did it go? Did they like it? What did they say?"

There definitely are days when temptation tests my maturity to throw away my "pastor" button, but I knew this was not the day. As she listened to my woes, she finally looked me in the eye and said, "Honey, you'd better go to your study and ask the Lord for help, because you only have until tomorrow morning to pick a new topic; and you still have to write it all up. So, sitting here bemoaning your plight isn't going to help!"

Determined to have a topic by the next morning that would be beneficial to our work with families and the educational world, I made my way to what had by now become my dungeon. My objective had already become solidified. I would pick three topics this time just to make sure one of them passed the test. Topic one and two were finished quickly, because I just wanted to be done with it! Yet, as the topics met the criteria for the work, I found myself pondering.

"Lord, You seldom cause such a block, unless You are seeking to open my eyes and ears to something completely different than what I have already done. What is it?"

In the quiet moments that followed, I found my eyes gazing through the double doors of my office library. I could see through to my wife's favorite little table where so many of our stimulating conversations took place. Studying her at a distance as she sat riveted to her book, I watched as she adjusted in her wheelchair. My lips pressed tight against each other, as I could see her grimace from the pain that accompanied her most of every day.

"What a remarkable lady, Lord," flowed from my lips as I thought about how precious she had been to so many through the years. The attitude that graced her even amidst the years of pain and suffering had been such an encouragement to so many.

In that moment, an idea surfaced, and thoughts raced through my mind. I began to write. In minutes the idea had formulated into a thesis that made my heart pound. Suddenly, I shook my head as I realized that to pursue this thought any further would require her utmost willingness to be involved. It would mean her having to relive the years that the "locusts had eaten." Further, could she bear the pain of what she did not know had gone on just outside her known world? Would she be willing to hear first-hand just what so many who loved her had encountered and learned through their associations with her?

Before going any further in my writing, I left my office to rejoin her in conversation. "Sweetheart, I have a rather different idea and if you don't mind, I would like to hear your thoughts. The topic involves us and you have all the right to nix the topic if you have any doubts or reservations. If so, then the topic and all the history with it would remain history. It is not worth having you go back and relive it all again."

The topic is "Physical Disability in the Pastor's Spouse: The Effects and Challenges Resulting from a Physical Disability to the Pastor's Spouse." I told her that there was much she was unaware of, much we kept from her, because there was no point or value in sharing such painful matters. I wanted her to know that this project carried the potential to resurrect those events and the pain that was buried with it. It had all the potential to reopen unaddressed hurts. Also, I let it be known that the project would as well come to an end if any of our four grown children would feel uncomfortable in their participation.

As she listened, I could tell she was contemplating her choice of words. When I had finished with the criteria and my intent for the topic, she merely looked at me and asked, "Do you think anything valuable and honoring to the Lord would come from this? Could people be helped and Christ honored?"

"Tom," she then concluded, "I would be more than willing to jump into this with you, if through this project there could be the opportunity to come alongside others who may be hurting and give them hope or offer to them, if nothing else, the story of how the Lord has carried me through it all."

I never forgot Dawn's response, as the maturity level of this beautiful lady was definitely on display. The outcome of our discussion led to a late night writing project, followed by a short rest and a journey back to stand before my distinguished colleagues. Anticipation and apprehension mingled in my mind, but this time I decided that I would move from the academic to the life story that set the whole project on its way. Yet, what I did not know or could not have anticipated was what would result from this shift in topic, and how it would change my life.

"I actually have three topics," I began, when I was asked to present my case, "because I am not leaving without one of them meeting the approval of this group. I never would have even thought this, but the rejection notice on my first try forced me to think again, outside my box of comfort." Knowing in my soul how this topic had already stirred my thinking processes as well as my wife's, I wasted no time in presenting it.

"The theme for my thesis is: Physical Disability in the Pastor's Spouse: the Effects and Challenges Resulting from a Physical Disability to the Pastor's Spouse." At this moment, I let the shift begin, as I knew that no single person in the room knew the story of my wife's disability and ordeal with chronic pain, nor that I was her primary caregiver.

"You may wonder why this topic can mean so much," I said to the group, "and what lies behind my thoughts, so let me begin by telling you a story of a dear lady, who happens to be a pastor's wife and whose physical disability, prayers and handling of trauma have been an inspiration to many, including myself. She is only one, but her life has been a great influence and inspiration to many already." Having successfully made the shift to tell her story in the third person, and leave the punch line of our relationship until the final note, I began.

Her Story

A plaque hangs on her wall "There are no wheelchairs in heaven." Another plaque finds the words of Jeremiah the prophet embroidered into it: "For I know the plans I have for you, declares the LORD, plans to prosper you and not to harm you, plans to give you hope and a future" (Jeremiah 29:11).

Her commitment to the teaching of Jesus began at the age of 20 in the spring of 1966 while attending a Billy Graham-sponsored movie entitled,

"The Restless Ones." Yet, her new faith would be challenged just seven months later, on a crisp, sunny November afternoon.

Vera, Dawn's mom, opened the door one more time to ask, "Donald, are you done? We have to go! Remember, we have to get to Diane's for Gy's birthday party and then get Dawn back to Tacoma to the hospital. She has to work tonight." Donald, Dawn's father, had been out early to prepare the equipment for the next day's construction crew in order to have it ready to start the job first thing in the morning. "I'll be right in, honey. I just finished."

After cleaning up, Donald, Dawn and Vera loaded into the '64 Thunderbird. Still a bit chilly, Donald gave the wheel to Vera and poured himself a cup of coffee. Grabbing the newspaper, he laid in the back seat to relax as they journeyed down the back roads from the little town of Randle, Washington, a little logging town nestled in the heart of the Cascade Mountains. Mt. Rainier stood to the north, Mt. St. Helen rose from the southwest and Mt. Adams, which was the family's favorite, filled the horizon to the east of their home tucked away in Big Bottom Valley Country.

Vera buckled herself in, and, then, as any mom would, turned to catch the glimpse of Dawnie, as they called her. "And? And?"

"Oh, Mom! Why do I need a seat belt? These things are a nuisance, and there is no law that says I have to."

"Well, let me put it this way. This car isn't moving until I hear the click and see it on you!" With a little smirk the click filled the air, and the journey down the mountain began. It was about a three hour drive to their daughter, Diane's, so Donald stretched out in the back seat, without having his seatbelt on.

Through the little town of Morton, where Dawn and her twin sister were born 20 years earlier, they made their way along the old highway pointing them toward a stretch of road that had become common turf for Dawn, as she travelled back and forth to the hospital in Tacoma where she was now a resident student. Three months had passed in her x-ray technology training and her hope had been reignited after her depleted funds kept her from returning to the University of Washington for her second year of college. The x-ray training, she knew, would serve her well as she saw its potential for providing the funds needed to further her quest for college and to become a medical technologist.

6

The sun's rays filtered through the tall timber, and the peace and serenity of travel through the majestic Cascades brought a calm that morning. Ahead, an oncoming truck waited with his wheels turned for the threesome to pass before crossing the two-lane mountain highway. Turning in his seat, the truck driver reached behind himself to adjust a back support that had accidently slipped. In that brief second, his foot slipped from the clutch of his truck, launching his already-turned truck across the highway and immediately into the path of Dawn and her parents.

Their car slammed into the truck at 60 miles per hour. Dawn's father, who had been resting in the backseat, was thrown over the front passenger seat. The force of his body drove Dawn's seat forward, breaking her seat-belt, snapping her spine and burying her face into the dashboard that simultaneously was being pushed into her.

An accident, derived from no ill intention, now in only seconds left Dawn fighting for her life. As the paramedics arrived, their assessment found her crushed under the dash board which had blown out her teeth and smashed her face. On top of that, the medics realized her spine was crushed and that any movement would require the use of sand bags, until the doctors could do a thorough examination at the nearest hospital back in the little town of Morton.

Lying in the entangled mess, Dawn knew that her state was serious. Yet, her only thought, she would later recall, was the well-being of her parents and their need for finding peace with God. It was then that she heard a voice, as if someone was speaking directly to her, "They will be okay, and they will know Me," leaving her with a private but stabilizing truth that would in later years be fulfilled.

Arriving Late to Work

Upon arrival at the hospital in Morton, Dr. Hogberg kept her sandbagged, but obtained remarkable x-rays, as the little hospital serving the national forest had a lot of skill from many logging accidents that were first brought there. Assessing the situation, he knew there was nothing more that could be done for her there. He had her immediately transported to the next major hospital, which was 80 miles away in Tacoma.

The day had faded in and out for Dawn, when the ambulance pulled into Tacoma General Hospital close to the time she would normally be reporting for work. She was quickly moved into the x-ray room, so they could acquire additional pictures of her spinal and facial damage. This time, however, she entered not as the technician but as the patient.

The room was abuzz, and, because Dawn had not reported for work, a substitute had been brought in. But the truth be known, Dawn had arrived, unnoticed by all. Her face and body had been so completely distorted from the wreck that the staff did not even recognize her. As preparations were being made, she lay quietly on the x-ray table. Finally, one of the technicians received the data about the patient from the medical transport team that had been sent from the hospital in Morton.

Reading Dawn's name, the technician was shocked to realize that her patient was one of her own. Slowly she walked over to the table and, looking into Dawn's eyes asked, "Dawn, Dawn is that you?" It was at this point that Dawn realized for the first time just how serious her injuries must be, since the staff who knew her as a co-worker didn't even recognize her. At this point the x-ray staff's skills were being put to use to help save one of their own.

Seven Month Stay in the Hospital

Within a few days, Dawn's condition stabilized enough that she could handle her first corrective surgery, a spinal fusion. Post-surgery, she was placed on a Stryker bed, which allowed her body to be flipped every two hours for what would be the next seven months. The flipping was done to facilitate healing and minimize any unnecessary trauma. Yet, still only one question lingered over her life, and faced the medical personnel. "Would she walk?"

It was in these months that an "angel of kindness" found her way to Dawn's bedside: a student nurse, Marj Oines. Their acquaintance as fellow students would grow into a precious friendship, and it provided Dawn with a regular visitor. Marj had a mature faith in Christ, which enabled her to speak words of comfort to Dawn, and to answer many of Dawn's faith questions. Over time Marj's visits helped to ground Dawn in her new faith in Christ, as well to offer stability in her loneliness. Ultimately, they became lifelong friends.

The day finally arrived to test the work and answer the question sought by the doctors and Dawn. Slowly they lifted her distorted frame and for the first time allowed the full force of her weight of 90 pounds to stand upright. Excitement and tears of joy filled the room!! It held!!! She could stand and even walk a few steps!!! How exciting!!! How amazing for them to be first-hand witnesses to the miraculous grace of God, who, through the skilled surgeons' hands and the healing ways of the body, caused her to again stand and walk.

A New Script

Due to her inability to lift and move patients, Dawn's dream of becoming an x-ray technician was demolished, along with the car. Home now became her life, so back she went to the little logging community that sported a population of 500 when the hikers were in. Confined to wearing a heavy back brace for the next year, Dawn's physical challenges, coupled with a sense of purposelessness and helplessness, as well as the frustration and financial exhaustion brought on the family while the lawyers sifted through their battles in court, took their toll. Her father, Donald, whose back was also broken, also wrestled emotionally for the next several years with the anguish and the guilt he felt for not being the one who had been behind the wheel, for discarding his seat belt, and for causing Dawn such anguish.

Dawn's recovery was slow, and it would not be until January of 1968 before she could arrange housing, and once again return to school, back brace and all. A small community college, in Centralia, Washington, some 60 miles from her home, offered the best living arrangements for her adjustments back to the world of education. As her time ended a year and a half later, she was again faced with the choice of a larger university to prepare her in her choice of medical technology. Though she desired to return to the University of Washington with their medical school, those avenues became blocked, leaving for her the opportunity to attend what she referred to as "the farming school" in Pullman, Washington. Surprisingly and begrudgingly on her part, she was accepted into their college of bacteriology and public health.

Her career choice had now led her from her secure family and close friendships that had become her web of encouragement to Washington State University. At four foot, ten inches tall and a history over the last three years that had left telling marks on her, she trusted once again her faith to be her guide as she ventured into a whole new world. Her surroundings were all young people her age seeking an education and the enjoyment that came with college life on a university campus.

Our Story

Let the Wedding Bells Ring

It was during these few college years that life would bring another change. It was there that she met and, after graduating in 1972, wed a young engineer, only to find that God would then call him from his engineering profession to pursue training as a pastor. Graduate school for her husband ensued at Western Seminary in Portland, Oregon, while at the same time Dawn's professional dream came true, when she found work with the bacteriology lab at the Oregon Health and Science University.

After three years her life would take still another remarkable turn, with her announcement of a coming child. Though her spinal column had been severely affected by the accident making her delivery more difficult than normal, in December of 1975 she gave birth to a healthy boy, whom they named Matthew, meaning a gift from God.

Then in 1976 with her first child cradled in her lap, the happy couple embarked on their first church assignment and the rigorous task for her as the pastor's wife began. Three other children followed, and for 19 wonderful years of marriage, of which fifteen were as a pastor's wife, all seemed relatively normal. The counseling and family ministry they led as a couple had grown in their community and extended regionally through their associations.

The Injury Resurfaces

In 1991 the effects of her wreck would plow into their married life, creating new challenges and questions for their family, ministry and church. A trauma cyst had formed inside her spinal cord at the site of her original injury, restricting the spinal fluid flow and causing one of her feet to drag. The ensuing spinal cord surgery left her disabled in one leg with heightened pain, thus requiring heavy narcotics to help control the pain. It would be a year before she could experience some degree of normalcy, only to have another cyst form in 1995. This required an additional surgery and further recovery. Another cyst in 1997 followed the same pattern, which the local neurosurgeons realized was beyond their skills to address.

What followed was the first of many trips down the I-5 corridor from Bellingham to Seattle, Washington. A hundred miles of driving found them waiting in the office of Dr. Sean Grady. As he entered, this gentle, middle-aged man sat and, looking directly at Dawn, began to ask clarifying questions, making it very apparent that he had a thorough understanding of her case. He had studied every part of her situation, pulled out scans that showed much of what was going on inside her spine, and then announced, "I have a plan." The next step though, was to consult with a team of doctors from the university to solidify and expand upon their ideas that might further help provide the best plan for Dawn.

A few weeks later, they laid out a plan. The surgeon explained that it would be an extensive effort conducted by a team of neurosurgeons and orthopedic surgeons from the University of Washington Medical School, to be done at Harborview Hospital in Seattle. The surgery would involve, in essence, re-breaking her back at the original injury site, cutting and removing the injured, deformed vertebrae, straightening out her spinal column and the spinal cord, plus adding titanium rods alongside the spine for strength, all with the hope that no more cysts would form.

To hear all of this and to agree with the plan, though it included the dangerous surgery and potential for further neurological damage, reflected the courage she carried in God and the skilled team of surgeons. It was truthfully more of a step of faith for her and her husband.

Surgery and a Remarkable Answer to Prayer

In June of 1997 her husband took up residence in the waiting room of the neurosurgery department of the hospital. Sixteen hours of surgery followed and by the time the doctor could relay the outcome, night had fallen over the city of Seattle. Unable to see her post surgery due to her condition requiring extended care in recover, he left, only to return first thing in the morning. Entering the room, he found a smiling young lady lying on her bed. One little glimpse and a "good morning" followed with their eyes catching each other's. Tears filled his eyes and joy filled his heart for the remarkable had been done, her spinal cord was freed, and her spinal column once again straightened.

A few days later, a "turtle shell" was cast for her body to hold her back and spine correctly while the healing took place. For the next five months, which happened to include their 25th wedding anniversary, it became part of her undergarments. Each day meant separating the two pieces that comprised her cast and rolling her out of her shell to clean her up and prepare her for the day. Then it was rolling her back in and refastening it all, covering her profound undergarment and getting on with the day.

Her eyes told her story. Amidst the ordeal, they communicated with everyone that she was doing well. The smile on her face and the fact she could walk meant that an end was in sight. Then, in October when the cast came off permanently, many tearfully rejoiced as she stood erect with a straight back for the first time in 30 years. Six years of trauma, medications, disability and physical challenges, seemed a mere story of the past. God had used some highly skilled orthopedic and neurosurgeons for His work of healing, thus bringing smiles to her face, as well as to many who loved her.

On one occasion while in recovery, Dawn grabbed hold of Dr. Grady and expressed what could not have been said better. "Would you do me a favor?" she asked. "When you get home would you tell your wife how thankful I am for her, and would you give her a hug from me. This must be after you give her your own hug. Then tell her, that none of this would have been possible if she had not willingly supported you in obtaining those special skills enabling you to do what you did for me. God has gifted you, and the devotion that you gave to be the best you could be in this field now works itself out as an answer to prayer. We had nowhere to go and no hope left until we were blessed to have met with you and your wonderful team."

Lightning Strikes

After the removal of the body cast, all seemed well, until three weeks later while in route to teach a parenting class, tragedy struck again.

"Do you have everything for the class?" "Yes," she told her husband. Their teenage daughter, Marjie, named after her nurse friend, piped up, "Oh wait! I forgot something for working with the kids." The small delay didn't mean much, as the parenting class which she would handle was only a few miles away at the church.

The early November evening was dark, and the fog had rolled in over the farm land. As they reached the end of farming land and approached a row of houses, the speed slowed to about 30 mph and the air cleared of its white soup. Out of the fog from behind them, her husband remembers seeing a flash and then hearing an explosion.

The next thing they knew, the van was lifted into the air, resting with the rear end on top of a truck hood that had sped out of the fog and was still pushing them down the road. The truck's estimated speed was in the range of 85 mph, and behind the wheel was a drunk, illegal immigrant with no insurance, driving a borrowed pickup truck from another immigrant. The impact had buckled the back of the van, and the force snapped Dawn's seat backward, thrusting her upper body back in her seat with such force that it broke the seat locks. In that moment, her husband found himself steering the front wheel drive of their van down the road as the force of the truck kept them going forward. Finally, the van and truck separated. Over a small embankment went the truck. The van came to a slow roll and ended in front of a house.

Emergency teams were called, and minutes later the night air filled with the sound of sirens. Neighbors brought Dawn, her daughter Marjie, who had been injured, and then her husband in from the cold outdoors. An evening at the hospital followed, and with the light of day, the opportunity to see the destruction to their van brought home the awareness that life was a gift.

Yet, for Dawn it was only the beginning of a new chapter. Shortly thereafter tingling in her back began and what she feared the most became a reality, as this second accident had caused the process of new cysts to form and once again traumatize her weakened spinal cord.

By early February of 1998, they were headed back to Seattle to the surgical team that had been God's answer to prayer. Sadly, all had been lost and they determined that another surgery was needed, though this time the outcome would not be the same. She left the hospital confined to a wheelchair, and even more extensive drug treatment was needed to handle her pain. Financial pressures added to the physical challenges and her mental stress and capabilities deteriorated due to neurological damage to her body, the use of the heavy narcotics and continual use of antibiotics to counter the reoccurring infections.

She was now physically disabled, and mentally and physically affected by the drug treatment for pain. Her life work with her husband was extensively hampered by her condition. Struggling just to stay alive, Dawn and all those who loved her, found themselves facing a new set of difficult questions. "What did she do to deserve this? And if it was nothing, then what kind of God would allow such rejoicing in the healing of her back only to let the months of prayer, hundreds of thousands of dollars and months of rehab be destroyed three weeks later?"

For me, I wondered, what truthfully was the point of more intense pain, more drugs, and further financial pressures? What was the intent of it all, if there was any? How does she, as a servant of the Lord, explain to her children that the Lord loves her and their family, and how do they explain that He will watch over them and protect them when the occurrence of such debilitating acts seems to make a mockery of this truth?

This is your Life

As I finished Dawn's heartbreaking story to a classroom full of doctoral candidates, I paused only to see 17 sets of eyes, many filled with tears, staring directly at me. With that last set of questions I had made my case for asking for such a thesis project; but before anyone could respond, I let the silence have its effect and continued with one last reason and set of questions that were needed to solidify my appeal for such a project. Again addressing the group, my words were now filled with my own emotions.

"What can be learned from the pain, suffering and weakness of this lovely lady, who happens to be my wife, best friend and fellow companion in life and ministry? What can we learn from our household and others whose lives are dedicated to the service of the Lord, but faced with a physical disability? What can be gained to help the households of pastors, their families and churches who face similar complications?"

Dr. Wan realized at that moment that the project was no longer just a fulfillment to the class. "This is not just about a project; this is your life," he said. No one in that room in all the times that we had shared had ever heard the story. Yet, now from their seats, they arose and slowly gathered around me; and placing their hands on me, they began to pray. It was not about a class or an assignment anymore. Now it was about friends who, upon hearing the news first-hand realized that our battle was ongoing. They together asked God for strength for the day and God's blessing upon what lay ahead for us as a couple.

In the shadows there stand men and women alike who have been given and have responded to being a caregiver. Old and young are numbered amongst them but for sure, their story involves learning how to handle an adversity just as their loved one who is part of their story does the same. Unsung heroes, for certain, as they continually demonstrate a strength of human character and blend it with a spirit of compassion.

Chapter 2
We are not Alone

Little did I know!!!

As the prayer time ended, I was a bit shaken. "What just happened?" I wondered to myself. "What is going on?" I don't remember my colleagues praying like that over any of the other doctoral projects. Seminary professors, Bible school teachers, directors within mission organizations, and pastors were now praying for this project that had originated in my office during a late night vigil.

Dr. Wan returned to the front of the class. He turned to me and asked, "What is your wife's reaction to this topic? Is she ready for it? Does she think she could handle such an undertaking?" His question carried such insight, for many who are disabled are sapped from having to go through it all over again, especially when they become the focal point of conversations.

"We've already talked," I responded. I told him of my conversation with Dawn in which I had given her the complete freedom to nix this idea. I never forgot that moment in that classroom. As I would later express to Dr. Wan that moment was a defining moment in our lives. The academic nature of the project had vanished and a passion was born that has fueled the birth of a life ministry to caregivers and the families of the disabled.

With the answer and explanation, a smile crossed the face of Dr. Wan, and he nodded with his approval. At that moment he offered the class a break.

As I was a bit overwhelmed at this time, I moved out into the break area only to find the interest for the topic had drawn many to continue the conversation privately. Little did I know how a topic like this would evoke such sincere interest!

A fellow doctoral student and native from an African country expressed how, "We encounter these types of issues in our country, which present for us real challenges as we are so different than in America."

Still another pastor from the states, waiting for some private time, approached and asked, "Would you consider addressing the issues of mental disability? I would really like to hear your thoughts, as I have a wife who has been diagnosed as being 'bipolar,' and there is no way I can let that out."

He could see the puzzled look in my eyes, so without me asking he continued, "People don't want a pastor whose wife carries the tag of being mentally ill. So we just keep it quiet." As I heard this, I thought, "How true and how sad." At that moment, I recalled my own upbringing. I had grown up in a home where she was.

"Your mom's crazy! Your mom's a witch! Your mom has no friends!" These were all memories stamped into my mind. The truth be known, she didn't have any friends, and the difficulties for my father and family sparked many dilemmas throughout all our upbringing. The handles forced upon us, the misconceptions, even the mishaps that come from such adversity, tend to create fear within people, especially those who are unaware of the intricacies that accompany such disorders. Blending theology with any disability is not easy, so many just choose to avoid the mentally ill or render them as belonging on the dark side of the spirit world, which only reinforces the need for keeping matters quiet.

Before the day was over a few more pastors expressed their concern for friends. In each case they were at a loss as to how to help them. By the time I reached the door of my home that evening, I knew there was something brewing in this project. At the same time, I knew that we are not alone. What I didn't know was how much it would reveal about how little I knew of the disabled world and their families and what it would mean for redirecting the ministry opportunities of our household.

Disability Defined

Pastor Robert Molsberry, a disabled pastor and author of the book, *Blindsided by Grace*, cites the definition of a disability given in the Americans with Disabilities Act of 1990 (ADA), which was revised in 2008 as follows:

Disability: a physical or mental impairment that substantially limits one or more of the major life activities of such individuals. This definition would seem to imply that a disability refers to something concrete and physical, some condition, medical or biological in origin that limits a person in an abnormal way.[1]

Molsberry further cites the work of Ingstad and Whyte who conclude, "The core meaning for most of us is a biophysical one. Blindness, lameness, mental deficiency and chronic incapacitating illnesses – these are prototypical disabilities."[2]

Katie Banister in her book, *The Personal Care Attendant Guide*, recognizes the definition but further notes that though the ADA recognizes two types of disabilities: physical and mental, she sees the breakdown as "physical, sensory, cognitive, and emotional disabilities."[3] She then offers an explanation for each type of disability:

- Physical Disabilities: affect a person's ability to move. They include: spinal cord injuries, cerebral palsy, spina bifida, muscular dystrophy and bodily injuries.
- Sensory impairments: affect a person's visual and auditory senses.
- Cognitive disabilities: affect a person's ability to mentally process information. These disabilities include: developmental and learning disabilities as well as mild or severe mental retardation.
- Emotional disabilities: affect a person's ability to interact with others and society such as depression, anxiety, bipolar (manic depressive) disorder.[4]

In the opening chapter of *Relationships in Chronic Illness and Disability*, the authors refer to chronic illness and disabilities as "conditions that result in moderate to severe restrictions in physical functioning and the performance of social roles related to work, leisure, family and friendships."[5]

So, though the term for disability may be bantered as being either an impairment or condition and though there may be two or four different categories of disability, the definition as provided by the ADA holds firm. As well, they all agree that a physical disability is an impairment that limits one's physical activity.

In addition, though all disabilities create daily issues for those affected by them, physical disability presents its own set of complexities due to its visibility and often bodily impairment or immobility that accompanies it. In addition, each condition may or may not be accompanied by the debilitation brought on by chronic pain that for many physically disabled especially, adds to their daily plight. Yet, in the case of most disabilities, somewhere in the shadows stands an individual who awakens each day to the added tasks of being a caregiver.

A Slow Learner

Sixteen years had passed since that initial trauma cyst formed in my wife's spine and now I found myself standing with the librarian at our local library seeking her help into a whole new world of research libraries. My interest into the world of the disabled had stirred my soul, for I knew the Lord had me here for a reason that would extend beyond our household. Yet, even before the door opened to those vast resource libraries, I found myself having my eyes enlightened to my own personal setting and that vast sea of humanity beyond our household that looked and acted just like I did.

I admit some of us are slow learners who find ourselves embarrassingly learning things that maybe most would think we would understand, but the realization that would come from the dialogue with the librarian was a jolting reality check. With the topic of physical disability in the pastor's spouse, the librarian went through what she could to introduce me to the vast number of works on the topic. Then she asked, "What other topics can offer us insights that will reinforce what you are researching; for example, the topic of caregiving would be closely related to disability." Looking directly at me, she said, "That is what you are, you know."

I am not sure if I looked puzzled or not, but hearing the word, "Caregiver," struck me funny, even though that is what I had been for 16 years. In all the adjustments and continual activity that required my attention I never took the time to consider it; but now I was hearing how many others viewed me, which actually took me a moment to grasp.

In those split seconds I wanted to deny it. I am just being what any husband would be. This is how any husband would act, or so I thought. Truthfully, I had to admit I had never thought much about it, because I just did what I had to do. Most people in crises do what they have to do, not thinking about being some amazing person or prepared or anything. I just stepped in to care for and to assist my wife, care for four children and still do my work in the community. I didn't really think much about what I was doing or what I needed.

Though it took a while to get used to, I found the term, "Caregiver," was not a bad word. In fact, it fit into my recognized community role as a pastor and shepherd, or "caregiver to a community."

So as the door opened to research a world pertaining to the disabled, what I found hidden in their shadows was a pathway that would lead me to see into the eyes of hundreds who were just like me and for whom my heart yearned to help. They were those referred to as Caregivers.

Caregiving Defined

Caregiving is such a strong and honorable word, that when one finds himself absorbed or even consumed by its activities, generally he finds himself in a devoted service for the betterment of another human being who God Almighty sees as precious. Caregiving, for sure, means giving a cup of cold water to someone in need. It means caring or looking after someone who is sick, and with whom Jesus himself identifies (or at least that is my take on his words) (Matthew 25:34-40).

Consuming? Fore sure! Strenuous and difficult? Well, we will deal with that in the coming chapters, but honorable and the right thing to do? Absolutely!

Disability comes into a life with absolutely no respect for whom it affects. Yet where the disabled person contends openly with a challenge that all can generally see, the caregivers will slowly discover an erosive wave of added responsibilities, depending on the type and severity of the disability that imposes its unwanted needs upon its unsuspecting victims. Spouses, parents, family and even extended family regardless of their stations in life, find themselves often in hospital rooms standing next to loved ones beginning a journey down a path unlike any other as caregivers - a path most often uncharted and unexplored, yet threatening in its scope.

Though the definition for being disabled can be debated, the consensus meaning for a caregiver is much easier to attain. In the broadest sense Beth McLeod, a practicing caregiver and noted author on the issue of caregiving, simply defines the act of caregiving as "the act of providing assistance to someone ill or frail."[6] This holds true for all caregivers whether they find themselves in it for a short period of time or for a lifetime. For those who are disabled, this person or these persons become the most important people in their lives, who they will learn to greatly appreciate.

Four types of caregivers

Acute-Care: It is worth noting the admirable qualities that accompany the skill and place of caregivers, beginning with the acute care caregivers that arrive with their medical skills. Invaluable at a time when skill is needed, these angels of kindness provide care during that critical initial state or times when the physical crises require skilled treatment.

Restorative-Care: Once the crisis subsides a second phase of restorative care caregivers enters the scene. These angels of kindness bring the occupational, physical, mental, emotional and spiritual care that carries the afflicted person to a complete restorative state or a position where restoration has reached its end and the disabled condition is now permanent.

Palliative: Taking into account the permanence created by the disabled condition leads us to the third type of caregivers who most often find themselves faced with providing long-term support that focuses upon relief and improving quality of life, rather than upon a cure. Where the medical world includes services and treatments described as "palliative," the vast majority of those involved in palliative care rests upon unsuspecting candidates who are enlisted into this service. Family members and loved ones, often times without even knowing it, join the ranks of caregivers or more precisely, "palliative caregivers," in that the long-term prognosis finds no immediate remedy for the one they help.

All their energy and all their work will be done with no foreseeable cure to the problem. This adds a different kind of stress, because from the beginning, barring a miracle, all the assistance one can give will not bring any rectifying solution to a person's disability or illness. The outcome is permanent, and for those caregivers it becomes a lifestyle that will now be metered out to them to learn.

Many of these same palliative caregivers will have the extra palliative care skills added to their already-ascribed responsibilities of making provision for their households. This means that for many caregivers, the weight of caregiving really is added on to the 40-plus hours that have already been dispensed to provide for the family. Spelling it out plainly, this spells S-T-R-E-S-S.

Hospice Care: One last form of caregiving comes when matters reach the final stages of life. Hospice care seeks to provide the physical, emotional and spiritual support to an individual with an expected survival of six months or less and it focuses on comfort rather than on finding a cure.

The Prevalence of Disability and Caregiving

Staggering Statistics

Lest we think we are alone, Pastor Robert Molsberry, who himself is disabled, draws our attention to the reality of the disabled and makes us aware that they are in our midst and cannot be avoided. "My experience is shared by millions of Americans, and hundreds of millions of people around the world. When Congress passed the Americans with Disabilities Act in 1990, it counted 43 million Americans living with disabilities. That's one in five of us."[7]

In 2007 Katie Banister reflected in her writing that there is a startling number of 58 million Americans who are now disabled.[8] Even the U.S. Census Bureau, published in a 2006 American Community Survey, figures that approximately 9.4% of the non-institutionalized civilian population in the USA, over the age of five, had some form of physical disability.[9] Please note that refers to the non-institutionalized, let alone the others who need continual care. A 2013 facts table from the Census Bureau had the number up to 12.6% of the non-institutionalized population of 312 million people to be disabled.

At the same time, "a 2000 survey by the National Family Caregivers Association found that more than 54 million Americans spend between 18-20 hours a week, on average, caring for an adult loved one. Most of these people remain caregivers for 1 to 4 years, though for some– 20 percent– the commitment lasts longer."[10] According to the National Family Caregivers Association, "In 2009 more than 65 million people, 29% of the U.S. population, provide care for a chronically ill, disabled or aged family member or friend during any given year and spend an average of 20 hours per week providing care for their loved one while 13% of family caregivers are providing 40 hours of care a week or more."[11]

Though the numbers can vary among researchers, one fact stands out. If the number for disabled and caregivers are added up, it means that approximately one in three non-institutionalized Americans awake to the issue of disability and caregiving every day. In short, **we are not alone**, and the number will only increase.

Why the increase? One reason lending to this number of people needing a caregiver stems from the fact that the "average life expectancy has increased from 49 years of age in 1900 to 75 years of age today. Chronic health problems have largely replaced infectious diseases as the leading causes of death. People are living longer, but they are living longer with chronic, disabling health problems."[12]

Dr. Sharron Guillet, PhD, and RN, in writing the opening chapter to *Care of the Adult with a Chronic Illness or Disability,* notes that the "public interest in chronic care is increasing for a number of reasons, not the least of which is… because the baby boomer generation is aging and living longer. Thanks to advances in health, nutrition and technology, increasing numbers of them are living with chronic conditions.[13] Even a *Reader's Digest* article on caregiving cited that, "There are approximately 50 million Americans who provide the majority of the help needed by relatives or friends who are elderly, ill or disabled. And those figures are only going to grow–the number of people 65 and over is expected to double in the next 40 years, and the number of those over 85, will more than triple."[14]

Once again I was struck with the fact of how little I know about a world that is all around me. Former First Lady Rosalynn Carter once shared a quote from a colleague: "There are only four kinds of people in the world– those who have been caregivers, those who currently are caregivers, those who will be caregivers, and those who will need caregivers."[15]

Quite encompassing I might say, but the challenge presented to families and to the church, if they want to see far enough down the road and prepare for what lies ahead, arises from these concerns. Caregiving already affects many and the probability that many more will face this task will present a heart wrenching challenge, while at the same time a phenomenal opportunity to help families and communities.

Compassion's Eyes

The Challenge of Caring for the Weak

As a pastor, these facts act like neon lights that draw my attention to a pressing social and spiritual dilemma that seems to go unseen. But the truth be known, compassion has eyes. It has eyes that compel one into action on behalf of another, which was the way of Christ. Recently I asked a leader from an evangelical institution of training what they had to offer in training for the leaders as they ministered to the disabled and their families. He said that the institution did not carry an interest in special interest groups like that, but they focused more on Bible, history and the languages.

The answer is fair in that he parroted the objectives stated by the institution's leadership, which I am sure are strapped, like many, with how they allocate their funds. Yet, the number of disabled within the United States approaches one in five, with approximately half of them, or 1/10 of our population facing a physical disability. Add to this the number of caregivers, and the accumulative number approaches about 1/3, if not more, of the US population that contends with the issue. Though challenges and pressures facing many of these families might be out of our sight, they should not be left out of our minds, especially when we know there are a staggering number of our neighbors who face disability or are called to be caregivers. For sure, it must be understood that, for the family, this number of people constitutes enough to not be considered some sort of "special interest group."

For the compassionate, the challenge to develop a ministry to families contending with disability and caregiving becomes an imperative to accomplish, especially when one considers that, for the disabled and the caregivers, just finding the energy to be able to attend a Sunday service can become quite an ordeal. Personally, I admit that I have had mornings where I have wanted to stay home. A difficult day, plus an exhausting night, or being awakened to the need for pain killers to just get my wife's pain under control, has a way of pressing the question, "Do I really want to go?"

On many occasions, I recall walking into the bathroom in the morning to see my wife's clothes all laid out to go to church. With a sigh, I lift my head to the Lord and cry, for her words only moments earlier expressed how she hurt too much to even try. Best laid plans, but it was not going to happen that day. There were also many times I waited, as she had spent two hours just preparing to go, only to find that, as we proceeded to the door, her body did not cooperate, or an accident occurred that delayed the process.

I cannot escape the fact that I am a pastor, which leads to another question that has forced me to rethink our approach to caring for the needy. "If they can't get to us, how do I get to them?" Here lies the challenge as to how we can invest our time and resources in responding to the cries of families from within our own communities who need us to come. Remember, if I have a neighborhood that meets just a simple cross-section of our country, I am talking about almost one in three people contending with this issue, which means that this is not to be taken lightly. If the challenge isn't enough to awaken us to the importance of caring for those who need help spiritually, then maybe getting a grasp of God and His take on the topic could awaken us to rethink our focus.

A Biblical Theme for Followers of Our Lord

In his book, *Hope Again*, Pastor Chuck Swindoll tells of a preacher who once said to a group of aspiring young ministers, "Preach to the suffering and you will never lack a congregation. There is a broken heart in every pew."[16] Sadly his advice has not needed to change much down through the years. Tragedy continues to claim victims regardless of their nationality, religious conviction, race or position in life. In many ways, "suffering is the world's common language. The question is not 'Will we face suffering?', but 'When will we face it?' Mistakes happen, relationships sour, we all age and have aches and pains, and we have all rooted for teams that lost in overtime."[17]

Illustrations of God's people suffering and facing adversity extends from cover to cover in the Scriptures, leaving the conclusion that in this world, even with God present, suffering will lodge in the home of those who are in a relationship with God. Let me assure you, being in leadership provides no exemption clause from adversity, even those types of adversity which become earmarked as long-term.

Most people would choose to avoid such situations, as they appear overwhelming. The uphill challenges brought on by caregiving responsibilities reflect a lifestyle which is similar to traversing the steep cliffs and rugged paths of the high places. Others turn to the One Who "makes our feet like hinds' feet on the high places" (Hab. 3:19). They turn to the One, Who offers surefooted confidence, thus enabling them to walk on those high places.

Personally, I would never desire that anyone should experience such a trauma as a physical disability or, for that matter, join the realm of being a caregiver. Certainly, I am aware that with any adversity of a long-term nature the unwanted results often carry a tsunami-like potential that can engulf its unsuspecting prey, even if they are a pastor. The cry for the security of the high ground and the quest to reach it reverberates through one's soul, leaving questions that often shake the strongest of men. This may be even more so when one's station in life comes equipped with the title, Pastor.

My position as a pastor in our community often targeted me as one to whom many turn in their adversity. The added fact of Dawn's disability and continued crises only furthered the requests from people to interact. Undoubtedly her dilemma provided for us a unique starting point on a journey that introduced us first-hand to the world of adversity. Our personal questions and search for understanding found resolution that gave us our needed strength and comfort. In turn, as we found our answers which helped us to survive in this crucible of pain and suffering, those we sought to help realized that the answers had been refined and filtered through our experience of tears and hardship. A spirit of empathy began to shape our manner and responses, preparing us to communicate as much in our silence as in our information. Looking back, I recognize how my journey morphed into a lifestyle earmarked with the words, "long-term," just as those who are disabled; but this long-term also included an open door for caregivers, the chronically ill and the disabled to enter.

Pain, suffering, weakness, persecution and tragedy I have learned, are a given in life. Yet, this theme takes another twist when the burden to be a caregiver is seen as a command to those who are followers of the living God. He cares for the weak, and that concern was transferred to His church, when Paul instructs them by saying, "...help the weak" (I Thessalonians 5:14). Again to the Church leaders, the Bible says, "...you must help the weak" (Acts 20:35). This is not given as a suggestion but as a command.

New Testament writers expressed such thought because it is the nature of Almighty God to identify, as well as to help, the poor and weak. Psalm 113:7 says, "He raises the poor from the dust and lifts the needy from the ash heap."

Elsewhere, there are passages that speak of the Lord hearing and responding to the cries of men. Exodus 2, for example, tells of the people of Israel in bondage to the Egyptians and crying out to the Lord, and having Him hear and respond. Psalm 146 offers a ringing declaration to care for the poor. God even had a way within His people's agricultural system to aid the needy with some dignity by allowing them the privilege to glean the fields. This continued in the church with the care for the visitor and the widow (Acts 4 & 6).

26

If this isn't enough, then Jesus' words concerning his mission in Luke 4:18-19 should solidify its importance. "The Spirit of the Lord is upon me," said Jesus, "because he has anointed me to preach good news to the poor. He has sent me to proclaim freedom for the prisoners and recovery of sight for the blind, to release the oppressed, to proclaim the year of the Lord's favor."

It would also be Jesus, who at a later moment in His life would identify with the poor and needy, as recorded in Matthew 25:35-40. "For I was hungry and you gave me something to eat, I was thirsty and you gave me something to drink, I was a stranger and you invited me in, I needed clothes and you clothed me, I was sick and you looked after me, I was in prison and you came to visit me.' Then the righteous will answer him, 'Lord, when did we see you hungry and feed you, or thirsty and give you something to drink? When did we see you a stranger and invite you in, or needing clothes and clothe you? When did we see you sick or in prison and go to visit you?' He replied, 'I tell you the truth whatever you did for one of the least of these brothers of mine, you did for me.'"

If he saw it as something so important, then why wouldn't I? Why wouldn't I take seriously the cry of the disabled and the caregivers and find a way to take to them the encouragement found in Christ. We must awaken this important ministry to those who live in our own neighborhoods and are not always visible because of their situation.

Throughout the Scriptures pain, suffering, weakness, loss and a host of infirmities have depleted the energy of God's people. Much of this pain was undeserved, while the suffering of others was an inevitable outcome. For my wife, two automobile accidents and fourteen surgeries, specifically related to her crushed spine, have left her suffering daily. She faces weakness and the loss of a normal, functioning body while she contends with all the effects of managing her pain. Yet, Dawn is well, if you can understand as disabled author and conference speaker, Marva Dawn, concludes that "well means finding rest in the Lord's tender embrace."[18] The radiance that often accompanies Dawn's time with people stems from communion with her Lord (Psalm 34:5). It is in His presence that her joy is found (Ps. 16:11). Her mind wrestles with new thoughts, as she reads profusely. Her sin nature has not been removed, nor has she found how to remove mine, but her heart flows with thanksgiving and she looks for any avenue of using her resources to help others.

Party Crasher and Open Door to the Weak

Physical disability crashed the party at our home. Uninvited and unwanted, it has presented many challenges. At the same time, God has used it to supplant our human logic with a silent impact in the lives of others, brought about by her powerlessness and her compelling concern for others. Our journey together as one disabled person and one caregiver has become a channel for the Lord to use to reach into the hearts of many.

Truthfully, Dawn's physical disability, as we have seen with all its struggles, must be seen within the Trinity's larger story, which came out of eternity past and extends beyond our foreseeable future. It implies God's intervention in coming into our world, calling us to accept His forgiveness for our sinful, selfish heart and then calling us to join Him in His movement of history toward its culmination. We will one day see an end to all evil, and His world restored to its intended creation in harmony with God. His story presents Him as the potter and us as the clay, jointly influencing people to come to Christ and His likeness. It is all about the restoration of a relationship between Almighty God and mankind. It is about our involvement in His unfinished story, which carries a mystery that leaves us to understand that the reason for our pain truthfully lies hidden in God. He has a reason, and it involves Him using our plights to impact the world to His glorious end. His story is our story and the fact that He allowed our crises to occur implies that He will enable us to use His story of His love for mankind. Indeed, as the Scriptures say, "My thoughts are not your thoughts, neither are your ways my ways" (Isaiah 55:8). In due time, or more rightly, in His time, we will understand completely; but until then, we will use our situations to open avenues to care for the weak.

In summing it up, the caregiver's world has many more members than it appears. All enter and abide under the watchful hand of Almighty God. We are not alone, and we will be joined by many more. Suffering, pain, weakness and the call to caregiving have been activities facing His people throughout history. As author Dr. Ronald Allen says, "It is only with a divinely given hope for the final victory of right over wrong, that we, as well as those who have lived before us in the faithful community, may relieve our sense of frustration at the ambiguity, uncertainty and enigma of our own existence. Unexpected, unexplained evils that come into our own lives, be they locusts or disease, war or disaster, are placed in a divine perspective when we have some knowledge of God and God's future dealings with evil itself."[19] Let's keep this in mind in the face of any disability and rest in the truth that God's future is our hope, while we do our part to care for the weak.

We are not Alone

On one occasion Dawn and I were asked to attend a banquet that honored some distinguished guests. Not knowing anyone and wanting to know more about this organization, we accepted. As we rolled in we found our place at a table. Since we were early, we waited to see who would join us. Three other couples joined our table, and one additional couple from the organization was assigned to serve our table.

As the night went on, and introductions expanded to include what we do, my wife explained her story to a middle-aged lady. As she spoke of our work with family ministries, she elaborated on how the work had opened up to include helping families with disability and caregiving. Within a few moments, this lady unfolded a recent chapter out of her life as she then told of her choice to care for her grandmother only three months prior. With good intentions and with hope that others would assist her, she soon found she could not attend church, except by alternating weeks with her husband, since one of them needed to be home with Grandma. Tears welled up as she expressed the stress and strain that she now faced.

Another couple happened to be the one serving our table. I would find in our conversing how he and his wife had to open their home to their newly divorced daughter, because she had acquired a chronic disease that led to her husband's departure. Contention and strain, he admitted, had filled the atmosphere of their home as their empty nest now had a "wounded chick" that needed their continual care.

For Dawn and me, this is a regular occurrence. Everywhere we go a family in need seems to surface in front of us. Maybe it is because we look for them; maybe it is because the Lord knows we will be an encouraging resource to them. Regardless, I know that these are but a few of the many, and to get to the rest will require some creative thinking and commitment to be to them what Almighty God has been to us, One willing to seek us out and provide the care our hearts cry out to receive.

But for sure, we are not alone!

29

Chapter 3
The Unsung Heroes

It the spring of 1998, Dawn had again undergone an extensive surgery at Harborview Hospital with Dr. Sean Grady and his neurological surgery team from the University of Washington. I had prepared myself as best I could for the potential complexities that accompanied this spinal cord surgery. Yet, when I heard him say, "Profound damage," it was like getting hit by the truck all over again. Amidst not only his but now, my tears, his words grabbed hold again as he turned the moment's pain toward the future. "I am sorry Tom," he said. "I am very sorry. The damage is profound, but please, hear me! Do not give up hope. So much is being done in the field of spinal cord injury, and what lies around the bend could prove helpful. Please do not give up hope!"

Alone at the time in a city 100 miles from home, I retreated to find my special table where I had spent so much private, quiet time, in the hospital cafeteria. A cup of coffee was about all I could afford, but as I sat there, I wondered and prayed. "Lord, what does it all mean? What hope? What does he mean not to give up hope? What confidence is there when the news is so devastating? What does he mean, 'in the future,' and just what does the future even look like?" Yet, for some reason I could not forget his words.

The coming months of rehabilitation and care for Dawn brought with them the ever-escalating and arduous task of caregiving. The wheelchair had become a permanent fixture, as did the rehab and physical therapy. Three more surgeries followed in 1999. An increase of Dawn's medications to curb her intensified pain levels began having negative effects. The side effects of the nerve deadeners, pain killers and narcotics, plus her body's inability to cope, the mental stresses and physical breakdowns began to wear us down. Infections followed one after another, finally prompting our family practitioner to admit that he was at a loss as to what to do. Having been in the medical field herself as a medical technologist, Dawn knew something had to change, and she felt she had to instigate it.

By 2001, however, that hope had become illusive, as her body was failing. She had difficulty digesting food, and often times afterwards she had to return to bed. Her pain levels had reached the point where 320 mg of Oxycontin and 2400 mg of Ibuprofen a day, plus nerve deadeners, did not work. To lighten the atmosphere, I can even remember telling her that, if she didn't mind, I could surely make some good deals on the street with all her meds. But that was often met with a stern look and a shaking of her head. Eventually, as our eyes met again, a smile mixed with the shaking of her head and I knew my goal of placing a smile on her face at least once during the day had been accomplished.

Hope Arrives

Dr. Margaret Burden, a family friend and fellow teaching partner, who often travelled with her husband as members of our family ministry team, privately asked Dawn if she would allow her to take over the case. Since change was needed, Dawn wasted no time in responding with a big, "Yes." Then she asked, "Would you be able to work alongside a naturopathic doctor, because I think I am going to need his specialties in order to contend with all my digestive issues and dietary problems?" Dr. Burden's willingness was immediate.

Dr. Joseph Wessels, the naturopath chosen by Dawn to help, soon offered his evaluation and commitment. "Your condition is very poor. In fact, there is no reason to explain why you are still alive, or if what we can do will work," he told her. "This many major surgeries create a tremendous amount of stress, which the body finds difficult to handle; but I am willing."

Shortly thereafter, the primary neurosurgeon from the University of Washington in Seattle, who had been so instrumental in Dawn's case, suggested another major change. Since the pain levels had risen exponentially, he suggested that Dawn accept his referral to a colleague and friend, Dr. Burchiel at the Oregon Health and Science University (O.H.S.U.) in Portland, Oregon. Since no more major surgeries could be done, the meeting was set up with O.H.S.U.

The plan was to experiment by taking her off all her medications and inserting morphine directly into her spinal column at her injury site. If the pain subsided, the team would implant within her abdominal area an intrathecal morphine pump that would mechanically inject morphine into the spinal column just above the injury sight.

In those moments when the test began, anxiety was high. So were her pain levels, as they had momentarily blocked the medications' ability to function. Shortly, though, the anxiety was gone. The test had worked. The morphine injection had blocked the pain and provided the assurance that her pain levels could be brought under control with the use of the pump, leading to the insertion of the morphine pump the next day.

Over the next six-month period, the weaning process from the Oxycontin was undertaken, while elevating the amounts of morphine through the pump to keep her pain levels under control. In the end, the amount of pain medication through the pump was equivalent to about one hundredth of the amount she had been taking orally, and it was being dispersed through a tube directly into the injury sight, reducing the effects that the narcotics had been having on her digestive system and her brain.

The next hurdle involved a marvelous working relationship between Dr. Burden and Dr. Wessels. Together they completely changed her diet, by removing and adding foods that calmed her digestive system, as well as providing needed supplements and reworking her remaining medications. Combined with the prayers of many, a slow, but methodical, change eventually brought improvement in her bodily functions, as well as her mental capabilities.

The fog that clouded so much of her thinking while under the influence of the heavy narcotics was lifting. Her cognitive awareness to all that was going on around her, even matters that were previously kept from her, was increasing. Her stamina and capacity to process information brought a welcomed change to her life and our relationship. The disability was still present tense--the wheelchair and walker were permanent fixtures—but after ten years of unrelenting suffering, hope had finally arrived. Once again, with the skills of some wonderful doctors, a strong determination, the prayers of many, and a wonderful support network, Dawn was re-engaging with life.

We Still Have Her and Her Beautiful Smile

During those tumultuous years between 1998 and 2004, life had become a blur. The world still spun, and life's blessings and hurts added accordingly to the household. Dawn's two brothers both died. Then her mother, who was very close to Dawn, passed as did my father, who, after

32

a year in a nursing home slipped into His heavenly Father's presence. Also, during this same period, our three oldest children graduated from college and were married bringing a continuum of joy to the festivities that accompanied those years.

Life was difficult since the pain and disability encumbered much of what we would have liked to have done. Still there were wonderful memories that to this day warm our hearts, douse the flames of pain, and bring thankfulness that her life had been extended.

Regardless of what one may read, I have not found one disabled person or their caregiver who did not wish that their conditions were different. Certainly there are those who have learned from their disabilities and even gained a better understanding about life. They may have become better people due to the disability, or even found a "true" meaning in life with peace and purpose with God, which they may never have found otherwise. Still, as the disabled Pastor Molsberry, states, "No one in their right mind would give up abilities they once had."[20]

Every disabled person, as well as the caregiver, would gladly accept a miracle or remedy, including us. In our case, no recklessness on our part led to Dawn's immediate condition, but now she lives in a wheelchair or in a position bent over her walker when she does stand. She cannot completely straighten out, even in bed, and is confined to one position when she rests. Mere observation reveals the difficulties, inconveniences, frustrations, burdens, embarrassing moments and losses that roll along with each turn of her wheels. Yet, it is a life to which we have learned to adjust and make the most of. It is a tragedy to see someone so beautiful and full of life overcome the initial trauma and have many of the effects solved by her last surgery, only to have another's unnecessary and heartless act blow it to shreds.

Still, the tragedy fell short of swallowing its victim when, by God's grace, her life was spared. We still have her. I still have her and that underscores my every day.

Welcome to Caregiver's Unlimited

Neither my wife nor anyone I know willingly entered "Disability World" thinking it was the greatest place on earth. Disability happens, and while Pastor Molesberry speaks to the disabled, I extend my thoughts to the caregivers who find themselves being given a lifetime membership card to "Caregiver's Unlimited." No waiting in line occurred, or will it ever be necessary, but a pen to write one's personal caregiver's story offers a starting point to a pathway that will either harden your soul or open your eyes of compassion to the world as it is.

"Caregiving for a loved one is an emotional roller coaster that can leave a person exhausted, bewildered, and dislodged, wondering how she or he can feel so helpless in a period so supposedly grown-up,"[21] writes Beth McLeod, author and experienced caregiver. She then offers this insight. "For some it comes like a bump in the night; for others, it is a realization of having already been swept away. We become caregivers by choice, by default, and by obligation; we assume the role because the alternatives are unacceptable. In a culture defined by short attention spans and sound bites, family caregiving demands investment for the long term, often an abrogation of dreams and a wholesale reconstruction of the future, one slow brick at a time."[22] This is what is meant by caring for someone, and what one does in sickness and in health.

The Caregiver's Message: Life is Valuable

The caregiving act is not some project to just "get through." It is not a competition or a philosophical test where, once learned, we are granted the privilege to graduate to something else. And certainly it does not have to be associated with a hardship or negativity.

Caregiving makes a statement that matters deeply, especially to its immediate recipient for it says loudly and clearly that life is valuable and to be honored. It personifies the love of Almighty God by its initiating action that supplies another's need. Indeed, if love, which so permeates the nature of God, means anything, it means involvement. Love initiates action toward another, as we use our eyes and feet to see and attend to another's needs. It brings a listening ear to hear another's heartfelt concerns, plus a consoling word that comforts another derailed from the simple functions of life. This could not be more recognized than in the involvements of those we call caregivers.

The Caregiver's Work: A Very Present Help in Trouble

Beth McLeod, further captures a truth learned by many who travel the road of being a caregiver. "Tears are the glue of the soul. When you weep with a friend, you bind your hearts to theirs."[23] Surely the caregiver's position and work present the opportunity for sharing boxes of tissue. At the same time, catching those tears that wet the caregiver's cheeks has a way of knitting together friendships. It just happens, because the experiences are so emotionally charged with appreciation, which in turn draws people together.

So, welcome to the front lines, where people hurt, including the ones who are often administering the care. Let's accept the fact that caregiving and ease are not synonymous, as well as the fact that most often, the work doesn't come as a matter of choice. Hiring someone to undertake this job on one's behalf may be a privilege granted to some. Yet, for the most part, it means rolling up one's own sleeves and jumping into the fray. It is a soul-crunching work, as one's inner makeup is taxed by the menial, but essential, requirements. It is spirit-bending, as the wrestling within one's heart to make sense of one's plight simultaneously competes with the necessity of loving another as Christ would. Called to care, to love, and to be a true friend, the work becomes a personification of Christ that portrays an unconditional and unfailing love.

Still, the work carries a toll with its body-wearing, day-to-day battle to learn the necessary skills that do not just come by reading a book. They come in the crucible of a hospital, in handling the agony of a late night spike in pain, as well as in the exhausting trips to find and bring relief. These skills are forged by learning what provides strength, comfort and encouragement for one who most often never asked for the dilemma in the first place.

Relief again is the hope and goal, and as the expressions of loving kindness achieve their momentary salve, the reward usually comes hours later in a shared moment and warm smile. Though forged in adversity's fire, the caregiver's life goes from day to day, lending energy to console a loved one but more importantly being to them what God is to all of us, "A very present help in trouble."[24] Here lies the cornerstone for building strong, intergenerational families. Here sounds the anthem that flows from the heart of God in His expressions of compassion. Here, by the mere actions of a caregiver, honor and love meet; the very honor and love that gives dignity to the disabled and captures the value that God had already placed within them.

The Caregiver's Ethic: It's More Than About Me

The honorable actions of a caregiver speak volumes, but the silence that often accompanies those same moments and deeds can be wearing. Let's not be fooled. It is not easy because if it were, we would not hear stories of desertion by spouses, and friends would be more seen than remembered.

As the clock rolls and calendar changes with the seasons, the unmet needs and constant demands mount, grinding at the caregiver's inner constitution. "God, what is expected of me? How much can I endure? Is there an end or even a reprieve? What about me?"

In one instant, the wear and tear can erode at one's commitment. At other times, the human spirit generates an inner strength, rising like a refiner's fire to purge the self-centeredness and to purify one's ethic with an attitude that is other-oriented. But it is that clash in the inner man that wears with an intense, continual challenge to our ethic.

I oftentimes find myself chuckling in these moments, for one might assume that, as a Christian and pastor, my choice to serve would sound like music to my ears, as it harmonizes so strikingly with Jesus' explicit expression that He came to serve.[25] Yet, in our western ideology the attitude that, "It is not about me, it is about others," finds its limits. Subtly, the culture--our collective beliefs that define us as a people-- exalts a system that pounds one's chest with production, accomplishment, beauty and personal achievement. Fame, fortune, power and pleasure come with being self-assertive and overcoming obstacles, but it was Jesus who mastered bringing about change by spending time among the weak and helpless. It is more than about me. In fact, Jesus' "others-focus" was on continual display throughout his life and many of his early followers.

This truth found expression when the Apostle Paul wrote to encourage and console a group of friends in the midst of their own trials. Recalling the encouragement and consolation derived from the love of God, Paul, who had by this time risked so much, drew upon the understanding that he had both experienced and witnessed in his friends and offered a challenge to them. If Christ has already brought so much, then let the gratitude you have well up within you to, "Do nothing out of selfish ambition or vain conceit, but in humility consider others better than yourselves. Each of you should look not only to your own interests, but also to the interests of others. Your attitude should be the same as that of Christ Jesus..., who made himself nothing, taking the very nature of a servant."[26] Here stands the core of the Christian's ethic. Parasites that take and never give, we are not. To combine responsibility and giving simply mirrors the attitude that Christ desired in his followers.

Literally, the choice of words by Paul "to consider others," meant to place value upon others. This would include anyone made in the image and likeness of God, which most assuredly includes the disabled. In short, as Paul wrote to the Philippians, he stressed the importance of having an attitude and ethic that was other-oriented. This is exactly what a caregiver personifies. In fact, what better word is there to capture that concept than the word, "Caregiver," as it best resembles those who are graced with such maturity? Though our world and the heart of man fuels a self-centered, narcissistic way, new caregivers can expect their consumer mentality to be refined, if not replaced, with a giver's heart.

Easy and caregiving seldom go hand in hand, and where one's religious convictions may desire highlights marked by blessings, the true caregiver and servant learns that is not always the case. Caregivers learn that they have a God-ordained schedule that does not usually mesh with the corporate ways, let alone their own. They also learn that they will face situations with limited resources. Tears may flow, and beseeching hands will be lifted to God asking for insight, but Shelly Beech acutely states what many caregivers have learned or will learn: "In an ocean of need, we have only the cup He has placed in our hands…The hardest thing is admitting that we cannot take away pain, protect our loved one from suffering, or stave off disease or death."[27] Yet, this type of constant demand that marks the caregiver can become quite taxing.

The Caregiver's Rightful Title: Unsung Hero

It is for this reason that Mala Ashok concludes, just as I, that the family caregivers deserve the title of, "Unsung Heroes."[28] Whether they are the primary caregiver, which occurs with a spouse, a parent to a child, an adult child to a parent or as younger children who step in as caregivers, or other relatives or friends, there is no doubt, they are the Unsung Heroes.

The word, "Hero," might sound out of place to some, but in my world as a pastor, counselor, caregiver and coach, I have had many opportunities to witness firsthand some of the most remarkable people one could

37

ever know. For the most part, these men and women, like any hero, are willing to put everything at risk in order to save or assist a comrade, drive back an enemy, or achieve and hold a position that modeled courage and determination. No one signs up to be a hero. One earns it at the intersection of happenstance and hell. Show me a hero and I'll write you either a tragedy or story of true grit. Introduce me to a man of valor, and I'll introduce you to someone who has been on the front lines, who, in a moment of time, risked it all for something or someone else, because they held a deep-seated conviction that life is a gift to all.

The military reserves the Medal of Honor for those who, in the thick of battle, demonstrate gallantry beyond the call of duty. The recipients of such an honor are always the first to remember their comrades who were not honored and to acknowledge those who made the ultimate sacrifice of their own lives. They will all tell you that they are merely the caretakers of the medal for their comrades left behind on the battlefield, and they will remind everyone of the cost of freedom.

The recipients, as they speak of their heroics, do so in simple terms. As one recipient put it, "I had a mission to complete and it seemed like the right thing to do at the moment." But a hero's actions are always extraordinary, because they are so contrary to the basic human instincts of self-preservation and survival.

My world has provided me the opportunity to meet some remarkable caregivers. I think of Pastor Brunner and Pastor Malmin, both of whom are from the Portland, Oregon area. One is a Lutheran and the other from a charismatic church, and both of them are remarkable human beings. Both are in their 80's and both at the time of my research work still served in their respective churches. The uniqueness behind them both stems from their love for the Lord and their unmatchable commitment to their spouses, who are disabled. I can remember interviewing both of these men, who were 20 years my senior, and in each case, hoped that, if God would allow me to live to be their age, He would enable me to become as gracious as these two. Each day they still care for their spouse with gentleness, kindness and patience.

This has been just as true for our dear friends, Ron and Carolyn, who cared for their son, Steve, who was born with cerebral palsy, until his precious Michelle made the commitment to be his wife. Another is

Mrs. Honcoop who had cared for her daughter, Kathy, who was born with spina bifida. Yet, she instilled within Kathy life skills which enabled Kathy to go on to become a self-sufficient adult. Then there are Larry and Kathy Ibsen who continue to care to this day for their middle-aged daughter, Laura, whose body has been overcome by scleroderma and lupus. Every day they have gone beyond the ordinary, because love does the right thing for another. Heroes? In my book, a resounding Yes, especially as we see the impact that marks their lives and all who surround them.

In the remainder of these pages, I write as a caretaker and representative for those caregivers who daily pay the cost by extending themselves to assist others. One desire of mine is to awaken our communities to the silent servants who generally say little, complain less and seldom realize the amazing work they do, merely because it often occurs behind closed doors. Heroes seldom wear their medals, so they often go unnoticed, just as caregivers seldom are noticed behind the complexities that their disabled loved ones face.

As a result, caregivers are hard to spot, but once again I hope my point is clear. If ever there were a need to recognize the unsung heroes of our day, we need look no further than those who fill the role of caregiver. Without their willingness to place one foot at a time on their new pathway, their family would easily have disintegrated. Even for me, I can easily conclude that without the care especially expressed by our four children, I would not want to guess where my wife and I would be today. They have left indelible imprints upon all our lives.

♥♥♥♥♥♥♥

Caregiving often relegates the caregiver to the shadows, embodying stations that seemingly make them beneath themselves, as if serving were some form of lower status in life. No servant need bow his head for what he does, any more than Christ did. Serving marks one of the four major qualities of any leader, along with being a sage, steward and seer (visionary). It stands as an essential ingredient to any leader worth his station; as any good leader knows, one never knows how to lead, until he knows how to follow. Is there any wonder why then the core of the Christian ethic revolves around having an attitude of a servant? It reflects God's way with man, and that is not demeaning in any way.

God's nature exudes with care and compassion toward those in need. With one simple statement He clearly delineates His own heart's desire for the needy with the words to us, "Care for the weak," which for certain involves the action of the caregiver toward the disabled as much as it does those who find themselves burdened down by their task of caregiving.

Once again I take liberty to honor the millions who have crossed the threshold of caring for a loved one. Long-term or short-term care does not matter. The caregiver's work underscores what truthfully makes this and any country great, for it quietly personifies God's way with us. Life is valuable and to be honored; and caregivers demonstrate that truth daily. Whether that person reaches a point of productivity or not, they carry an intrinsic value given to them by Almighty God. The act of caregiving captures and expresses an ethic which is like Christ, willing to give, not for what one receives in return, but because life is valuable and to be honored. No Purple Hearts or Medals of Honor will be administered, but the hearts that these unsung heroes touch will be forever grateful.

Chapter 4
The Four Corners to Puzzling Events

It was the fall of 2001, and while the communication waves throughout the country continued with the aftermath of the September 11th Twin Towers' tragedy in New York City, another not-so-noticeable scream sounded through our household. It was early evening when I found my wife in the bedroom, her big beautiful eyes filled with a look of pain and trauma that I will never forget. Screams and moans sounded from her beleaguered body that at the moment rolled back and forth on the bed, looking for a position that would bring relief.

After giving her an additional breakthrough pain medication, in hopes of regaining some relief for her, I reached out just to hold her, with the hopes of consoling her weary mind and body. A sharp shriek filled the room with a glare that needed no interpretation. My mere touch of her body had set off the nerves in her back that escalated the pain levels to a state that for her was unbearable. An hour would pass, the tears would cease and finally a moment of relief was found that would enable her to find rest and quiet as the medication took effect.

My office study in our home had become a haven, as it was there that I did most of my own crying out to the Lord. No internet connections made it to this room, only the emergency line to my wife, my secretary, and my private line to the One who said, "Come to Me, all you who are weary and burdened, and I will give you rest."[29]

As on many occasions, I walked into that room, sat down and found myself probing through the Scriptures like one forging an uncharted course through a wilderness. My heart's cry I am sure, was heard in heaven. "God, I can read your book in both Hebrew and Greek, but please speak to my troubled soul and make it in English, because I think that's all I can understand, and even that is questionable."

It took only minutes of seeing just words on a page before I succumbed to the overwhelming hurt and lay my head in my arms on my desk and wept.

On that particular day I remember thinking how her ordeal was such a seemingly useless cross to bear, as a victim of two car accidents.

She asked for none of it, and now her plate was full every day with the repercussions of others' senseless and careless actions. Not only was her plate full, but the added effects, responsibilities and challenges that flooded over to me completely filled any unused time in my schedule. Permanent relief seemed as likely as reinforcements to the Alamo. I was also sure that she couldn't miss the anguish that her situation caused. Yet the solace of the moment was the same. I had a line to the throne of God which stilled many storms. Though my tears flowed, and as difficult as it was, I took great comfort and found myself very grateful for one thing: I still had Dawn.

I have relived this scenario, scores of times, just as any caregiver to some degree encounters. When asked on different occasions what I have found with her disability is the hardest part to handle, I generally refer to moments such as I just described. The personal anguish of watching a loved one suffer rips you apart. In my case, I have learned that we will make it through one more time, and we will still have each other, God willing. Yet, those around us did not necessarily understand the full extent of the effects of the disability upon both of us, and, quite frankly, I am not sure how much they could have helped, even if they had understood. For us, it had become a way of life that often destabilized many of our best-laid plans.

My time alone in my study between the tear sessions found me reading and asking questions of the Bible and its Author. One major question that surfaced often was, "How Lord am I to understand and handle crisis and adversity in life?" In fact it was this question that surfaced from within the church where I served during that tumultuous time surrounding September 11, 2001, that has framed much of how I have come to handle adversities.

I sought more than the simple, man-made explanations formulated by man's psychology and theology books. Though I could not escape the plight I faced continually, my objective was not to establish my philosophy of pain and suffering. My challenge was to search the revelation given to us by God Almighty, the Bible, to unlock the truths that would stabilize our souls, frame our thinking in adversity's face and drive us to the Lord, rather than away from Him. I sought to hear from Him what He felt I needed to know in order to handle the real life encounters for which I was trying to make some sense.

As the late nights and early mornings provided the atmosphere for my study, thoughts began to materialize that gave needed anchors for stabilizing a life that contends with adversity. Simultaneously, I found those same answers formed a pattern that focused my thoughts without jeopardizing my faith in Almighty God. Over and over again, four repeated themes rose from the pages, and over and over again I wrestled with how to present what I had learned without having to address the many complex questions that arise when the primary topics are tragedy, adversity and disability.

It was then that one of my wife's harmless, but cunning, practices struck our home and provided the idea that offered a word picture that encased my findings. Though I have refined my thoughts over the years since the original idea was literally dumped on my desk, it is this same picture that will frame much of the remainder of this book.

The Four Corners to Puzzling Events

It all began when, during one of our winter hibernations, Dawn grabbed a big puzzle - a thousand pieces plus - and threw it out on a table, and drew in every bystander to assist her in putting it together. Fresh brewed coffee and hot cocoa aromas lured us to join her. As for me, my phenomenal, probing intellect involved me just long enough to separate out the straight edges from the rest and find the four corners of the puzzle, plus get my coffee. Finding those corners assures me that a picture will occur over time that will make sense out of the scattered mound of baffling forms.

On one occasion, my wife was amazed that this enormous puzzle was not the puzzle pictured on the box. The only similarity was the number of pieces listed on the box. When she made the discovery, "Take it back and get another one!" was my cry. But she responded, "Oh no! This one's a challenge!"

The words, puzzle or challenge, may be an understatement, when it comes to a pile of pressed paper pieces meant for reconstruction in order to make a picture. Nevertheless, these same words are very appropriate when it comes to facing any adversity or being pulled into the ranks of the caregivers. Such events surely resemble a pile of puzzle pieces. Yet, the seriousness of this type of challenge can engulf its victims, not only with the issues surrounding loved ones, but with all the perplexing challenges of one's inner journey as a caregiver.

These challenges affront our attitudes and convictions about life and faith. There have been many times when I have heard a caregiver's cry find its faint whimper in the words, "Lord, I want you to take this one back." Personally, there have been many times that these same words filled the hollows of my emptied soul and, like Job of old, moved my thoughts from the philosophical to the reality of what awaited my next breath.

Nevertheless, when crises hit, fitting all the pieces of life back together, though it is an overwhelming challenge, seems feasible, especially if only the four corner pieces, some of the straight edges and perhaps a small cluster from the picture's centerpiece can be found. It may seem simplistic but when your world has been shattered, stability comes and anxiety is dampened when we can rely on what we know to be certain.

By no means do I want to simplify complex issues, but for my own inquisitive mind that has contended for over 25 plus years as a caregiver and some 40 plus years as a pastor, holding the corners to adversity's puzzle offers some semblance of order to an otherwise baffling mystery that accompanies crisis. As the crisis of my own wife's disability thrust me into the realm of caregiver, the stability that I finally gained was brought about because I knew I had enough of the puzzle to know how to handle my situation a step at a time, and that centered on my relationship to God.

As we journey together in learning to care for ourselves as caregivers, as well as in ministering to the caregiver, we do so with the full intent of addressing two questions. The first is, "How are we to understand and handle adversity?" The second is, "What can be done to help provide the care that will sustain the caregiver?" My hope is to give each reader the four corner pieces to a puzzle and maybe a little glimpse into what it means to commune with God. These stabilizers, I have come to realize, are what God seeks to make clear amidst the darkness and blurred understanding that accompanies such trials. Here lies the starting point for preparing a caregiver or in caring for the caregiver.

To prepare us for what lies ahead, I return to my trying year of 2001. In early November, I began a short series to the congregation entitled, "Why Does God Allow Crisis?" The combination of the recent national tragedy in September plus the concerns that had affected our home brought people to ask, if I could address the issue. The opening engagement started on that first Sunday morning the message began by my bringing and dumping out on a table before the church one of my wife's massive 1000 piece puzzles. With all eyes focused, I then explained my wife's empowering ways to lure us into her puzzling ways and how my part was limited but focused. I then redirected the message to the questions that supplied the challenges that would be the content of the next few weeks of messages.

Each crisis brings with it a set of questions that demand a reply, and normally those questions are directed at God. Why does God allow crises? How, Lord, are we to understand and handle crises and adversity in life? What is at the heart of such difficult moments? As I lifted the puzzle pieces to accentuate the 1000 pieces, I began doing what I do well when this massive mess lies before me. I sipped my coffee and looked for the four corner pieces to the puzzle, which for the sake of time, I had already removed and held in my hand.

What those messages unveiled and what will be discussed in the following chapters is what each corner piece presents. What we will uncover is that four repeating themes occur in adversity in the Scripture that lead us to one central truth, namely...

In this world, adversity comes to draw us to God and his likeness

At the outset of any adversity, we will find that all the participants find themselves awakened to the hidden, painful side of life with certain immediate and unwanted adverse effects. Such effects become somewhat overwhelming, when they begin to pile up one on another. The compounding nature of such effects and the severity of the problems that arise present a series of challenges that necessitate our need to adjust, even before the long-term effects are firmly established. Adjustments are not change, but they ultimately lead to our own internal transformation, which ignites an impassioned mobilization toward God and others in need.

45

When a crisis (disability) hits, it...

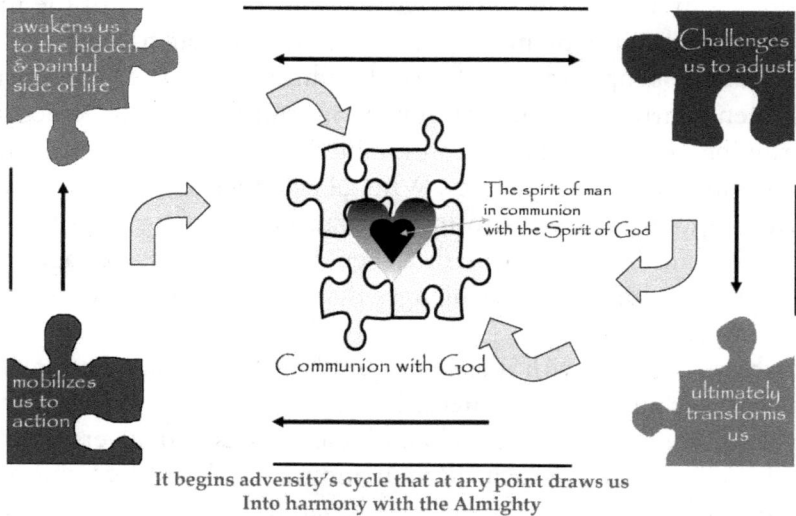

awakens us to the hidden & painful side of life

Challenges us to adjust

The spirit of man in communion with the Spirit of God

mobilizes us to action

Communion with God

ultimately transforms us

It begins adversity's cycle that at any point draws us
Into harmony with the Almighty

At the same time what we will find is that in facing adversity, the four reoccurring themes carry a common thread in that each of them opens a pathway to draw us into harmony with the Almighty. As well, mere observation enables us to see how the four themes fit together to make a cycle of adversity that accompanies any hardship. This becomes strategic in helping to understand where one is in their journey, as well as helping each person make sense of his unique setting and his progression in the midst of their hardship.

♥♥♥♥♥♥♥

Chapter 5
When Crises Hit

As the search for the corners begins, the first corner appears as quickly as the diagnosis or the sound of sirens cease. Puzzled and bewildered, the news finds you in a setting you would never have chosen in your wildest dreams. Nevertheless, the facts do not change. "She has MS," "She has polio," "He has cerebral palsy," "It's the early stages of Alzheimer's disease," "She is paralyzed on her right side," "She may live, but she will never walk again," or "There is profound damage, but don't lose hope." When you hear these words, they resound through your psyche, leaving you numb and bewildered.

As shocking as the news may be, and as much as the medical personnel, friends and family offer their assistance, what has transpired finds you standing on the first corner piece of a life-sized puzzle. Before long, you cry, "What has happened? Where do I go? What do I do? God, how did I end up here?"

Suddenly you are awakened to a world that you no longer recognize. It may happen suddenly or slowly, but either way you are awakened to a pressing adversity that alarms you to the truth that something just happened, and your life has been shattered, or at the very least permanently affected. It is only the beginning.

Corner Piece #1: Adversity Awakens us to the Hidden and Painful Side of Life

In those split seconds, which revert to slow motion in my mind, I recall the sight of lights in the rear view mirror, and before I could utter a word, an explosion that not only buckled the back of our van, but lifted it into the air and back again on top of the truck's hood that hit us and was now propelling us down the road. Separation and safety would come only by taking advantage of our front wheel drive, which at the right moment pulled our van from its attacker. Adrenalin rushes in those moments, and the thought for the safety of loved ones totally occupies one's mind. As matters settle, the awakened sense of having just escaped death alerts one's inner being to one's mortality. Crises have a way of doing that.

Sirens sound in the distance only to cease when the help they carry jumps into action assessing the setting, asking questions, and trying to make sense of the picture that affronts them. Before long paramedics are loading my wife into an ambulance, while our daughter and I await a second ambulance to arrive.

The journey ends in a familiar place for a pastor and caregiver: the hospital. How many times I had entered the local hospital to attend to another family's need, I could not count, but now the tables were turned. Strapped to a table as a patient, I not only hurt for someone else, I hurt myself. Soon, my eyes catch a glimpse of our younger son entering the room, having been called to meet us at the hospital. Tears surface as thoughts of different scenarios underscore how thankful we were that we could still interact, and that his mom, his sister, Marjie and I were still alive.

After a series of tests, we were released from the hospital. All of us seemed to be okay, though we had many aches and pains. Later that evening, we found ourselves sitting together in our living room. Now the questions mounted almost as though all was surreal. "What just happened? How could this happen? How could this happen only three weeks after getting Dawn out of her body shell in which she had lived for the last five months? Lord, how could this be? What is going on?" So many questions, yet as we looked at each other, an overwhelming sense of thanksgiving dominated the room.

Immediate Effects that Accompany a Crisis

At the very outset of any adversity, all the participants find themselves alerted to certain immediate effects that come to life in the early moments. Some occur within hours, and some take days, but the barrage of alarms that reverberate through one's mind, even before any major decision needs to be made, often carries enough weight that one looks just for a place to sit down. The adrenalin flows, the heart beats faster, and the mind shifts into overdrive as the truly painful side of life becomes a reality.

Crises Awaken Us to Our Own Mortality

What happens within individuals when crises hit? What effects are immediately generated when adversity's unwelcomed consequences crash the party? There are no doubts that crises, especially when you have just passed through them, alert or awaken us to our own mortality. Each

48

participant will find that a brush with death only stresses the fact that we are mortal beings. If the setting actually involves the death of another, our heightened sense of mortality becomes noticeable with the tears and shock for those who remain behind, on the edge of the "valley of the shadow of death." As only moments before life flashed in front of us, the immediate effects of such tragic moments find us overcome, not only with a sense of our own mortality, but also the realization that we are not in control.

Crises Awaken Us To an Awareness of a Numinous Being

At the same time crises awaken us to an awareness of a numinous being, whom I refer to as God. When the vehicle finally came to rest and I could see all were still alive, the words uttered from my mouth expressed my complete awareness of the living God. "My God, what just happened?" I asked, even before I made another move.

C. S. Lewis states that "In all developed religion we find three elements, the first being the experience of the Numinous."[30] This numinous or numinous being refers to a deity of a spiritual nature that inhabits another world outside themselves. When you think you are in the presence of a numinous being, "You would feel wonder and a certain shrinking sense of inadequacy to cope with such a visitant."[31]

The second element of developed religions like Christianity that Lewis mentions is "the consciousness not merely of a moral law, but of a moral law at once approved and disobeyed...All men alike stand condemned, not by alien codes of ethics, but by their own, and all men therefore are conscious of guilt."[32] Yet, the third element follows when men link both the moral experience and the numinous experience. Here, "the numinous power to which they feel awe is made the guardian of the morality to which they feel obligation."[33]

In the Garden of Eden following Adam and Eve's dismal quest to become godlike (Genesis 3), they found themselves shamed and filled with fear at the thought of being found by God. In Adam and Eve's case, their self-made crisis of fear and guilt arose in the face of their choice to be like God. Guilt and shame marked their moment, alerting them to the awareness of God and before whom they sensed their own failure and obligation.

It is here in the face of one's crisis that the awareness of this numinous being and our sense of obligation and accountability shapes our thoughts.

With adversity's interruption, a divine encounter occurs and our sense of moral accountability screams with thoughts that seemingly fall on deaf ears. "What did I do to deserve this?"

And Then There is the "Why God?"

"Why God?" These two words have been expressed by countless numbers of people, including those who have made their life pursuits living with and for God. But what possible answer could restore the damage that has ransacked the life energy of a precious loved one. We also know that no answer puts us back "in control" which often is the reason we ask such questions. Somehow in our independent selves the thought of life being out of our control leaves us with an insatiable drive to answer the question, "Why?" Otherwise, we are left to acquiesce and admit our interdependence on someone or something other than ourselves.

Yet, the shrieks and screams of "Why God?" that commonly associate themselves to adversity actually alert us to our awareness of a numinous being. It is almost as though each human being has a vacuum within their soul that seeks attention from God. Even emptiness finds some relief in just expressing, "Why God?" in that it at least constructs the thought that maybe someone, other than myself is in control.

Please hear this, because on more than one occasion I have found this point to be instrumental in helping channel people's energy during the opening moments when all is being sorted out. "Why, God? Why weren't You there? How could You let this happen?"

These expressions have often been directed at me as a pastor and caregiver, and I have responded by affirming their question as a great question. In many cases I acknowledge that, "The mere fact that you ask, acknowledges that there is someone other than yourself who is greater than you who is in control. That is a phenomenal statement for someone whose tear ducts are on the verge of running dry."

I then turn their thoughts to the fact that we need much more time to address that question, but for sure the underlying statement communicates a degree of truth that they can hold onto, in that their question acknowledges a numinous being more powerful than themselves to whom they can direct their thoughts. Yet, for the moment there is an even more pressing question, and that is, "How do we handle this crisis?"

I have found that it is in these moments, solace is found merely by being in the company of others who, with a sense of thankfulness, bow to God for what they do have. Yes, the anguish and uncertainties of the moment still need to be addressed, but even our household bowed for what we still had—each other—which brought in itself a restorative calm and security to us all. Making sense of the problems offered nothing, but knowing the personal presence of God and holding each other meant everything.

The why question that so easily flows from torn hearts is a very legitimate question. It also happens to be a great question asked by many great people. The author of many of the lament psalms in the Bible was King David. Psalm 22 was quoted by Jesus Christ on the Cross. Add the other hymn writers like Asaph, the sons of Korah, Moses and of course Job, Isaiah and Jeremiah, and I must admit it sounds like pretty good company asking or acknowledging the same concern.

In the hymnic literature of the Bible, the lament psalms sound out the anguish that accompanies those encountering trials and adversity, often by using very similar questions that face us in our adversity. Psalms 6, 10, 13, 22, 46, 60 and 142 are just a few of such psalms that cry out to God.

- Ps. 10:1 "Why, O Lord, do you stand far off? Why do you hide yourself in times of trouble?"
- Ps. 13:1-2 "How long, O Lord? Will you forget me forever? How long will you hide your face from me? How long must I wrestle with my thoughts and every day have sorrow in my heart? How long will my enemy triumph over me?"
- Ps. 22:1-2 "My God, my God, why have you forsaken me? Why are you so far from saving me... O my God, I cry out by day, but you do not answer, and by night, I have no rest."

Yet the same lament psalms generally feature a vow of praise, leading us to understand that though the question expressed the sorrow in one's soul, the writers found solace in their acknowledgement of God. In fact these very vows proved to be the source that lifted my spirit amidst the tears.

- Psalm 10:17-18 "You hear, O Lord, the desire of the afflicted; You encourage them, and you listen to their cry, defending the fatherless and the oppressed."

- Psalm 13:5-6 "But I trust in your unfailing love; my heart rejoices in your salvation. I will sing to the Lord for He has been good to me."
- Psalm 22:22-24 "I will declare your name to my brothers; in the congregation I will praise you. You who fear the Lord, praise Him! ... For he has not despised or disdained the suffering of the afflicted one; he has not hidden his face from him but has listened to his cry for help."

Crises awaken us to a numinous being, Who in our screams and demands, often bears the title, God. So as we pour out our souls, the uniqueness of those moments finds that He is listening and that in some way He is one to whom we feel obligation and, in turn, somewhat expects the same. Somehow our scream links to a quest that His unfailing love will make sense of the ordeal, and His fingerprints will be found making good to come out of what at the moment seems the opposite.

Crises Awaken us to the Fact that Something is Wrong with the World

An accident, a birth defect, a genetic disorder, a miscarriage, severe illness, random disease, an earthquake, a natural disaster and death--to what do they all point? A political system losing its moral compass, an economic system falling prey to man's greed, a religious system adulterated by the gods of fame, fortune and power, along with a social system that fuels self-centeredness and independent self-sufficiency--to what do they all point?

Even a natural law that storms relentlessly out of control, striking mercilessly into any misfortunate soul who happens to find his pathway mistakenly facing this fallen and broken expression of natural law--what message ultimately hits the recipients whose headlines are full of such catastrophes and illicit actions? Is it not the message that there is something wrong with our world?

Sin has brought a curse to the world. The world has fallen just like man. In the beginning as Colossians 1:16 states, "all things were created by Him (Christ) and for Him,"[34] which implies, "that initially all the powers were created for good."[35] Yet, just as sin entered the world, so did its effects on creation, and creation now groans in waiting for deliverance.[36] As a result we now find a world system, and "the working of principalities and powers at a level of evil that is often misunderstood."[37]

Awakened to the wrong of the world does not mean that we need lose heart. Marva Dawn again speaks a note of encouragement to this darkened fact of our world:

"We are encouraged to know that none of the powers (or principalities) can ultimately keep us from God's care for us. Romans 8:38-39 underscores that nothing in all creation, particularly the powers, will be able to separate us from the love of God in Christ Jesus Our Lord. Since we know that God is on our side, we have more courage whenever we have to engage in combat against the powers, and we know that God is with us even if we can't do much about them."[38]

Marva Dawn then offers this insightful distinction to the sources of evil. "The Biblical vocabulary shows that the principalities and powers are neither unearthly entities nor simply human beings operating in devilish ways. Rather, the powers are on an intermediate level and combine elements of the other two — exhibiting supernatural power, but linked to human institutions or cultural fabrications."[39] She then acknowledges the three levels of evil often referred to as the world, the flesh and the devil, but does so by referring to them as "the supernatural forces of evil resident in the spirit world, the principalities that are superior powers in our world and our own sinful inclinations."[40]

What does it all mean when facing a tragedy? The forces of evil are at work, and many of these forces are outside our control. We can do our best at combating them, but recognize they are a large part of the explanation of why there is something wrong with our world.

Crises Awaken Us to the Fact that Something is Wrong with People

The last of the three evils mentioned, namely our own sinful inclinations, offers us a less popular observation--that people have a problem. They are sinners. This does not nullify that they are incapable of loving and doing good, but from the opening chapters of mankind's history as given by God Himself, He reveals when and how sin found its first victim. As well, the book of Romans reinforces that there is no human being, apart from Christ alone (II Corinthians 5:21, I Peter 2:22) who did not come under sin's influence and curse, just as the Scriptures and history have clearly displayed since that fateful day in the Garden. Clearly, says the Apostle Paul, "All have sinned,"[41] and from Adam to present man a sin nature with its sinful inclinations has been passed from parents to child, leaving all in the same woeful condition. "Just as sin entered the world through one man, and death through sin, and in this way death came to all men, because all sinned,"[42] spells it out pretty clearly.

The consequence to that action was separation from God, which, from God's vantage point, was caused by Adam's actions. It seems rather harsh, until you recall that what Adam sought was equality with God. His instant desire for knowing good and evil meant knowing everything. It meant being equal to God Himself. Pretty brazen on his part, but, in truth not much has changed.

Understanding that the creation account of man being made in the image of God, underscores how God made man as a volitional being: a free moral agent with a capacity to make choices for good or evil. This freedom carried a great risk that man could make the wrong choices. Personally, the thought that God could create a being that had the power to accept or reject Him of its own free will astounds me as to His creative ability. Yet, once sin's ways were chosen by man, for God to erase all the consequences and to stop all bad choices, He would need to remove the capacity for man to choose, and that would no longer make us free agents. Either that or He flat out removes evil, which would mean that we and our sinful ways must come to an end.

So, where does this leave us, but to conclude that there is something wrong with man? "I want it my way—and I want it now," fills his utterances, while deep within the drive for satisfaction in life man's way controls his thoughts and propels his actions. Selfishness as a purpose distorts his legitimate longings and ultimately deceives him.

Think with me about what God recorded for our instruction. Once He revealed that sin had entered into the heart of man, look at the effects of this upon others. Cain did not like his brother and made a choice to kill him, resulting in the death of Abel (Genesis 4). Sarah mistreated Hagar and her son Ishmael (Genesis 16), contributing to the animosity between the Jews and Arab world. Joseph, son of Jacob, would find his brothers selling him into slavery (Genesis 37), resulting in years of imprisonment and slavery. Pharaoh refused to honor the demands of the Israelites and God, bringing upon the Egyptians the plagues, destruction of animals and finally the death of all the first born sons (Exodus 7-11). Jesus' birth in Bethlehem prompted Herod, in a fit of jealousy, to slaughter all the children under the age of two who resided in Bethlehem (Matthew 2). What did they do to bring this despicable destruction? Saul, who later became known as Paul, ravaged the early church, even holding the cloaks of those who would mercilessly stone a man for his beliefs in Christ (Acts 6-8).

Add to these stories the situations told and retold of abusive parents, rebellious children, a drunk driver, a druggie, a greedy business man, a broken relationship, a jealous spouse, an illicit affair, a hatred for a race or religion, a genocide, an Auschwitz, a New York Twin Towers, slavery, among so many other examples, and it awakens you to the horrific pathway of destruction and pain that permeates mankind. If this is not enough, add to this Satan and his demons with their powers to control peoples' minds or crush their lives, as in Job's case. Because of the evil and sin in the heart of mankind, choices have been made that produce a mourning that awakens us to the fact that something is wrong with people. Crises reveal that we live in a broken world, inhabited by broken people, broken systems of power and rebellious spirits.

Crises Awaken Us to the Fact that Something is Wrong with Me

Lest we get caught pointing a judgmental or critical finger at all the illustrations that demonstrate how people have problems, it might be worthwhile to make sure that we do not lose perspective by realizing that in the minds of other people, we are numbered among those people with whom something is wrong. I am saddened to say that some crises we face in life are self-inflicted, not just because of our wrong doing, but as well our ignorance or inadequacy. Yet, the very self-centeredness ruling the hearts of those people who have supplied the examples also has a residence in my own soul.

It is I who can choose to break the rules and find myself in a crisis with the law, the school administrators or the boss. I can choose to drink excessively or use drugs, and find myself in a crisis with a melted brain. I can choose a free and uncontrolled sexual lifestyle and find myself facing the news of an STD or unexpected pregnancy. I can choose an internet site that erodes the trust of a spouse. I can choose to harbor a wrong, only to waste away in self-inflicted bitterness: or I can embellish a thought or gossip behind someone's back only to find my relationships vanish.

Maybe the choices start on a small scale and are even innocent, but with time habitual bad choices grow into full blown addictions and lifestyles. Families face a crisis intervention and the reason is simple: there is something wrong with me.

Crises Awaken Us to Our Innate Longings

Crises also bring another type of alert which awakens us to something deep within our souls. Think of a recent news flash of an earthquake, a flood, a hurricane, a school shooting, the collapse of a building, an automobile accident, or the news of cancer, and one recognizes a familiar tug at the heart. Oh, Lord, that could be me or my family! How can I help? How can I be of assistance? What can I offer to bring a moment's security or restore a sense of dignity to someone devastated by their mishap? Tears well up for someone you have never met and even more so when it involves those you know. It does not matter as we find ourselves identifying with others whom we know reflect the very same longings that drive us.

At the same time, a friend might reject you (Psalm 55:12-14), a sense of hopelessness overcomes you (Psalm 60), or grief grabs your heart strings with the loss of a loved one. Darkness surrounds you (Psalm 88), loneliness becomes your bed mate (Psalm 6:5-7), and the silence of God oozes a tearless sorrow, while you pen in your diary your heartbreak to God. When the cries resound from within your own soul, the unfulfilled quests for genuine security and the desire for meaningful significance reveal the legitimate, God-ordained, innate longings in those made in His image and likeness (Genesis 1:27).

Yet, amazingly, when we stand face to face with a crisis, whether as an onlooker or as one intimately involved, a strength of human spirit arises and fuels the desire to jump headlong to offer assistance. This is common among those confined to the world of disability and caregiving. Crises have a way of exposing our softer, caring side. Intense action may be required, but it comes encased with a sense of compassion, kindness and genuine concern that often surprises even those whose actions can only be summed up with the words, "It just seemed like the right thing to do." Indeed crises awaken us to what constitutes the heart within all of us.

That night upon arriving home from the hospital, I remember us all sitting in the living room. The evening's events had definitely found us all awakened to the immediate effects that come hidden among the more contemplative moments such as we were now sharing. The questions that so accompany such crises had woven themselves into the conversations, especially as the news spread that the incident stemmed from a drunk, illegal immigrant with no insurance. Interwoven into the conversations, were the phone calls from friends and neighbors, family members and medical personnel pertaining especially to Dawn's condition, which mirrored the heartfelt longings and concern of others for our family. Yet, for the moment, a spirit of gratitude filled the atmosphere, and it appeared that all that was lost was replaceable.

Indeed, I know when the effects are more extensive, the anguish rises proportionately. Little did we know though that what seemed frustrating and destabilizing would soon, escalate. In only a short period of time, Dawn had intense discomfort, raising fears that she had not escaped unscathed. Further medical attention became necessary, and as the ill effects clouded any family plans, those same immediate effects with their heart-wrenching questions once again mockingly reentered not only our own conversations, but the many who were close to us, wondering as we, what was the point of it all? Once again we were faced with the fact that adversity awakens us to the hidden and painful side of life. Once again the barrage of alarms with their unwanted and annoying stresses reverberated through our minds:

- To our own mortality
- To an awareness of a numinous being
- To the fact that something is wrong with our world
- To the fact that something is wrong with people
- To the fact that something could be wrong with me
- To our own innate longings for security and impact

Chapter 6
At Least I Still Have Her!

Dawn's eyes welled up with tears, as her body, now bent over and somewhat rigid, made every effort to put her arms around my neck. Titanium rods and fusions of the spine made for stiffness in her posture and slowness to her every move. Positioning myself on a stool to enable her to see eye to eye, I held her cheeks in my hands while gazing straight into the same set of eyes that for 39 years had shared so much. It was our anniversary and in that moment, not only were the pain levels high, but the needs for her well-being had grown. Financial pressures were extreme, as were her pain levels. For many this would be a day of celebration. However, it now found her muttering the words, "I am so sorry." As the conversation continued with what would not happen that day, the tears rolled down her cheeks.

Finally, I reached up and placed my finger upon her lips bringing a silence to the moment. "Stop!" I said. "Don't do this to yourself. You didn't ask for this. No one asked for this, so do not think for a minute that I am going to pile on more hurt to what you already endure daily. WE will make it, and WE will enjoy the day. Happy Anniversary!"

The words, "Til death do us part," were part of our vows 39 years ago to the day. Yet, when those words were exchanged, our understanding was limited, especially when unwanted adversity took up a permanent residence. Genuine? Yes! Heartfelt? Yes. On this day we could say how thankful we were that we both still had each other.

Nevertheless, once again I could see in Dawn's eyes the same expressions I saw in the wife of my youth with whom I have shared so much. Even with all the trauma of the last 20 years, the joys, celebrations and privileges stored in our memory banks greatly outweighed the pains. Though momentarily overlooked, they were brought back on line to regenerate a grateful spirit. As well, I had the tiny slice of time to gaze into the person behind those eyes to whom I made a vow and from whom a vow was given. Here lies one of the hidden secrets we hold together: the person to whom we joined our lives resides in the inner person. To me, she is the same wonderful person, and though the adversities continue to mount, I am thankful to say, "At least I still have her."

No one asked for this just as in all adversities. No one asked for a child to be born with spina bifida or cerebral palsy. Dementia or Alzheimer's were never part of the goals for life nor did anyone hope that they could someday care for a loved one riddled with cancer or any other debilitating disease. Mental illness and chemical imbalances were not planned any more than my wife waking up one morning and planning an accident or for that matter, two. On the contrary, what was now her burden was as much mine. What confronted her confronted me. It goes with the turf. She didn't ask for it any more than I did. But now the words, "Til death do us part" took on a whole new meaning that involved addressing the adverse effects that accompany her plight. It is daily, if not moment by moment; and it is not easy.

Adversity and the Place of Palliative Care

Adversity is rarely described by the terms, pleasant, enjoyable, fun or welcomed. More often than not, terms like anguish, loss, pain and grief latch on to those faced with adversity. As we have already seen, the immediate effects of adversity stir and challenge a man's inner, mental and spiritual state. Yet, adverse physiological elements are often simultaneously tearing at its victims. Pain is real, and irritated nerves draw attention to the fact that something is out of order. Even for the caregivers, the myriad of unpleasant emotional states arrive, clashing with the need for a clear frame of mind that will be needed in making decisions that provide care and comfort for a loved one.

The more recent term used to capture what faces caregivers is the term, "palliative care." This refers to the care provided for those whose affliction is incurable. Consider those people who care for someone with a physical or sensory disability. Then add the number of those who care for terminal patients, or those facing mind-altering situations or emotional problems that require constant care. In most of these cases caregivers operate in a scenario where a cure is non-existent.

Remarkable medical assistance provided by dedicated acute care physicians and assistants has arrived in Dawn's life, bringing relief and hope. Yet, as our home has experienced, there has been no cure, and, as in so many cases, there is no foreseeable cure this side of heaven. For us, a healing is not necessary to validate our faith, and the amazing presence of

59

our Lord has brought a joy and peace that has inspired many. Endurance, indeed, has been provided by Him, and as Dawn has shared with many, when she contemplates all the suffering Christ did on her behalf, her suffering is nothing, if it brings for Him the opportunity to use her in sharing the marvelous love of Christ. Ultimately, our rest in the Scriptures assure us that someday in a place called Heaven, "He will wipe away every tear from their eyes. There will be no more death or mourning or crying or pain."[43] For that day we await.

The difficulty lies in this momentary time frame that occupies life today. Here we grapple with the ill effects of adversity, which most often includes pain. From the opening scene in Dawn's life on that disastrous day in 1966, the effects were instantaneous for her and those who would become her caregivers. Though a seeming recovery would be reached, the later devastation and damage from those complications, as well as the second wreck, turned my wife's care into a palliative state. Maybe crises tend to be titled crises because of the adverse nature that permeates the atmosphere of all involved. Life is altered as one knows it, and this applies both to the disabled and those who bear the load as caregivers.

If one is to learn to be, or care for, the caregiver, it means one must understand each caregiver's situation. As we enter into this section on the adverse effects of crises, I have (with Dawn and my family's blessing), opted to "drop my guard," in hopes that it can help bring understanding to some of what caregivers encounter. Each adversity is unique, however. What accompanies one does not necessarily accompany the next, so as a word of caution: Don't superimpose upon every caregiver that their world will face all that follows. It very well may end up being true for them, but some caregivers have disabled spouses who do not sense the adverse effects of chronic pain. That is a big issue, even as one disabled lady told me, "I may have been crippled for life, but I don't suffer like your wife." Still, other caregivers may find their circumstances filled caring for a child whose dependent condition creates so much more uncertainty. So what fits one caregiver may not fit at all for another.

It should also be understood that the real life stories I share are just snippets of the reality faced over time. A story most likely occurs on a regular basis as opposed to a one-time event. Each illustration reflects a host of other expressions that could have been used to make the point meant to be explained. Adversity is referred to as adversity, because it engulfs more than just the event. It brings lasting effects that mark life, long-term.

As we start, we will begin to recognize some of the adverse effects upon the caregiver personally, emotionally, and socially, and then we will move to the added marital and family effects (Chapter 7), which also add to the social and financial dynamics facing the caregiver. We will then end this section with some clarification to the spiritual dilemmas that potentially arise.

The Adverse Effects of a Disability for the Caregiver

Learning to Live in the Disabled Person's World

Effective caregiving from the very onset involves entering and seeking to understand, as well as possible, the disabled person's new world. From the opening moments, the caregiver will sense his own world being pushed into a corner, as the adverse effects hit one after the other. The moments give way to the day-to-day experiences that solidify into a lifestyle with no apparent end in sight. With the dawn of each new day, the caregiver awakens to a friend, a relative, a parent, a child or as in my case, a spouse who lives in a world much her own. What would be seen as normal activity for an able-bodied person is no longer normal for the disabled person. They become absorbed by their limitations to accomplish even simple activities, such as preparing for the day. Minutes for you and me turn into hours for them.

This new reality begins to define the caregiver's world and requires the caregiver to seek to understand just what will be required of them. Pastor Molsberry, when referring to his disabled world, offers a general perspective which is worth understanding. He describes it this way:

"In spite of the variety of disabilities we live with, and the severity with which we experience them, still we share some common experiences. We have to claw our way into a world that is arranged and organized for people who can walk and see and hear. We tend to be hired at a rate that lags far behind the general public. We are four times more likely to be poor. When churches post signs that say 'All are welcome,' they may not be talking about people with disabilities who can't climb their stairs or hear their sermons or read their bulletins. Only in the last thirty or forty years has it dawned on anyone that the disabled community, sharing a common experience of stigma and discrimination, can rightly be seen as the largest minority group in the country."[44]

61

Now add the internal tensions stemming from our culture's infatuation with overcomers. "You can overcome,"[45] "You can do it," confronts many who wish that was so. Still many today think that medicine and hard work can make you better, but this is not always true.

In addition, the culture communicates that to be a success requires you to "be young, healthy, independent and financially able to keep up with the neighbors."[46] Success means you rise to the top, you overcome. Where do such thoughts put the person sitting in a wheelchair, whose spinal cord and neurological system has been so damaged that apart from a new body, no recovery will be found? Enter their world and there comes an immediate adverse clash with the social norms for success.

Please do not misunderstand what I write. My wife and many whom we know have overcome immense obstacles in their lives. Completely changing diets, dealing with the side effects associated with drug therapy, regimenting therapy in order to retrain the body to lost functions, as well as completely readjusting to lost physical abilities are but a few of the obstacles to hurdle. Hard work and endurance play an important part to all situations, but for my wife to put on her shoes still requires help. She needs props to get around. She cannot drive. Her pain levels can squelch a day's activities. The wheelchair can be difficult to get in and out of the car. Yet, do any of these deficiencies make the disabled person less of a person? Does their ineptness make them less valuable, because they are not productive in society's terms? Even for those who do overcome, is the overcoming what substantiates their place in society?

"Can I go to the grocery store with you?" she asked. Reading between the lines while looking into her petitioning eyes, I realized what was really being communicated was that she wanted to feel like she was part of caring for her family. "I would like to participate meeting the needs that will be a part of their every day. I would like to feel like I am contributing to the family."

Yet, I also knew that her requests meant that I would need to adjust my schedule, as she could only go during the warmer parts of the day. It also meant that a one-hour job would now take two hours. Pushing her in her wheel chair while I pulled a grocery basket behind me was always a sight, I am sure. However, living in her world, including her in routine activities, and seeing her smile when she found a good deal or purchased items that she knew would be appreciated by her family awakened us to a world that was so similar in desire for any of us, but so much more difficult for her to reach.

Caregiving and even understanding how to care for the caregiver demands a consideration of the disabled person's world, both in entering his particular world and being the one they need to meet his needs. Their care will vary to the degree the disability allows, but the limitations, the personal, legitimate desires and our culture's imposed measurements for success cause a unique pressure, not only for the disabled but those who carry the title, "caregiver."

Heart-Wrenching Losses and Gut-Wrenching Anguish

A trip to the Oregon coast provided many wonderful memories for our family. Tillamook, Canon Beach, and Lincoln City along with Fort Clatsop, Fort Stevens, Depot Bay and Seaside all carry unique highlights that can be resurrected in minutes. Add a walk on the beach with the cool evening breeze blowing in your face, the gorgeous sunsets, and a warm cup of coffee while the surf rolled across the sands in front of you, and the memory banks were full. Hand-in-hand while dodging waves or step-by-step through the tide pools, the enjoyment of recalling such events, warms our hearts.

Then there was the family cabin on Mt. Hood, which, to this day draws the family back to enjoy and now share with their children the host of activities that filled their younger years. Nestled in the middle of the national forest at the base of Zig Zag Canyon between two mountain streams, the time we spent at the rustic 1920's cabin brought many memorable moments. Hikes along the old Oregon Trail or up to favorite fishing holes known only by locals, plus games and even puzzles with the hot cocoa and coffee were priceless. The morning chills, which were an everyday occurrence even in the summer, were broken only by the crackling wood burning in the wood stove. Family gatherings with siblings and cousins filled the atmosphere with laughter and stories that were most always marked with smiles.

Yet today, those events are limited. A trip to the beach finds Dawn's highlight just being able to be there. No walk on the beach for her, and as for me, most walks are taken alone where the majesty of God's creation refreshes my own personal state. The same is true for the mountain, where, for the most part, I go alone to get my writing done. The memories are refreshing and reawaken thoughts and smiles to my face. But because the mountain chill sets off nerves in Dawn's legs that only inflame those same nerves into channels of excruciating pain, I cannot blame her for not wanting to go to the mountain.

"Let's take a walk," are words that are not expressed. "Let's go out to a ballgame," for her meant sitting in the car alongside the field of play, in a place reserved for her to be able to see. If people who knew us came over to visit, which was often, the venture was at least made worth the effort, as prized interaction with others compensated her efforts.

When one loses mobility and contends with pain just by happening to be hit by a breeze, the losses are measureable. Yet, even the preparation for such an event entailed much more than throwing stuff in a nap sack and rushing off on a spur of the moment. For her, it required carefully, considered plans that entailed certain preparation and timely acts, just for her to be comfortable enough to try.

The most excruciating effect that tore at my heart, flared up with having to witness the anguish that riddled Dawn's body. Being around people often was a therapy for us, as her being occupied with people seemed to mask the pain even from her. Yet, as people left, and her body became aware of what had been done, the only persons there to see it and help were her caregivers, in particular, me. It was a heart-wrenching price to pay, but it was a normal occurrence.

In the early times of her disability, optimism carried me through the ordeal. Over the years that optimism slowly eroded, especially after the second accident. Loss of her mental clarity due to drug therapy and expressions of pain that created times of helplessness and hopelessness all had their erosive effects on both of us. Gut-wrenching are those moments when I realized my limitations and those of the medical field. Even more crushing was the realization that I personally have no restorative ability whatsoever. The helplessness can overtake one, and the emptiness can find its only solace in those quiet moments where the tears could flow privately with God.

Shattered Dreams and Exhaustion

Another personal side effect extends into the caregiver's career and passions which, for us, took a direct hit. Our work focused on restoring and establishing homes that would honor the Lord, and our family ministry that found us helping families on a regional scale. Yet with each surgery, our responsibilities and commitments beyond our own community slowly diminished and finally came to an end. God chose to use others now, which was His privilege. Yet with each step backwards, it seemed that a dream was shattered, and the sense that we had been beaten by an unseen enemy was as real as my wife's disability.

I was still involved in doing the work I loved as a pastor, though Dawn's needs required my attention and limited some of my extra community involvement. The counseling, addressing crisis issues with members of the church and community, as well as the teaching responsibilities were still every day. Yet, as my public commitments decreased, due in part to my added activity of caregiving, so were some of our personal dreams set on a back burner.

Then came the subtle and not-so-subtle discriminations which often times made their way into our hearing "I don't know if we are getting the best bang for our buck by having him as our pastor anymore. We should be talking to him about stepping down so we can get someone else."

One colleague of mine shared how he was actually forced to step down following his wife's ordeal with M.S., as the church could offer no help. On the other hand, another expressed how fortunate he was to be part of a larger church and denomination that saw to his disabled wife's and his wellbeing. That is not always the case. So in short, all my education, all my experience and success in the same community for over 25 plus years did not stop some couch critics from finding ways to express their short-sightedness toward us, who already had enough on our minds. Welcome to the world of disability!

While we encountered my wife's hardships, life went on. We had four children, and three of those chose to marry within two years. With the added care and finally the deaths of three of our parents plus Dawn's two brothers, within a four-year spread, our load and sorrows increased. Remember, I was the pastor that they turned to. Also, since I had to perform tasks that used to be Dawn's, found me often late at night, after teaching a class or attending a meeting, scurrying off to the grocery store or drug or hardware store to obtain our family's needs. Yet, this is the way it was. This was the nature of our household. This is what our everyday was like.

Constant demands, plus hard decisions, especially when they involved another hospital trip or revised medications, had a way of wearing on especially me. Each surgery meant that another vacation would be spent as a bystander at a hospital, usually in Seattle which was 100 miles from home. Late nights finishing my work or addressing the household needs filled my times. This often found me becoming exhausted and hoping that it would soon pass. Yet once again, the palliative care my wife needed, meant that there was no end in sight, just further adjustments.

False Guilt, Debilitating Grief and Anxiety

Exhaustion brought on by the constant demands goes hand-in-hand with caregiving. Then guilt, plus its cousins, grief and anxiety, add to the personal toll measured out upon the caregiver. Even though their journeys begin while they are reeling from being personally shattered, they find themselves thrown into a setting where they are called upon to make decisions that affect loved ones. These decisions require the need to understand the disabled person's condition. In my case, fortune had it that my wife was in the medical field and had a medical understanding far superior to mine. She understood terms used by medical people and already had verbal exchanges that involved words that I could not even spell. Yet for me right from the beginning, the mental readjustments were demanding.

The need to be available compelled me to be "present tense." Being responsible to provide what she needed to start her day, make it to a physical therapy session or meet with medical people all were added, as we learned how valuable two sets of ears were to provide clarity. Day after day, week after week, surgery after surgery, the responsibility to be involved brought an end to what many refer to as "spare time."

When the medications reached the point of affecting Dawn's mental state, I needed to exercise caution in how much information I shared with her. One friend confided how he learned that love does not always share everything. If the information would harm his disabled spouse or create unnecessary pressure, then why share it? Love doesn't do that. Love learns to bear the load.

Spinal cord injuries can sometimes be accompanied by paranoia. Matters could seem under control one minute; but several hours later, she could become fearful or guilt-ridden for becoming such a burden upon others. Information that was meant to keep her informed had now fueled within her a diminished sense of value that generated a false guilt. Sadly, I was the cause.

In those moments, frustration welled up within me and guilt overtook me because I had caused such discomfort for her. Already tired, the added guilt found me crying out about how unfair the setting was, not only for her but for me. On more than one occasion, I said, "O.K. Lord. I have learned the lesson, and patience has been gained; so You can stop. You can remove this."

Time has a way of making you smarter and less prone to succumbing to the false guilt that attacks you, but I still hurt when my actions lend to her momentary discomfort.

"Hope deferred makes the heart sick," says the writer in Proverbs 13:12. As the effects kindled by a disabling adversity begin to be realized, the caregiver, especially when it is a spouse, finds how true this proverb comes to life. Shattered hopes and dreams, the loss of companionship, security and even intimacy, along with the financial pressures and diminishing hope for recovery are all experiences which one would not even want to dream up; but now they are real.

The envisioned ideals and dreams that accompany the words, "I do," start to resemble a child's wishful thinking at Christmas. Recognizing the deferred hope or grief now adds to the caregiver's plight. What was anticipated and valued becomes replaced by this exhaustive emotional state of grief that surfaces in the form of shock, denial, anger, resentment and bargaining that flows from those affected by the loss.

Some might question the idea of "Bargaining." In an interview with Pastor Brunner, from Lake Oswego, Oregon, he tells about how, on the first Christmas at his new assignment, his wife Glenna who had already been struck and affected by M.S., had a grand mal seizure and viral encephalitis. Though her life was spared, her voice was taken away. After further diagnosis, a CAT scan revealed that there were sections of her brain that were damaged and would never recover, including much of her short-term memory. Pastor Brunner said,

"One miracle of God, though, occurred just about four weeks later in a return visit to my former church. Because of the damage to her brain,

Glenna was unable to remember many of the songs that we used to sing together. So I bargained with God, though you shouldn't. 'Lord, if you will give me her voice back, I will not complain or gripe for the rest of my life.' On the trip I asked her to sing with me (knowing full well she couldn't), and I just began singing all the songs we used to sing together. Then out of her mouth came the words in answer to my prayer that, for me, would be so meaningful."[47]

Tears filled his eyes as he told the story and a little laugh, as he confided that he had found himself honoring his commitment to not complain. I must admit our conversation left me realizing that I stood before a man who modeled a life worth following. The point is that grief finds expression with inadvertent bargaining that, in actuality, comes really close to exposing the honest truth. Grief also involves moments of frustration and anger over our blocked goals for life, and, as these effects well up from within, it will fall upon the caregiver to take the time to lament and grieve.

The caregiver must understand that legitimate dreams and desires have been crushed and that these losses do not equate with being selfish. Simultaneously, anxieties created by the unknown outcomes also require time to process, and that time is limited, as one's caregiving responsibilities beckon for any free moment. Nevertheless, the need for the caregiver to process grief and lament the losses is essential. This entails an honest cry time with God, as well as finding a trusted confidant with whom they can express their soul.

Being Alone and Lonely

When my wife required surgeries that took me to cities that were not our home, I found myself among scores of moving bodies, all seeming to know what they were doing and where they were headed. Life surrounded me, but truthfully they had no clue or concern for what took me there. Smiles and courteous nods that at least acknowledged my existence momentarily warmed my soul. During some of the extended hospital visits, there were those who inadvertently reappeared and struck up conversations, but even with all the people I knew and with the ability to make friends quickly or update family and friends via my cell phone, life at that moment sitting at the little table reserved for my breaks made me aware that I was very alone.

And it did not end there. It came home with me, where amidst all the household responsibilities and personal care that enveloped my time as a caregiver, the sense of being alone gave way to loneliness. For many caregivers and the disabled, they sense a loss that feels like abandonment. Activities and social involvements that saw friends stopping by or impulsively seeking me to join them on the spur of the moment became fewer and fewer or ceased to occur. Right along with that, the phone messages and request to join friends for an activity that would present a possible challenge for Dawn found me being left out altogether.

In short, due to the disability, relationships destabilized, in part because of the restrictions and limitations brought on by the disability. Time restraints that can constrict the disabled, often detoured invitations. Inconvenience also stopped people from developing relationships, as was expressed by one who felt put out because Dawn's condition required someone to transport her. If they wanted to interact, they had to come to our home. But others, who knew their homes were not disabled-friendly, went out of their way to accommodate what would be needed to develop a friendship.

Yes, there are people who would prefer this quiet, sedate lifestyle, but for "people-persons" with people-genes in their DNA, plus those who find loneliness a form of punishment, the sense of confinement over time is wearing. There is no one to blame for the emptiness of the moment because it comes with the turf, but for many caregivers and the disabled, when it becomes more of a regular occurrence, the relational or social losses begin to mount and a subtle form of rejection is experienced.

A Consuming Service within a Consuming Process

Let's not forget that the caregiver's main role has them consumed in service to another. In a culture that recognizes the top dog as the independent one who tells everyone what to do, how, then, does the confinement to being a caregiver act as anything more than being an anchor to one's personal objectives that would bring personal fulfillment?

The disabled also find themselves battling their thoughts as they try to make sense of their situation. Questions rage and at times even "present a struggle between reality and fantasy."[48] And all the time that disabled individuals take to adjust to their world, there, serving in the shadows facing struggles of their own, are the caregivers. For both it is a process, a time consuming process, where thoughts and questions surface, are squelched, and then resurface at a later time. It is a process that requires honesty with the facts and time to think, rethink, experience, handle any setbacks and then further time for further rethinking.

Therefore, in caring for the caregiver, one must recognize the uniqueness confronting them. They live in the shadows, but those shadows define their personal story. They live with one trying to process adversity's plight, while at the same time they face a process of their own. Questions also arise within the caregiver pertaining to the adversity of their loved one. Impulses, both legitimate and illegitimate, seek to find expression. Further complications set their needs on the back burner only to resurface when the difficulties are brought under control.

The Need for Help

The caregiver and those coming to the aid of the caregiver need to recognize that they, together, form a vital support team to the disabled person. Some who assist may only be temporary, as is common with those called upon to respond in the acute-care-state of the disabled person; but they are vital to the process. Yet, their time ends until the next acute-care necessity arises, and the responsibility rolls over to the primary caregiver and those who further come to help. Whether that primary caregiver be a parent, a spouse or a grown child, aid or help to them will be vital. "Teamwork makes the dream work," is an old saying I used on the ballfield as a coach. Truthfully, it applies just as much in a family successfully handling a disability as in any field of play.

The team captain comes by default to the primary caregiver, but the secondary caregivers, which involve family, friends, church associates, medical personnel and even newcomers to the household, all have a place. To recognize their place and to be willing to draw upon and even seek their assistance rubs against our independent ways, but the necessity of doing so far outweighs going it alone.

I can testify to the angels of kindness who entered my wife's life. Even now, I cannot express enough how appreciative I am for them and how they so tenderly taught me to accept their gestures of kindness.

70

The Need to Talk

Yet, what many find, whose life story involves living in the shadows of one rocked by adversity, is that like me, they don't recall speaking much about what they encountered. The reason, at least for me, was because I did not want to bother people with my problems. I knew Dawn's were so much more severe, and that I was on constant 24/7 call to be there for her. To whine about my minor stresses could only be seen as unloving and selfish, or so I thought.

Another reason I surmised was that since my work involved counseling and being available to people in their need, I did not want to present a picture that I was not available. I did not want people to think I was so tied up that they could not get the proper assistance they needed. As well, I wanted to go on with life and not have Dawn's issues be such a focal point. But, the truth be known, they were an issue. So, welcome to life in the shadows.

An underlying reason for my silence, I would later acknowledge, stemmed from the fact that I knew very few people with whom I could interact privately, who truthfully understood my complete scenario. Though my world involved public speaking and facing adversity as a pastor, it would be years before I would understand that people wished that I had openly addressed my situation more than I did. Looking back, I must admit that they were right. It would have helped immensely: All of us.

Early Arrival to Old Age

It is a realistic assumption that there are problems that will arise with a disability. Loss of mobility or bodily functions slows life down. In many cases, one could easily conclude that old age has arrived early, as the losses seem to pile up. On the flip side, disabling situations can produce what many come to value in their latter day experiences, namely a reprioritizing and authentic placement of values on relationships and what is truly important.

For those disabled at a younger age, this is often common; for within these individuals and their families, the placement of value upon relationships comes at an earlier age. Their desire to relate about matters of importance often finds a higher priority in their dealing with people. Though disability can most assuredly offer a major threat to relationships, it does not have to. Renee Lyons, Michael Sullivan and Paul Ritvo, in their work, Relationships in Chronic Illness and Disability, reinforce this idea when they suggest,

"There is also evidence that through even the most severe, life-threatening illness, social relationships can be preserved, effectively restructured and even improved... Illness (disability) has a way of removing the window dressing of everyday life to expose those elements that are of central importance. People often take stock of priorities, including the value they place on close relationships. Energy is reserved for people and things that really matter."[49]

Beth McLeod, from her own experience as a caregiver in the book, *And Thou Shalt Honor, the Caregivers Companion*, expresses that, because of caregiving, she "has been blessed with the opportunity to discover what really matters. I have been witness to a personal transformation in the midst of suffering. I have seen the spirit of humankind shine bright again and again."[50]

As simplistic as it may sound, living in a caregiver's world brings a reality check. Many tell of such an experience in their working in third world countries. Personally, life among the disabled, for any extended period of time, presents a similar, if not more profound, scenario. In this world, one learns that life is not easy and the difficulty that affronts the disabled and caregivers sooner or later reflects a normal part to the cycle of life. Yet, the importance of people as individuals and the relationships we share, the privilege of service, commitment, the value of being other-oriented and God-honoring, all rise on the priority list.

Uniquely, arriving early to old age, facing disability, or being a caregiver breaks the self-imposed protective walls we often build to escape or avoid conversations of a spiritual nature. Conversations about God, His values and His ways permeate and are often most welcomed, because life near the valley of the shadow of death brings the Great Shepherd into focus. Hope eternal becomes more than an ideology or a doctrine. It becomes real.

♥♥♥♥♥♥♥

The initial effects of any crisis carry the ability to alter one's life as they know it. This applies both to the disabled and the caregiver. Sadly, the initial effects are usually adverse in nature, with the more adverse situations making the headlines in the news media. Yet when the media runs to its next story, and the disabled contend consciously or unconsciously with the adverse effects, the caregiver's journey finds his or her starting point clogged with unwelcomed sensations, unwanted adjustments and diverse challenges that do not necessarily have an end in sight. As we have already witnessed in the immediate effects to a crisis, the newcomer to this journey awakens to a plethora of questions that demand resolutions mentally, emotionally and spiritually. Yet, those immediate effects are only the beginning of what lies in store for the caregivers.

Life is altered. The caregiver's world, though much of it looks familiar, now stretches to include the adversity that has overtaken their loved one. Caregivers find themselves literally thrown into a school that requires them to understand and assist in providing the necessary care and comfort that will test their inner constitution to the fullest.

For the caregiver, heart-wrenching personal losses relationally and the anguish of witnessing a loved one suffer or struggle take a toll. Shattered personal and professional dreams require immediate adjustments and are only accentuated by the exhaustion and demands that now awaken the caregiver each day. In my case, the false guilt, debilitating grief, anxiety, sense of abandonment, plus the confinement and loneliness, wore upon me. Consumed in a process, needing another's assistance, plus realizing it meant I needed to come to grips with what makes me tick and find the strength to articulate it, found me making an early arrival to old age. Yet, I can still say, "At least I still have her."

Before we turn the page, I hope one can understand why I refer to caregivers as the "Unsung Heroes" of our day. In most cases, I find them to be remarkable people marked by compassionate spirits that quietly do what they know to be the right things to do. Generally speaking, this is what forms the foundation of whom they are. Is there any wonder why this country is what it is, when one reflects on the 63 million non-professional caregivers, if they have captured even just a little of that compassion?

♥♥♥♥♥♥♥

Chapter 7
What Touches One Touches All!

In the face of personal adversity, I found over and over again a strength of human spirit welling up from within me. Caregivers, just as the disabled, find a focused energy set on handling the circumstances that confront them. I found myself tirelessly there for my wife and wanting to do all I could to see a resolution. Simultaneously, adversity's tentacles quietly extended beyond my conscious concerns by wrapping their life-sucking ways around those for whom one has made a commitment to love, to protect and sacrifice their all: my family. I was not the only one hurting. A whole household was left waiting and wondering.

"When one member of a family is disabled… it is as though the whole family is crippled."[51] As one family therapist noted, "Families can be likened to a baby's mobile that hangs over a crib. When one of the objects on the mobile is touched, all of the other objects are disturbed."[52] There is no escape; it is beyond one's control. Slowly, the primary caregiver comes to realize that what touches one, touches all.

We caregivers find ourselves standing on the first corner to understanding puzzling events. Yet now, we are not alone. Our tear ducts for sure have emptied, but now our hearts begin to rip open as even more adverse effects crash into those whom we dearly love. Domestic issues, affecting the marriage and each child separately, economic loss, professional misfortune, and what would seem to be even a loss of God, add to a growing list that painfully lies waste to each of us. Our personal strain multiplies, and all we can do initially is watch as adversity's effects plow into all who helplessly stand in its pathway.

Adverse Effects upon the Caregiver's Family

In August of 1991, I stepped into my wife's recovery room from her surgery in the second wave of surgeries focused upon her crippled back. Word had it that the surgery was a success in that the trauma cyst that was growing within her spinal cord had been shunted, which would allow it to drain. Though the prognosis was good, the surgical effects were alarming. Sitting beside her bed, her concerning words drove home the seriousness of her condition. "I can't move my right leg."

She had come out of the surgery but she was paralyzed on her lower right side, as apparently nerves in the spinal cord were damaged. Where her nerves were deadened, my nerves came alive with shock and disbelief. As I left the hospital later that evening, I screamed in silent denial, even though no one heard it but God and me.

Over the next few weeks, medications were added to her daily diet that brought noticeable side effects, which made her body swell. Once again, I was all the more awakened to the fact that my precious, precious wife's condition was serious. Thoughts of her mortality battled within my soul, and frustration voiced its silent demands of God.

The loneliness pierced my heart, but as the adverse effects continued to mount, I found myself plodding through unfamiliar ground, while familiar voices were asking genuine but strange questions.

"Daddy, is Mommy going to die?"

"Is she ever going to walk again?"

As adults, we might put off such thoughts and offer a quick, "NO, NO." But from a child's perspective, the questions were as real as life. Four children ranging in age from eight to 15 years, sensed the gravity of their mom's plight. As the discouraging news became ever more real, and the questions from extended family, close friends and the community found us continually rehearsing the setting, the seriousness grew even more noticeable.

Wanting to deflect the exaggerated force that accompanies the repeated rehearsing of her condition with well-meaning friends, meant a constant guard on my attitude which I knew influenced the whole home atmosphere and thereby the family's sense of security. The desire to protect came naturally, but the need for all to be informed was essential. Experience and understanding offered much to bolster my confidence, as I again would find in the repeat surgery on her spine in 1995. But then came the surgery of 1997, followed shortly thereafter by another in early 1998, following the second accident. This time the effects were even more obvious, as she came home confined to a wheelchair, as well as extreme pain and an intense drug therapy. This time, she would come home to four young adults, ages 15 to 22. They understood, without a word. They sensed the dilemma, and they felt it, as they would later unveil.

Impaired Family Activity, Peer Discrimination and Hidden Fear

Physical disability in a mother impairs family activities and sparks fears. Again, touch any hanging piece of a decorative mobile and the whole mobile moves. Touch a family member, and all the family is affected. Pastor's family or not, the impairment and loss due to the disability extends much further than to just the disabled person.

The next few stories I share were taken directly from our family's contribution to research that constituted my doctoral thesis. In the case of our family, we asked for their willingness to participate. A questionnaire addressing what it was like to be the child of a disabled parent, plus a group interview, were given to them. The ground rules surrounding the interview involved me asking questions and letting them respond without any rebuttal whatsoever. I may have sought clarification later, but what I wanted to know was how it really was for them. So, with my mouth closed and my tape recorder on, I listened and now share what they encountered. Please note that at the time of their response they were between the ages of 27 and 34 and they had had much time to process the effects the disability imposed upon them.

A disability means that all are affected, but when life revolves around the disabled person, it can easily breed resentment when a family member's personal desires conflict with the added responsibilities connected to caregiving. Being amongst the ranks of caregivers can be and usually is exhausting, especially when you are a family member and the disabled one is your mother. Though "at first, children may love responding to requests, later on they'll resent it, if they feel they've become the errand runner."[53] This was truer for the younger children who, when the older ones left home, found the caregiving chores escalate.

In one situation one of our caregiving daughters, while dealing with a disabled and highly medicated mother, found herself in tears as her place, she felt had changed "from daughter to that of almost being a sister." This kind of stress is difficult and exhausting and best expresses the true meaning of selfless ministry, which now marks their lives.

One child shared that from the earliest recollections of Mom, "I remember thinking Mom was physically fragile,"[54] while another notes that, "where we were involved in sports, playing outside, some hiking, fishing, etc, Mom wasn't able to do many of those things to the extent she probably would have enjoyed."[55] "The weakness, I think, was we couldn't do other things that were fun together that were physical, that we could do earlier in our life, like hikes and camping."[56]

The truth was the disability left her unable to be overtly active. As a result, "It was annoying, frustrating, and eye opening, but for sure it revealed to me a bit of my own selfishness."[57] Still another responded,

"I was kind of embarrassed. I remember watching other kids who had parents involved in the classroom, but Mom couldn't. I was jealous for a mom to be able to go on field trips, but again she couldn't. At the same time, I didn't want her around, due to the fact that she had a cane. I was embarrassed, and I didn't want people to know what was wrong or face all their questions and staring."[58]

The stigma associated with having a disabled parent was felt more when they were in the company of their peers. For the children and their mother, many shared activities were impossible or at best complicated. Making lifelong memories between themselves and their mother was now relegated to trying to describe to her what they had personally encountered without her there. Sure, there were some events that they could enjoy with her present. These were special, but many events were impossible and, thus, the shared experiences were lost.

Hidden fears and even anxiety fostered by uncertainties also lingered in the backdrop as expressed by one child. "As I started high school, I always feared that Mom would die. It wasn't death that I feared, but the fact of having to go through life without a mom. I was scared of the responsibilities I'd face if Mom died, for I saw myself having to take on her role."[59]

Awareness to an Unjust, Unfair World

Physical disability alerts children to an unjust, sinful, selfish world. To say that handling a disability is easy or that joy or sorrow filled every moment would be a total misrepresentation of our lives, for that matter with anyone who has wheeled or crawled along these paths.

Every day meant every day, and long-term meant a long time. One driver accidently loses control of his truck, and a young lady spends years recovering from this mistake. One drunk selfishly drives down the road, crashes into a vehicle, and maims this same young lady for life, robbing her family of her involvement and her resources. Regardless of what many may think, life handling a disability is not easy. Every surgery, every treatment, every therapy, every new drug and every infection wore us all down.

As one child expressed, "Every surgery affected my heart more than anything. It was scary to have Mom go into surgery, not sure what could happen."[60] In short, the family became aware of the ugliness and pain created from the sinful ways of a selfish world. It seemed unfair that they continued to reap the consequences of others' actions, but its effect upon the family reverberated continuously with the realization that life was neither fair nor just, apart from God.

At the same time, each of them learned the beauty that arrived when the angels of kindness showed up at the door. These people marked the lives of each child. Still, the inability to prevent them from the onslaught of hurt weighed upon me as a parent, as I witnessed their struggles and heard the anguish they felt for their mom.

The Loss of Quality Time and Disrupted Role Function

Few realize the added responsibilities confronting not only the primary caregiver, but the family, when a spouse/parent goes down. Picking up all the pieces requires a consumption of the already-limited resources of time and energy that the caregiving spouse has left to give. Each child still needs a parent's constructive interaction, and when a parent like me is perpetually called upon to fulfill his place as caregiver, that quality parental interaction can be lost.

In settings like our home, where their mom's condition could vary from point to point in the day, the need for flexibility became constant. Family activities that normally saw Dawn actively involved, such as preparing a meal, often required someone taking over or assisting. Even a simple task like going to church was a hardship, as her body did not always cooperate. Unplanned bodily mishaps would often occur, which lent to many delays and the need to readjust one's attitude before entering the church with a mindset to worship.

Family vacations were indeed limited, especially due to the fact that there were nine surgeries over the ten-year spread of 1991 to 2001. Tack onto this the added limitations created by her disability and the financial burdens that accompanied us that found us broke or taxed to the hilt, and one can understand the pressure that families such as ours encountered. In short, family recreation declines.

When one lives in a world of constant adjustments and change, a sense of security and stability can be somewhat illusive. Imagine each child with each surgery wondering what was going to happen. Imagine not really having even a dad at home for a period of time during that whole episode, because he was a hundred miles away caring for their mom and his best friend. Remember no one asked for this. Thank God, we still had her, but the adverse effects that reduced quality time supplied a source of instability to our home.

The older youth, especially when they reached their teen years, were given the roles of caring for the younger siblings when I had to be absent, due to surgeries, appointments and the like. The chores still had to be done every day. School had to be attended, and even with great guidelines given to them all through the years, the placement of older siblings in control led to potential crises amongst the siblings. Though they were only a phone call away, they made the choice to hang onto matters rather than unload them on a weary dad whose plate was already full. Did it contribute to their momentary instability? How could it not? One daughter put it this way, "Maybe some of the sibling gripes could have been talked out rather than carrying on into later years. We love each other, but sometimes we were not able to figure out how to relate, because we each took everything differently."[61]

In hindsight, I must admit I should have known all this, but when I returned home and thought all was well, I did not try to uncover things. There were situations in which we did take the time to talk through to a solution. Yet, there were many that I missed, not because I was an incompetent father, but because I had to attend to the needs of my precious wife. I simply could not "handle" it all, but if I had it to do over again, I would have pressed for the cold hard facts of what really happened in my absence. I would have recognized that the personalities would clash, just because they did when I was present. Personally, I know I could have done better.

As this section about the adverse effects upon our family winds down, I am reminded of how, at the end of the third movie in the "Lord of the Rings" trilogy, when evil had been defeated and the rightful King was crowned before the whole world, everyone bowed, even the four Hobbits who had such a great part in bringing an end to evil's attempt to crush the world. At this point the scene shifted to the king approaching the four hobbits, and gesturing them to stand he said, "You have no reason to bow to anyone." Maybe our children were not all master communicators, but I can admit if ever there were those whom I personally number among the true unsung heroes of this world, it is Matt (Laura Jane), Beth (Travis), Josh (Karen) and Marjie. My hat goes off to them, as do my praise and thanksgiving for them. I thank the Lord that I have been fortunate enough to be a part of their lives. Their kindness and help for their mom and me have been and are still absolutely overwhelming, and they will never hear me express anything but thanks for the mature and loving ways they continually help. In my book they stand tall for the compassion and kindness that have come forth from them, even to this day.

Our focus so far has been upon the immediate and adverse effects that appear to engulf a family when adversity strikes. If we are not careful, the mere sharing of such complexities can discourage those who are presently entering into such scenarios by painting a picture that only heartache awaits us in the future. I am here to say, please do not lose heart at this point. It is no sin on anyone's part to have missed addressing a problem or to find the adverse effects and heartfelt questions have been overlooked. Even with all the difficulties and adjustments that were required, it is amazing how the creative juices did not stop flowing. In fact, the experiences probably pumped it up a notch, as Dawn's condition required all of us to think a little more about how we could include her in activities, because that is what families do.

Adverse Effects upon the Caregiver's Marriage

If the effects on the family and the personal effects were not enough, the interpersonal downspin between the husband and wife can also be very affected by the complications brought on by disability. I want to state up front that I have saved one whole chapter to express how we handled our marriage. Our approach to marriage focused not so much on role function, which is most common among the traditional mindsets of many people, but on being best friends together serving our Lord. We married because we were best friends and we felt that we could do so much more together in service to God and others by being married, which for us ended up being true. This friendship was nurtured and maintained as the crux of our relationship. It was not just random thoughts, but stemmed from a study in the Scriptures that gave us a fresh look at the Master's Dream for building an atmosphere of a lasting friendship in our marriage. Our "hallmark marriage" focused upon our being best friends, that framed our thinking around the question, "How can I help you?" Every day there was a desire to be together and a willingness to do just about everything together. There is so much more but I will save that for later. so

That being said, in our scenario 19 years had passed from our wedding day to that crushing first back surgery in August of 1991. We had time to establish the purpose between us that formed the hub of our thinking and actions as a couple. We had built the friendship which created an atmosphere within our home that made it a place we and others enjoyed. I enjoyed coming home, and we enjoyed growing together as best friends should. It did not become some kind of role or duty to fulfill, but an enjoyment that would be tested to the fullest in the years following the adverse effects of her surgeries and disability.

A Miscarriage of Marital Hope and Dreams Leading to Depression and Bitterness

Once again the proverbial writer finds his ancient words striking a cord, "Hope deferred makes the heart sick."[62] As one by one the dreams and marital hopes that framed our lives together were seemingly dashed, there arose the potential to fill that void with a life-sucking bitterness or an overwhelming depression. Tough as we may be and as strong as we think we are, these merciless emotional states can eat away at our very souls, as well as the relationship, if we allow them to take root.

As a pastor I have watched families face the finality of a loved one's battle with a deadly disease. Time may allow us the sense of feeling prepared for that inevitable day when loved ones close their eyes to this earth, but in their departure the finality evokes a consuming grief that has to be one of the hardest emotional states a person can encounter. The reason is simple. Finality is just flat-out hard to handle, primarily because we sense its permanence. Someone valuable and loved is gone from this world, permanently. Hopes and dreams are dashed, permanently, and when we think we are prepared, we are shocked to find our loss feels overwhelming.

In the same vein, because of my wife's disability, many of our marital hopes and dreams were extracted from our thoughts, permanently. To say it did not hurt would be untrue. Dawn used to love it when we would wedge into our schedule time to putter in her garden or prune her flowers. How many times, though, after the disability, do I remember coming home primed to get her fingers dirty only to find her tucked away in bed trying to get her pain under control?

On more occasions than I can count, I would arrive home from a full day to find no dinner, and no thought as to what we were to have for dinner, leaving me to pull up my shirt sleeves and jump in. It does not sound like much, but when the incidents add up one upon the other, they take their toll upon one's ideas of marriage. We could not do what we were used to doing. Even the pleasantry of cooking together and talking over the day's activities became less and less. Her condition stole those moments from us. A small thing maybe, but for sure it can be subtly erosive to a relationship.

Small dreams that had seen us develop a ministry to help families that extended regionally throughout the Northwest and Western Canada offered dreams, not only for us, but the team assembled to work with us. Yet, following the second wreck, those dreams and our connections nationally faded. Teaching and encouraging church leaders was a blast. Making friends around the country was rewarding, but so were the little excursions that accompanied each trip and made for wonderful memories with my beloved wife. Now, those thoughts are only history, and any foreseeable memory making experiences are illusive.

The awareness that our marital hopes and dreams had been stolen permanently made each encounter with the past or any lost activity and dream seem like we were standing at a crossroads. Pity and sorrow waited with open arms to welcome us down the pathway of depression and bitterness. But that bitterness was self-inflicted, stemming from the realization that someone has robbed us of what we considered to be legitimately ours.

The finality to the miscarriage of hopes and dreams presents a battle to which one must learn to adjust, and we will address this in the coming chapters. In my life, even as the losses crashed into my consciousness, the simple truths that, "She didn't ask for this," and "At least I still have her," both served to anchor my mental state by giving me the convictions that pulled us together. Just as all my questions for God were not answered as of yet, I knew that the loss could be creatively replaced once we were allowed to assess our remaining capabilities.

The Unmet Legitimate Needs Reserved for Marriage: Companionship and Intimacy

Shattered hopes and dreams often find caregivers busy with the added activities of providing the care needed by their spouses. Being busy doing and doing has a way of crowding out one's honesty with the heart's cry oftentimes until the pain hits, revealing the symptoms of a heart failure. Uniquely,

Longings for Security & Significance

Security   *Significance*

each human being is made in the image of God and comes into the world with innate, legitimate longings which are expressed as compelling needs or natural, inborn impulses that comprise the core to our hearts. The first is that of security or knowing that I belong. It surfaces in man's innate desire to be loved and secure. As an inborn impulse, this quest for security and love seeks for a meaningful relationship and identity, in which love and security are sensed and communicated. It seeks the safe embrace and convinced awareness of belonging and "being totally loved without needing to change in order to win love. It longs for a love that is freely given by another, that was not necessarily earned, and therefore something that one can rest will not be lost."[63] The second inborn impulse is that of significance, worth, impact or knowing where I fit in this life. It surfaces in man's fundamental longing to know one is worthwhile and what one does brings a meaningful impact on one's world, especially if that impact is upon another person.

It entails one's personal sense of value and purpose and acts as the source of enjoyment and fulfillment when expressed or accomplished. It seeks the realization that, "one's engagement involves a responsibility or cause that is truly important, and the results of which will not evaporate with time but will leave a lasting legacy, even if possible, for eternity."[64]

By God's initial design, one key primary social relationship intended to provide those unmet legitimate needs centered on the establishment of an interdependent, marriage relationship between a man and a woman, which brought a meaningful security and impact for both the man and the woman. This marriage relationship was formed in the freedom of interdependence, which encircled each of them in an atmosphere of strong affection, respect and loyalty with a person designed to be their best friend. At the same time marriage offered a meaningful companionship, sense of value, worth and impact as a couple moved in forming and experiencing together the accomplishments and enjoyments that accompany this unique union.

Yet, in the aftermath of a life-altering adversity, any marriage will be tested to the fullest as it contends with the loss of companionship, security and in some cases even intimacy. Add the mounting financial pressures and diminishing hope for recovery, and we have sensations which one could not even dream up, but now find as real. Marriage moves along in blissful ignorance until, as Beth MacLeod notes, "the unthinkable happens and the future blurs. Although it is illogical, illness or disability can feel like betrayal, a miscarriage of marital hopes and promises, and the well spouse grows angry that so many years have been taken away and resents losing control over life."[65]

The hard part following a life-altering adversity is that the envisioned ideals and dreams that accompany the words "I do" now resemble a child's wishful thinking at Christmas. Companionship can clearly be in jeopardy, sometimes more because of the ineptness in handling the adverse effects. Intimacy can be replaced by the added requirements necessary for survival.

Another precious facet to the marriage that can be greatly affected is the physical intimacy issue. Remember, that God was the author and creator of this very form of expression, so we need to see it as a gift to the marriage relationship from God Himself. Amazingly, when intimacy within marriage is the subject, thoughts usually revolve around the topic of physical intimacy or the sexual act. The truth though is that the sexual act is not a step that establishes deep intimacy, but rather it is one that presupposes it. Physical intimacy stands merely as the last step in personal exposure in a love relationship that has nurtured social, emotional, intellectual and spiritual intimacy.

Without these intimate associations in place the physical relationship slowly deteriorates into a self-centered use of one's mate for the sake of personal pleasure or a form of recreation. But when the physical union of a man and wife flows out of a committed friendship, it takes on a much larger meaning than just momentary pleasure. The purpose of the sexual relationship grows out of the deep personal desire to express love to one's mate, so that he/she experiences a sense of maximum personal fulfillment. For the man this means receiving a genuine sense of worth from his wife. For the woman this means receiving a real sense of security with her husband. Therefore, it becomes a form of important communication between a husband and wife, while providing a delightful recreation and a means of reinforcing their love relationship. Again, it is the last step in their communication that maximizes closeness, love and heart-harmony.

It is not uncommon when I sit privately with individuals who are asking about our situation to find them wanting to know about intimacy in our marriage. Though I find people are more intrigued by wanting to know how and what we do, I often find a graceful way to inform them that there are private issues intended for only a couple alone to discuss. This is true even for healthy marriages that do not face adversity. Physical intimacy happens to be one of those issues, contrary to the American way of thinking. I seldom find women, including my wife, who desire the intimate matters with their spouse to be public knowledge. Personally, I appreciate that stand and dearly appreciate not having people look with disdain that I do not publically flaunt what does or does not happen in the privacy of our friendship to each other. I will say that the one truth I have continually communicated to my wife is that she didn't ask for any of this pain and for sure I am not going to add any unnecessary additional pain for her to bear.

On the other hand, there are those whose neurological or physiological damages lead to limited activity or even total abandonment of any sexual activity. Place yourself in that situation, and ask yourself if that would be an adverse effect brought on by the disability. Absolutely, and its absence can be the first step backward and act as a primary cause for disintegrating a marriage or fragmenting a family. Remember, sexual activity or physical intimacy by God's intent presupposes an established personal intimacy and serves to express that intimacy.

Counselor, pastor and husband to a disabled spouse, Keith Korstjens, author of *Not a Sometimes Love*, addresses this issue by recognizing the fears that accompany the situation and the discovery process that becomes required for growth in this area of the relationship. He notes how he discovered, "That there had been a deep, unsatisfied longing within me all those months in the hospital just to be with her in the privacy we could experience... In this realization were the seeds of an understanding about the need a husband and wife have for each other that is infinitely more than sexual."[66] He goes on to conclude that, "I've found that a characteristic of sexual responsiveness is that it cannot remain at high levels of stimulation when fear or anxiety intrudes." They must be addressed privately by the couple as the ability to perform sexually is lost when fear permeates the atmosphere. What it reinforced was the discovery process, which is exactly what a couple must address.

Disability does not necessarily preclude that sexual activity is over. It is certainly affected, and this alone calls for the couple to build their friendship. Yet it is here that the best advice any of those I have met would conclude, and I would echo is: Addressing sexual activity requires that the couple talk, talk and talk some more. The sexual involvement of a couple in the confines of their marriage was designed by God. With the activity being negatively affected by a disability, couples need to interact. Where creative involvements can be utilized within the framework of acceptance by both parties, then the door opens to learn together. Still the end should be the same, in that sexual intimacy is designed as a final expression of their love they share with each other.

In many cases where the activity has been made impossible, the message still is talk, talk and talk. Remember that marriage is a ministry that does not always mean both the husband and wife are on the receiving end of ministering to each other. Sometimes ministry to each other affects only one, but the end will be understood by both that the best of what God had designed was met. If the stress and strain continues to heighten in frustration, then consulting with a trusted confidant or counselor is highly recommended. There is no doubt that left unaddressed this legitimate expression of love between a couple can escalate into a massive, blocked desire. This can lead to inappropriate and even damaging activity or hurtful expressions toward one's spouse that threaten to empty the relationship of any sense of security and worth. Ultimately, such internal emptiness that accompanies such actions leads to dismantling a marriage.

The Hidden Personal Impairments: Economic Drain, Network Reduction & Spiritual Disorientation

The unmet legitimate needs for companionship and intimacy add their adverse effects upon a couple. On one occasion I had gone home from the hospital only to have the staff call me to get my approval for a procedure for my wife. They informed me of the added cost to me personally, but saw it as important.

The facetiousness of the request left me chuckling upon hanging up the phone. The surgery was already into the hundreds of thousands of dollars. Everything I had beyond my insurance was spoken for. I could not even count as high as the amount I owed, so what was another little procedure? "Why of course," I responded with an affirmative, "Yes."

Consider for a moment what a major surgery, if not 14 major surgeries on her spine alone, would cost. Add to this the therapy and the durable equipment necessary just to get her up and going in the course of a day. Later years would add a colostomy and pelvic catheter to her daily necessities. Then add the pharmaceutical need, the necessary supplements to counter the adverse effects brought on by drugs, and we begin to capture the economic drain that can open beneath a couple. One word captures the typical outcome that faces the typical caregiver: Broke.

I have heard and encountered so many times the economic drain that impairs and weighs upon caregivers and their families. Insurance is a blessing, but insurance seldom handles everything that is needed, especially when the scenario involves someone who is older in age.

For a couple, the added pressures that can send them into a tailspin simply occur not so much in the immediate, but over time. People sense the difficulty facing a couple whose world has been rocked by disability. Inability to participate or respond to simple requests by well- meaning friends eventually results in an end to the requests. The inability to participate in activities because of the disability brings an end to requests coming at all. The outcome generally emerges finding the couple's social network noticeably reduced. As well, relationships destabilize as activities become numbered by the restrictions. If the personalities involved are already introverted, the adversity can now become the excuse to avoid people, which is just as true of the disabled/caregiver couple. In each case, the network is reduced.

One more side effect that quietly impairs a caregiver brews in the dark and serene moments when wrestling with God occupies their time. It is there that they have time to think and even wrestle through their thoughts with God, in hopes of making sense of the added burdens that now encumber their lives. "God, I don't understand. How could this happen? How am I supposed to handle all of this? How come it all seems so bleak with no end in sight?" As their heads lie motionless on their pillows with only the darkness in front of them, the sense of being caught in the silence can lead to a spiritual disorientation captured by one of the psalmists in one of his darkest laments. "Darkness is my closest friend."[67]

Consciousness of God still occupies our thoughts but the truth is that one's faith can be accompanied by a shaky sense of hope. Unfairness, frustration, being awakened to our unjust world, or even being disoriented about God's ultimate purpose in these types of crises in life are all very real challenges to the thinking mind. Prolonged pain wears one down, and the heart's cry for security and meaning generates the need for divine assistance in making sense of such events. Needless to say, a momentary spiritual disorientation fills these moments, and for many of us the rescue that overtakes us with what we call sleep is most welcomed.

♥♥♥♥♥♥♥

At this point I am personally glad this chapter is over. Like a wound reopened, the pungent reminders and simple rehearsal of the adverse effects expressed in this chapter brings tears welling up in my eyes. Caregiving is no simple task. One does not just wake up and find it gone, making it all the more real as a spiritual practice that places one's heart on display moment by moment. Overwhelming at times, but with each test of the heart's values and beliefs, a spoonful of compassion seemingly is added to vibrantly supplement this caregiver's inner man. Energy generated from God still proceeds to adjust my thoughts to the responsibilities at hand. There is no denying the source, as my own selfish nature would have responded so differently. It turns so many moments from a rote duty to an honorable practice that makes one conscious of a dynamic that cannot be scientifically explained.

Each daily encounter with adversity's draining ways beckons the caregiver to tap from God's storehouse of compassion. This compassion works its curing ways and then with time, as we shall see later, transforms the caregiver to being a source of such compassion. What one found to be such a chore, becomes a welcomed lifestyle.

As we move on, let me prepare you. Instant maturity on this journey is not easily found. Preparing for what lies ahead as a caregiver begins by getting a proper approach to the task. What this means was captured by Beth McLeod in her address to caregivers in general. You will need "...to see one's caregiving role as a calling rather than as an obstacle to achieving personal goals. Caregiving truly is a spiritual practice, a non-linear path with the heart."[68]

❤❤❤❤❤❤

Chapter 8
Behind Closed Doors

In a moment of time the caregiver finds his world reeling from the effects that have slammed into life. Sitting at her bedside and hearing a diagnosis carries an impact that leaves you a little out of balance. In each case, one common denominator fixes itself to the designated caregiver—the need to adjust.

Most often, it is not a choice of our own, but a happening that typically requires a response. With an accident, some adjustments come immediately. If it is packaged in a doctor's diagnosis, like with a disease, one might be able to ease into the adjustments. In the case of prolonged complications, as in a permanent diagnosis where recovery is not immediate, if at all, the word, adjust, becomes all the more fitting. To adjust, adapt, accommodate, alter, modify or rearrange—whichever word one wants to supply to the situation—implies evaluations, time and decisions. For the caregiver, it also happens to be the second corner piece in learning to handle puzzling events.

The first corner piece accentuated how adversity awakens us to the hidden and painful side of life. It also comes loaded with genuine questions that for the moment are kept at bay in order to allow the caregiver's full attention to be focused upon the essential question: how do I handle it?

In truth the philosophers and theologians can wait their time, as the pressing question that takes precedence necessitates the need for the caregiver to make the necessary adjustments.

Corner Piece #2: Adversity's Challenges Necessitate the Need to Make Adjustments To A New Normal.

When a person becomes disabled, a small task like a shower or preparing for the day becomes a time-consuming activity. Preparing meals and making sure the household chores had been done meant much to Dawn. When we made adjustments to handle the need, it reinforced the atmosphere that life, as we now knew it, was being handled. Complications due to infection, a small mishap, as well as the added daily pressures of Dawn's disability necessitated our making adjustments to become a way of life. Let's not forget there was the need to make time for physical therapy appointments, visits with the doctor, and late-night run to the pharmacy and grocery store that required our involvement. With each adjustment, the security she needed was accommodated and served to bring some semblance of order to her life.

For me, just as with many other caregivers, it was only a short period of time before the idea of palliative care transformed from an idea to a reality. The likelihood of a remedy began to fade, as the responsibilities for her care were added to my plate. In fact, what I, like most caregivers, came to realize is that the complications were like ocean waves that steadily and repeatedly crash against my world. Sometimes the tide was out, and the effects were minimal; but on other occasions, the high tide taxed my patience. A new diagnosis, a new complication or a new drug is all that was needed to prompt more adjustments.

Like the sounds of an old choo-choo train's groans as it pushes its way on its early morning run, each request sounds out its ominous challenge to "Adjust, adjust, adjust and adjust." With each chug, a whistle sounds. For we caregivers, we know that it means, "It is not about us." Over and over again the whistle sounds with each request. "It's not about us. It's more than about us." With each whistle another adjustment is made that few will notice, but the ones that do, are the ones that matter.

As the subtitle to the book acknowledges, this entire book seeks to provide an inside look at being and caring for caregivers. This means that one has to go behind the closed doors and address the challenges which the caregiver finds himself facing daily. What follows addresses five major adjustments that a caregiver at some point will encounter behind his own closed doors. These cannot be avoided, or they will compound problems. Each adjustment will often take time to work through just as the disabled loved one works through his or her adjustments.

I did not say, "change," which may come in time. I said the caregiver must adjust, merely because the situation demands it. As we shall see, change may or may not happen, but without the adjustments, there would be no hope. For now, let's focus upon what it means to adjust. What does adjusting necessitate or require of us?

Non-Negotiables of a Caregiver

Adjusting To Being A Caregiver...

1. Necessitates Our Embracing the Commitment to Care for the Weak

As caregivers, we soon learn we cannot run. We cannot feign that we do not hear or see, although we can try. It's all happening, whether we want to acknowledge it or not. By default, we as spouses, parents, children to a parent or family friends, become involved.

Adversity's effects, then translate into challenges that show up on our doorstep demanding attention and a need to make adjustments. This need to adjust introduces a ruthless pressure that tests the caregivers like nothing else. It often demands immediate action, no matter if one is prepared or not. It necessitates our embracing a commitment to care for someone in a weakened, but often frustrated state, who would just as soon not be in this condition.

I recall the first occasion in which Dawn was being released to my care from the hospital. She could not walk, as her right side was paralyzed. On another occasion she arrived in a body cast, and still another, her condition was marked by excruciating pain, heavy narcotics, a wheel chair and the fact that she could not walk. Each case, though progressively more difficult, found me reaching our driveway and accepting the fact that it was all now up to me.

Home typically means security and normalcy, but with a disability and chronic pain, the word, 'normal' becomes purely subjective. When someone comes home who cannot walk, and there are stairs to navigate to get into the house, normalcy is already in question, though, for Dawn, finding her own bed did help every time. Simultaneously, the innate desire for security sends out its sensors the moment the house becomes visible and again when the front door opens. Yet, the key to that house offering what the disabled person needs, rests squarely on the caregiver's shoulders.

I may not have had all the answers in those beginning years and trials. However, I knew enough to get an honest assessment of our situation, make the decisions I could, admit when I could not, and pursue the help from those who did know what to do. At the same time, I knew that my attitude set the atmosphere in which my wife would rest. Therefore, when I made the necessary adjustments, and, worked through each challenge with her, it reinforced the atmosphere she needed to be stable. My presence, my involvement and my willingness actually served to establish an environment that not only she needed but I knew God wanted established for her, anew and afresh. For that to occur, it required my commitment to care for her in her weakened state.

Dawn's crisis in each case was met with an assessment that included recognizing that her 4"10" frame with one side severely affected meant she could not get into the cupboards or cook. She needed medications every few hours, and that required a regulated discipline. Initially, all four kids needed to head off to school, and none of them drove yet. Still, there were four children who loved their mom and were more than willing to give a hand. However, it would not take long before the novelty wore off, and they began to feel that they were the errand runners, rather than sons and daughters.

Any visit with a therapist or doctor, I learned quickly, required my presence and assistance. I needed to hear the facts and ask the clarifying questions. It amazed me how one would think they were hearing something correctly; but by having another set of ears, they discovered that what was actually said differed.

Embracing the commitment to care, meant being willing to sacrifice. It meant that my energy would be expended and exhaustion expected. Resources would be consumed, and any ability to respond in a moment's notice would become part of our household lifestyle. Did anyone notice? Maybe, maybe not! But you will know, and, like any hero you will conclude, "It just seemed like the right thing to do."

Caring for the Weak Implies a Call to Encouragement

A key component to embracing our commitment to care for the weak finds expression by the caregiver becoming one of the chief encouragers in the afflicted person's world. Many will not know it, and even the disabled may only realize it over time. Yet, one of the reasons I admire the unsung heroes of our day is because it is most often the caregiver's encouragement behind closed doors that strengthens and energizes the disabled to press on.

When I speak of encouragement, I am not referring to just being positive. Encouragement most successfully proceeds from an understanding of the Godhead of the Bible, and I have found it most applicable as a husband, father, pastor, and as a caregiver. If ever there is a constructive exercise that serves to portray and enhance the commitment to the care of the weak, it is captured in this one quality known as encouragement.

Fear and rejection accompany so many in the face of crisis, and the one essential desire that of its victim is having a friend whose words ring with encouragement. Yet there is more to this word than what our western culture implies. When we see its meaning, we can understand why this concept, when enacted by a caregiver, has such a profound impact. The problem for us English-speaking people is that the New Testament Greek word actually needs four English concepts together to do justice to its meaning.

The main Greek word used for encouragement throughout the New Testament is the verb, παρακαλεω (parakaleo), or the noun, παρακλησις, (paraklesis). It literally meant to be called alongside someone, and depending on the context, its meaning expanded to include all four elements at once. So it is with encouragement! Each of the four expressions carries specific emphases that collectively give meaning to the word, encouragement. It is this meaning that I refer to when I attribute or speak of it as a key component for the caregiver's embracing of his commitment to care for the weak.

For the sake of teaching I usually present my case by drawing a square and speaking of the five sides of encouragement. I then present the four concepts captured by the word, to encourage only to finish by speaking of the fifth side, that connects the encourager to an inside source other than himself, namely God.

The Five Sides of Encouragement – On the Wings of a Dove

Side #1 - To encourage means... To strengthen, To put courage in – Hebrews 10:25; I thessalonians 5:11

The first side to encouragement means to strengthen someone or to renew strength that has been lost or deadened. It is to offer positive reinforcement via word or action that serves to motivate and empower a person to go beyond what he was able to do on his own. This may sound a bit simplistic, but the word carries within it the basic idea of putting courage into

The Five Sides to Encouragement

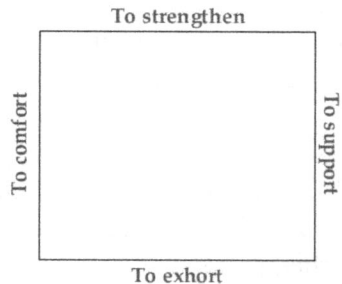

To strengthen

To comfort

To support

To exhort

someone. It involves more than just saying positive words, but also saying words from which the listener derives a sense of strength and courage.

In short, it means to strengthen or to put courage into someone, and it is used to address a person's fears, or to give him courage to carry on or overcome what causes him to fear. This quality, as well, implies that one knows the recipient plus their situation and what it will take to strengthen them or stir up in them the courage to accomplish a given task. Paul gave this command to the entire church in his writing to the Thessalonian Christians, "Therefore encourage one another, and build up one another."[69] The writer of the book of Hebrews calls us to "stimulate one another to love and good deeds,"[70] and we do that by being committed to come alongside people and offer those words that strengthen them in their daily battles in life.

At the same time to encourage someone meant to provide the affirmation or expressions of appreciation for another's actions or achievements. This same quality has an ability to renew strength that has been lost or deadened. When a disabled person loses heart, it is the encouraging words and actions that help to offer a brighter outlook. Encouraging words provide positive reinforcement via word or action that serves to motivate and empower a person to go beyond what he was able to do on his own.

Sometimes we think of courage as an extra burst of energy in which someone accomplishes a feat at tremendous risk or potential cost to themselves. However, courage is often nothing more than the continuous fulfilling of a given responsibility, especially those that we did not ask for. For over 20 years, the responsibility of being my wife's caregiver has had tough, as well as, easier moments. Between the years of 1997 to 2005 there were many moments when the responsibilities mounted, and the hope within her grew dim. The touch, the gentle hug, the straight talk and open hand to take her by the hand coupled to a smile or a short, "thank you," and the courage to carry on that emitted from these gestures became the encouragement that she needed, and vice versa. How many times I took her to her therapy sessions or meeting with doctors I cannot count. Yet the reason was simple. I wanted to hear what I could reinforce. Her mind often heard matters differently than I, and the clarity that I could bring offered her a renewed sense of strength.

Yes, there were times that I would love to have traded away my caregiver's button due to the fatigue. What made the difference? What enabled me to go beyond? What renewed the depleted energy? A gift in kind flowed through her hand as it grabbed hold of my hand bringing my eyes to catch a glimpse of her precious smile. Her "Thank you" was framed around the softness of her loving eyes that said it all. "I know I am not in this alone. I am so fortunate to have you as a husband." As my finger touched her lips, it was there that the reminder of the gift of life was sensed. "Sweetheart, you don't quite understand how fortunate I am to still have you." Encouragement goes a long way to bring the best out of another and the enjoyment of seeing her excel, personally, yielded enough of a reward in itself.

Side #2 - To encourage means... To comfort - II Corinthians 1:3-4

"Praise be to the God and Father of our Lord Jesus Christ, the Father of compassion and the God of all <u>comfort</u>, who comforts us in all our troubles, so that we can comfort those in any trouble with the comfort we ourselves have received from God."

The second word used to capture the full extent of this idea of encouragement is the word, comfort. This can also be interpreted as the word, consolation, (II Corinthians 1:3-4). This form of encouragement masters the use of being the late night helper when all is falling apart. It steps in to clean up a mess or offer the consoling words or actions that communicate hope (confidence) in the midst of loss or turmoil. This quality exudes genuine warmth often with a hug, while at the same time communicating through one's eyes an awareness that someone understands. "This momentary trial will end and good will come from it," can be heard by the mere presence of such encouragers. In these moments, or when words are at a loss, the encouraging caregiver creates an atmosphere about their dear one that offers the needed comfort for which their heart cries. In those moments, a consoling sense within one's soul rises to calm the troubled waters.

One's presence in a hospital room, a gentle cuddling of her broken body or grabbing of her hand and bowing in prayer, form only a few of the many ways that the comforter redirects his loved one's thoughts back in the direction of the master comforter. It always astounded me as to how the

Lord showed up to touch the deepest part of her spirit, as only He could. Indeed, He was a "very present help in trouble" and often as a caregiver, I found my involvement as being part of that wonderful experience.

Side #3 - To encourage means... To exhort - Romans 12:8; II Timothy 4:2; Hebrews 3:13

"...he who <u>exhorts</u>, in his <u>exhortation</u>." (NASB)

The third way of expressing encouragement portrays one who comes alongside someone and, with a firm hand, redirects his steps back to where they should be. It is translated by the word, to exhort.[71] This can be done through the use of correction or in a challenging sense, but it involves assisting a particular course of life or conduct.

This form of encouragement comes in the constructive conversations that empower people to move on and not lose hope. Usually more corrective in nature, this exhortative side of encouragement offers a strong, but firm, hand that correctly redirects someone in a direction of life or new or needed conduct that he was not intending. The right concept, as well as the right way to do it, needs to be expressed, while at the same time the long arm of the encourager must encircle their loved one in order to redirect him or her toward the correct goal. Interestingly, the exhortative caregiver may find himself getting "bit" by the very one whom he is exhorting. Resistance can be expected, and a determined refusal may need to be countered; but there are times as a caregiver that it is necessary. Nevertheless, all along, it is the caregiver's continued presence that fills the atmosphere with the reassurance that the new course of action will be worth taking.

Side #4 - To encourage means... To be one's advocate or support - I John 2:1

"I am writing these things to you so that you may not sin. And if anyone sins, we have an <u>Advocate</u> with the Father, Jesus Christ the righteous." NASB

The fourth side to encouragement is expressed in picturing one as an advocate who comes to one's defense when one is weak. It is the advocate who stands ready to provide reinforcement when life collapses. It is the advocate who is there standing beside a friend giving support with no intent of leaving, while at the same time offering what is needed to carry one through the moment. The mere thought of being an encourager finds the caregiver as an actual personification of this very idea. If anyone is going to be an advocate to the hurting and disabled, it is going to be the caregiver who will just be there, because that is what they do. It is no assignment. It is just the way it is. Caregivers are there ready to provide the needed reinforcement. For the advocate, it is not so much a sacrifice, but a residing responsibility that they just know is the way it will be.

Side #5 To encouragement: The Inside – On the Wings of a Dove

To strengthen, comfort, exhort and support provide four expressions of the same word used by the New Testament when it speaks of encouragement or those who are known as encouragers. It is not one of the above four expressions that mark the encourager, but it encompasses all four. In given settings the encourager knows just how to utilize his words and manner to be the one who comes alongside others to strengthen them. When the gentle cry for comfort pours from the hurting, it is the encourager who appears and brings a presence that calms the The Five Sides to Encouragement atmosphere. Then, if a firm hand is needed, the same individual will firmly offer their caring ways to move matters along a pathway for needed recovery. For sure, who is there throughout to provide the needed reinforcement, but the encourager?

Yet, the distinguishing mark to the New Testament understanding of this word comes to light when we look at the inside or source of such encouragement. Uniquely, a common New Testament expression used by the Apostles and even Christ Himself finds the manifestation for the Triune Godhead was expressed by the Greek word, "Paraklesis."

The Five Sides to Encouragement

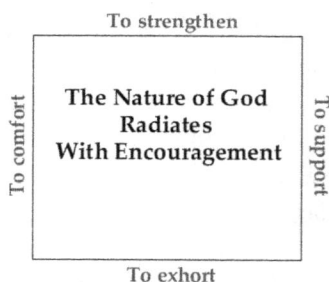

To strengthen

To comfort

The Nature of God Radiates With Encouragement

To support

To exhort

Particularly referring to the nature of God, the word paraklesis finds itself used when referring to God the Father. "Praise be to the <u>God and Father</u> of our Lord Jesus Christ, ... the God of all comfort (paraklesis)."[72] This same word is also used in reference to the nature of God's Son, Jesus Christ. "If anyone sins, we have an Advocate (parakletov) with the Father, Jesus Christ the righteous."[73] Lastly, Jesus' own words connect the Spirit of God to the paraklesis, "But the Helper (parakletos), the Holy Spirit, whom the Father will send in my name."[74] What we can conclude is that the very nature of the Triune Godhead (Father, Son and Spirit) radiates with encouragement, especially for those who are weak. Encouragement exudes from the entire Godhead which in turn overflows into any who turn their ways to rely upon the Almighty to help in their place of need.

The encourager knows that for a lasting, penetrating encouragement to be expressed, it will direct the one in need to the One who touches deep into the very spirit of man. We can then conclude as the Scriptures that the fifth side to encouragement, which speaks to the inside or heart of encouragement, finds its true source of strength from the One who Himself permeates with encouragement: God Himself. For those who have learned to direct their loved ones to rely upon this One Lord, have found His nature radiates with encouragement and His encouraging ways touch even the deep places of the heart. What I conclude from looking at the Scriptures then is that,

Biblical encouragement means:
    To be called or come alongside an individual
        In a time of grief, needed guidance or a difficulty
    To strengthen or reinforce that person in a course of life
        By causing him to look to the Lord & His Word for Counsel

True encouragement, the implied activity of the caregiver in embracing his commitment to care for someone, involves coming alongside the weakened family member in a time of grief, needed guidance or in a difficulty in order to strengthen or reinforce them in a course of life. Recognizing encouragement to be part of the very nature of God Himself, it makes all the sense then that the strength and reinforcement happens by causing the afflicted one to look to the Lord and His Way for counsel. It is this idea that the New Testament writers understood when they used the word, encouragement.

Picture the caregiver as the one whose arm is outstretched, ready to grab hold of someone in need. Encircling his object, he grabs hold and pulls him to himself, offering a reassurance that the afflicted one is not alone. Depending on the need, this same encourager opens up to strengthen, comfort, exhort and support one whose setting or heart needs that extra boost.

Actually, we all need this daily. We all need encouragers who offer a fragrance of God with their words and actions. For now, let's understand that adjusting to being a caregiver necessitates that the caregiver embraces the commitment to care for the weak which implies being an encourager.

Adjusting to being a Caregiver...
2. Necessitates our willingness to redefine and reconstruct our lives

Author and writer, Alan Rucker, in his book, *The Best Seat in the House*, was stricken with a rare disease in his 50's that left him paralyzed from the waist down in one day. Looking back after nine years in the chair, he offers some straight talk about the need to adjust as a disabled person.

"The beauty of it is that this is a creative problem, not a follow-the-rulebook problem. You're not changing the oil. You're reinventing your life. You're a little messed up, sure, but you're also given a license to redefine yourself. You will concoct the solution, whatever it is, all on your own."[75]

Stressing the importance of the hard work that lies ahead for the disabled, he highlights how, in making the adjustment to one's condition, it will require the need to reinvent life. In a similar tone, for caregivers everywhere, it is imperative that we understand that adjusting to being a caregiver necessitates the willingness to reconstruct our lives. The adverse effects, losses, physical limitations and exhaustion plus the depleted resources financially, all take a toll that cannot be allowed to define one's identity. In every arena of our lives, we are now being sought to provide care for others, while at the same time this same crisis calls us to adjust every relationship, our direction in life and many of our established activities.

For those of us who have children, each of our children needs attention. A mother-in-law persistently asks for information concerning her now-disabled daughter. Friends ask for some genuine ways that they can be of assistance. As well, a plethora of added responsibilities consumes every amount of our spare time. As the situation becomes more routine and the news less acute, our responsibilities, which had been momentarily set aside or absorbed by others, are added back into our lives.

For me, counseling appointments were part of my pastoral work. Caring for people, writing, teaching and the administrative tasks now waited their turn to be addressed. Certainly, there are those who are of great help, but it soon comes back to: Who owns the responsibility? The necessity to rearrange life was again, front and center.

It was not long before I realized that there was not a way in the world to operate and live as we did previously. As each encounter was handled, and a new wave of problems mercilessly slammed into us, the overall toll forced us to continually take time to reconstruct what was left. A new normal was needed, and what that looks like rests upon the caregiver.

Redefining and reconstructing our lives implies an honest assessment of life, our purpose and our passion

What are our resources now? What do we know to be our ordained purpose from which we could anchor all that we have? What passions were not sucked out of us? Emptiness overwhelms us, but the insatiable quest that by the mere fact that we breathe means that we are part of what God had ordained for the day. Therefore, the questions bid that answers be sought. What is left for us to use to direct what energy we have? What remains absolutely invaluable to our household and imperative for us to preserve? Both at home and at work, these were the types of questions that were generated and to which we had to have answers in reconstructing our lives. What is dispensable and what isn't? What dreams must be weaned or completely released? What obstacles are really insurmountable, and what do we understand from this ordeal that will lead to perhaps a new direction in life that we could have never seen otherwise?

Even as these questions formed the base to reconstructing our lives, responsibilities could not be avoided. We were still parents, and at the time adult children to parents who now needed us. We headed a family ministry within our extended community and I was still a pastor. We had to adjust our lives. There was no choice; this included further assessing our situation and rethinking just how we could do it.

For me, this led to changes in my morning schedule, so that I could handle morning responsibilities for the family, and especially my wife, before heading to the office. Certain matters I needed to know, and it required me to make concessions in my work schedule to find out what exactly was needed. Readjusting my schedule by allowing me time to read and study in the early morning or at night, after the household chores settled down, was essential. In order to grant me the opportunity to not be overwhelmed or appear too overpowered by our condition, I quietly established Thursday of each week as the day where I had absolutely no appointments that could be scheduled, except by me. As my week usually began on Sunday and had many spontaneous encounters that would demand my time both at work and home, I knew that I could adjust to help in a situation because, I had Thursdays open.

Slowly, but surely, some degree of stability and order was regained. Answers to our questions were gained. What we stood for as a household was reestablished. What I stood for as a husband, man, father, pastor and now a caregiver formulated to my satisfaction. As difficult as it was, the adjustment process necessitated that I endure the mental, emotional and spiritual disciplines that would lay again the foundation of our household.

Following each major surgery in which her life was noticeably altered, the necessity to adjust and reconstruct life was an exercise that took time. The only thing I can say is that after about the seventh adjustment, the time needed to adjust and reconstruct our lives has gotten considerably shorter.

Adjusting to Being a Caregiver...
3. Necessitates the sensitivity to refine and nurture our own inner journey

The external trauma to one's family and revision to one's career would be enough to rock anyone's boat, but adjusting to being a caregiver also necessitates the caregiver's sensitivity to refine and nurture his own inner journey. It strikes deep into that part of man that is unseen. It exposes the real you with your convictions and attitudes. It surfaces your sensitive side, the personal longings that contrive one's inner being. There is no escaping it. One tear betrays your sense of being invincible and in total control. One tear drops you into the realm of being human, and now, if it has not already happened, introduces you to the real universe. Here is where the illusions and dreams developed in your mind come face to face with a world that knows truth. Here, pain, suffering, evil, the ugliness of man's sinfulness clash with the presence of a relational God who seeks you and who longs for you to turn to Him.

Adversities have a way of dethroning our sense of self-sufficiency and exposing our inner need for God, His love and His sense of value, purpose and worth that comes by being related to Him. As the need arises from within that "requires us to summon the courage and flexibility to relate to life in an unfamiliar but more expansive way,"[76] we find a source in harmony with the real world, with the real truth, that places us rightfully before the one who truthfully holds the title and position of God, and who I have come to know to be Jesus the Christ.

Our external facades can only last for so long in the real universe, because they are connected to our inner man, which is real. If your inner journey was shallow, you will find yourself pressed to make changes. Here is where we face our greatest challenge, namely turning to God Almighty, Who is the only one who can touch our inner spirit to such a degree that we have a source of strength for any to draw upon. And the explanation for why we need God is simple. Everyone looks for the same relationship with God for their strength.

One man who knew me and our family well told me, "I had to see you succeed, not for you alone, but for all of us. If God did not help you navigate through this ordeal, why would I think I could find help when it hits me?"[77] God deals with us, and when He does, it will forever mark our pathway. Adjustments will be necessary and eventually so will change, but "to give good care to others, we first must take care of ourselves."[78] If this doesn't throw us on our faces before Almighty God, nothing will!

Refining and nurturing our own inner journey implies a time to mourn and accept our calling to honor the Lord

Once again I bring to mind the questions I humbly unleashed at the throne of God following the second accident. "What did she do to deserve this? What truthfully was the point of more intense pain and drugs? What was the intent of it all, if there was any? How does she, as a servant of the Lord, explain to her children that the Lord loves her and their family? How do we explain that He will watch over you and protect you when the occurrence of such debilitating acts seems to make a mockery of the truth she states? What can be learned from the pain, suffering and weakness of this lovely lady, who happens to be my wife, best friend and fellow companion in life and ministry? What can be gained to help the households of families and churches who face similar complications?" Mourning the loss, while witnessing Dawn's excruciating suffering, left me totally identifying with the poets of old, who penned into existence the famed hymn book of Israel, known as the Psalms. They hurt, just as I now hurt. They found themselves fighting the thoughts of their dreams being crushed just as I. They cried out to God. They mourned just like I, and on so many occasions found myself wiping dry the tears that traversed my cheeks. Dreams were being demolished, though I fought the thought. The stake of loneliness pierced my heart, and the silence was deadening to my soul. Days and even weeks would pass and my only words were, "God this can't be happening. Not again and again and again." How many times I walked away identifying with the psalmist who mourned out from the silence of a cave, "There is no escape for me; No one cares for my soul."[79]

Yet I must admit that 'in His time' I learned afresh that He heard. He bottled each tear[80] and He sent His angels of kindness to comfort my soul and absorb the loneliness that plagued my thoughts. And then there were the times that an even quiet presence arrived to remind me, "I will never desert you, nor will I ever forsake you,"[81] reassuring me once again that He is "a very present help in trouble."[82] He makes His appearance just as He says He would. Yes, crisis awakens us to a new journey, but at the same moment it awakens our spirit to the presence of His Spirit.

As one comes away from such an experience with God, we may do so without all the answers, but we recognize the pathway has changed. We plod through unfamiliar ground with many voices asking genuine, but strange, questions. "Is it too much for Dawn to handle the stress of the ministry? Do I need time away?" "Do I think I may need to step down so that the work of the Lord will not be hindered?"

Let me just say that instant maturity on this journey is not easily found. Preparing for what lies ahead as a caregiver begins by having a proper approach to the task. What this means was captured by Beth MacLeod in her address to caregivers in general. You will need "…to see one's caregiving role as a calling rather than as an obstacle to achieving personal goals. Caregiving truly is a spiritual practice, a non-linear path with the heart."[83] It is a practice that carries an overriding sensitivity that will refine and nurture a life that will seek to know, enjoy and honor God.

Genuine emotions, legitimate pain, controlled frustrations, and time to wrestle with our own selfishness will await the journey. Questions and even demands like Job of old will flood our minds and quiet dealings with God. May I encourage each of you regardless of your education, to utilize a designated quiet time to draw upon God! In the real universe He resides at the center. Do not go back to a world of illusions that will only disintegrate and disappear when confronted by the next adversity or ultimately death. Let your pains remove the veil that surrounds the fortress of our rebellious souls and blinds us to our own insufficiency. Let them introduce us to a grace and presence of God that settles the inner man with a peace and assurance that He is there, but He will, in His time, turn our mourning into song.

One last thought involves learning to live in the present. Any time one continually pushes the rewind button and relives the horror or recounts how much has been lost, an ugliness can emerge that soon permeates our lives. It is a trap, and everyone loses. Any preoccupation with the past, blaming of others, or overreaction with an anger that is out of proportion to what has happened, can fuel an underlying bitterness that consumes a person and pushes people away. Even though mourning is appropriate, there remains the need to adjust our thoughts so that we learn to live in the present. Jan Cox, in her book *Coping with Physical Disability* reinforces this thought and offers healthy advice for making this happen.

"When memories come bring them to the present and contemplate what those memories mean to you today. Learn to set your new goals in light of your new strengths."[84] The past will stay with you but what we do with it now affects the inner journey we walk in the present. "Take every thought captive to the obedience of Christ,"[85] said the Apostle Paul. In the same vein, "as you go through the process, allow others to go through the same. Give them the chance to react with shock."[86]

Now dream and dream again but let our dreams realistically take us to join God in what He is doing-not the other way around. Let us open ourselves to new passions that we know come from God, because He gives them. Problems will still arise, as evil has not yet been eradicated from this earth; but remember, just as one setback can plummet our best-laid thoughts and plans, the truth that God knows can act as our life default and keep us balanced. God knows, and He has allowed it to be; and therefore He has a plan for our welfare and not for calamity to give us a future and a hope.[87]

Adjusting to Being a Caregiver...

4. Necessitates acknowledging the need to accept support, validation and even relief for ourselves, our disabled family member and our family.

When we hear that "No man is an island," we generally nod with approval, but venture away from its wisdom-until adversity knocks. Being reduced to being human before God, though, should help us to recognize that to be human means we do need people. We are designed to be inter-dependent. We need what each other brings to life, and when someone voluntarily steps into your crucible, it is amazing how a friendship ensues.

The caregiver's journey, we have already acknowledged, is not without its own personal pain. There were times that I hurt so much that my faith was weak, or it was like I had no faith at all. Yet, it was then that I needed friends to come alongside. I needed someone to lean upon or to share the strength of their faith with me. It was in those times that I found the faith of these dear friends providing the substance for my faith. It was their thoughts which they offered that helped me keep perspective. It was the regular personal time together that maintained an accountability that stabilized my lifeboat in the rough waters. Their faith became mine, and it aided in carrying me through it all.

An old wise man stated, "Two are better than one, because they have a good return for their work: if one falls down, his friend can help him up."[88] I have found, on more occasions than one, this is very true.

Accepting the need to accept support and validation implies the need for a trusted confidant and support network

This adjustment for the caregiver necessitates acknowledging the need to seek someone who can be a trusted confidant, as well as those people who can provide validation and even relief when possible. Such friends may initially appear from among one's already-developed relationships and particularly those who may have encountered such situations. But, hear me well! To have someone who will willingly stand by your side, and with whom you, the caregiver, can retreat and talk to without fear of repercussion or jeopardizing his position, is priceless. Any caregiver's setting calls for having a sounding board who can help him sift through the rubbish of his days. It requires one who will be willing to stand as an encourager, friend and prayer partner and provide the reinforcement that every caregiver desperately needs. "What caregivers need most is support and validation,"[89] says McLeod. Having this trusted confidant provides that.

Having friends who empathize with us and voluntarily come to our assistance is invaluable. At the same time having those who can sympathize with our situation offers us the opportunity to draw helpful insights from those whose experiences have been mutually traversed.

My personal experience included a meeting with a group of gentlemen for breakfast every few weeks for years. All of us were caregivers, though others joined us on occasions. In my case, one of the men was a doctor who had a son who was disabled from an automobile accident. The other was an executive engineer who was a father of a son with cerebral palsy. The conversations were invaluable and energizing, and our friendships grew. The discussions provided assistance to questions that pressed on all of us, though not all our time was spent addressing problems. No words can underscore the value that filled the conversations that were exchanged over a breakfast. We challenged each other as friends. We rejoiced with each other as friends. We cried and prayed for each other on issues that were important to us as men, which kept us from being entrenched by our own little dilemmas. Over time, the greater need for just support was met. Even though we have moved from that location, the friendships remain priceless to this day.

Another invaluable resource that we realized could further assist caregivers and would be vital for those encountering such issues as we had, was people who had encountered similar issues themselves. People who are hurting attract those of their own kind. It has already been mentioned that the need for support and validity for the caregiver is essential. We found that a support network among caregivers was most helpful. For us, we learned that meeting once a month was wonderful and about all the time any of us had for such a group, as our on-going responsibilities limited our time. Opening our home, we invited caregivers to an evening of interaction, enjoyment and dessert. For my wife and I, it meant being creative, but what resulted made the time spent a valuable source of encouragement and friendship for all the participants. As McLeod noted, "For many, these circles of support are simply a place to begin questioning. People first come for answers to solutions for their problems. After a while the reason for the support group is the support. We don't have pat answers, because each case is unique; but we help people take the road that works for them."[90]

A tear to share together, a shoulder to let it soak into, a source of "the comfort with which we ourselves are comforted,"[91] are all part of the support that is needed. Often the respite itself acts to recharge our passion and love, as rejuvenation may require much more time to wrestle with all the issues. Let's understand that it is okay.

On top of this, one can make it a point to go the extra mile. We kept it simple in our meetings, but every so often, we just spoiled the caregiver's support group with a special dessert or evening of entertainment designed just for them. Oh, the enjoyment of caring for the weak and watching the smiles lift on beleaguered cheeks, as they mouth the words "Thank you" for the support that has been offered! Truthfully, it is rewarding.

Accepting the need for support and validation implies the need to see that the family gets support

For me as a caregiver, the fulfillment gained by such trusted relationships extended itself to recognize the same requirement stands for the disabled and their families. Adjusting to being a caregiver necessitates making sure the same support is readily available for them. Disabled individuals need friends who understand and who can intelligently interact about matters that confront them. Also, they just need friends. How thankful I was for the many who worked in our family ministry who loved my wife and made sure to include her in all the events! As two gentleman, Dr. Jim Fickel and Chris Seal said, "She is part of us, and if it means adjusting our time schedule a little to have her participate, then adjust we will."[92] Can you imagine what that meant to her?

I was personally grateful for certain women who made a special emphasis of meeting with my wife weekly. In fact, I encouraged it, as the brightness on my dear wife's face following their meetings refreshed my soul. Sure, they talked about life and its hardness, but they also just talked about life, being a parent, flowers, events, and all the things that they wanted to talk about. Uniquely, I found that each of those women (though I know I had to have been part of the conversation piece), ended up showing me the utmost respect, which I can only attribute to their maturity and my wife's way of addressing issues that never discredited me as her husband.

Accepting the need for support and validation implies individuality in parenting and developing healthy communication skills

Our children were inducted into the secondary caregiver's role by default. Here lies another challenge for the caregiver / father. Amidst the adjustments that are required of him come the voices from those in his own household who call him, Dad. Each of them has concerns. Their perspectives can vary as to how they view matters, and certainly their personalities, age and maturity level play a big part in how they will make their own adjustments to their mother's disability.

As stated prior, the caregiver's / father's mantra is to take precedence throughout his thinking. "It's more than about me!" "It's not about me!" Each mantra must find expression with each child. If the mere raising of children is not enough, the addition of helping them adjust to a disabled mom will push him to his limits.

The age, the degree of relational development, and individual personality of each child were all factors that had a bearing on each one's adjusting to the new setting. Each one of them looked at our situation differently, and rightfully so, since each one was different. The relational ones-who loved the quality time, responded differently than the task-oriented ones. The older ones remembered an active, engaged mom, had a completely different feeling than the younger ones. Thus, there are big challenges to the healthy and able-bodied parent to understand the child's need for information that suits each child, which is not always easy.

A disability will challenge the family to develop healthy communication skills. Stress, strain and breakdowns that accompany a disability expose the need for healthy communication skills. Beginning with the parents, each adjustment requires that they interact, so that they can be of support to each other. It means that healthy communication skills need to be in place.

This is just as true for the children in one's home. The security that the parents' relationship provides to the home atmosphere requires adjustments every day. This necessitates healthy communication that addresses the children's fears and provides clear and age-appropriate explanations for each concern. As well, it warrants that the children need to speak openly and honestly with their parents and comprehend the facts given to them.

It must be kept in mind that in helping children to comprehend the setting and articulate words that carry clear thought, while in a stressful

109

state, takes time for each child. It is a process of growing as caregivers, and for each child, it is a learning process that will have successes and failures from which they need to learn and improve upon.

As a family pastor and dad, I know the importance of being a parent; but the taxing strain that presses upon each day when a mom is down found great reinforcement, when other adults whom we respected took our children under their wings and talked. Even now that our children are grown, those same adults are now numbered among the people they still appreciate and enjoy, as do we. Uncle Ron and Auntie Mary Anne, Auntie Jeannie and John, Uncle Mark and Auntie Sally, Uncle Jack and Auntie Audrey, Dr. Bruce and Donna Rae, Ron and Carolyn, Jim and Marggy and a host of others, are all outside the blood lines, but endeared to our grown children's hearts. All had memorable and lasting impact on our family.

Teachers, coaches, pastors, church friends, and neighbors, along with the many family members all have a part. Encourage your children to find a few with whom they can interact. You do not need to know all that they talk about, and it may even display an area where you have not communicated in depth; but at least they will have people whom you trust, who have done their part and filled the void on your behalf.

Disability will challenge the caregiver's ability to communicate. Regardless of the relationship, the caregiver finds himself daily facing challenges to master the art of communication. His wife will require it. His children will depend upon it. Extended family and friends will appreciate it as will one's work relationships.

Of all the challenges that will drain energy from the caregiver and father, the challenge of keeping people up-to-date with what is truly necessary, coupled with the skill and time required to interact with those he loves, will weigh upon him. How much does he say? To whom does he say it? How does he communicate what is necessary? Are there trusted people who can speak on his behalf, so that he is not consumed by the process?

These types of questions call for an adjustment that begins by having to talk about oneself and the pressures brought on by the adversity. It calls for an adjustment that extends to even one's work. It calls for the transfer of information to people who need to know not just for the sake of being informed but because they legitimately want to know how they can help.

Make new friends and keep the old, One is silver and one is gold.[93]

110

Adjusting to Being a Caregiver...

5. Necessitates our initiating invitations to new relationships and involvement in outside interests

There is always the possibility that people will avoid either the disabled person or the caregiver, but that does not mean that the disabled person or the caregiver needs to avoid them. The caregiver will be called to show a greater love and initiate contacts when he wishes to break down the walls between the physically disabled and their socially-disabled counterparts. Further, if fears are going to be dispelled, the disabled must be willing to talk. Although every conversation will not focus upon the disability, it needs to be understood that when a person looks bewildered or acts unsure about approaching a discussion pertaining to the disability, the disabled person or caregiver should be the one to ease the atmosphere by helping to initiate the discussion, if possible.

Any conversation on the path to developing a relationship needs to focus on the other person, and the assumption is that they are just as desirous in developing the relationship. Finding areas of commonality becomes essential to the development of a relationship. This means showing an interest in their concerns, desires, family and activities. The physical disability may limit one's ability to do specific things, as well as limit one's availability to meet at a particular location; but creativity shines best when the limits grow tight. A small gesture from a disabled person and her caregiver carries an unforgettable impression, merely because it is often so out of the ordinary.

For the disabled person, this could definitely be a hardship that will require the assistance of one's spouse or family to pull it off. The limits of the person's disability must be considered in the time required for any meeting or event. Yet, even if one wasn't disabled, the same would be true. In our household, Dawn found that having people over for dessert was about all she could handle comfortably, especially with groups of people unfamiliar with her condition. Nevertheless, the desire on her part to be hospitable and reach out to others made these types of settings easier to manage. As her caregiver, I came to understand the value of having people in our home, especially to keep her in touch socially. It is indeed a challenge, and given the time plus the willingness to be available, the home can be full of life.

111

Even though the hospitality and openness to people go hand in hand with the caregiver and his wife, they will need to recognize that not every person's perceptions of one's disability are the same. In Dawn's case, because she could interact and operate individually within her own boundaries, it created a perception on the part of some that she was not disabled. Seeing her strength to tackle a situation became more of an inspiration and a shining example to those around us. This was evident while listening to her respond to questions in a classroom. It revealed an intact brain that still spelled out valuable help for parents.

I will admit that one large adjustment that went totally unnoticed, that aided our development of new relationships, was my wife's continued involvement with me on family matters. Even here, most would see her sitting in a chair and did not perceive her as disabled. Nevertheless, we did not hide it. In fact, every speaking engagement required a special person designated to give my wife immediate help, since the malfunctions within her body could create a distressing situation within minutes.

Even though my wife was able to get out, her abilities definitely were limited, and mine were not. Guilt could easily take over in matters like this, especially when it meant I would be leaving her behind. And so another factor surfaces the need for the caregiver to find a channel of refreshment. The key to being able to pull this off rests in both knowingly sharing in the activity.

My wife saw it happen every spring. She knew the local public high school would beckon for my time as a pitching coach. Not that I had the spare time, but she knew my involvement was more than just playing ball. It was my therapy. It refreshed me, as it provided an opportunity for me to be away from it all and with people, which for me was a therapy in itself. Her sacrificial love and desire to return to me what I gave to her came through her encouragement that I coach baseball. It meant a great deal to me to have a spouse who knew that I needed this activity.

♥♥♥♥♥♥♥

Adjustments are in response to the challenges that attach themselves to the effects that come with any adversity. The caregiver's inner journey undoubtedly stands front and center to the well-being for the disabled, himself and his family. As has been mentioned, pain brings us to the edge of real life. Our nature and inner impulses to avoid pain are strong, but here we find that our situation necessitates that we adjust.

Simultaneously, it beckons us to open our eyes to the one who has sought a relationship with us long before we knew He was even there-God Himself. Sadly, in this world because of our own self-oriented natures and the winds of evil that we avoid, pain introduces us to the real, but ugly side of this world. Illusions and self-made dreams that curb our appetite for God build for us a bubble in which we can escape.

Yet, from the sounds of silence, there comes a hand and a still small voice that says, "Come to Me, all who are weary and burdened, and I will give you rest."[94] As our tears begin to dry enough that we can focus upon who said such words, we find someone who sees deep within our own souls. It was Jesus who offered these words, and Jesus who stands behind them.

For the caregiver, then, adjusting to being a caregiver...
- Necessitates our embracing the commitment to care for the weak
- Necessitates our willingness to redefine and reconstruct our lives.
- Necessitates the sensitivity to refine and nurture our own inner journeys
- Necessitates acknowledging the need for support, validation and even relief for ourselves, our disabled family members and our families, and
- Necessitates our initiating invitations to new relationships and involvement in outside interests

Finding ourselves waking up in a crucible being ground upon by life's adversities presents a suffering which may be different than the physical strain the disabled one faces. Yet, the emotional anguish, and the mental and spiritual turmoil that rolls through our inner man definitely makes caregiving a trial. Avoiding pain and distancing ourselves from its sources cannot happen unless we flat out quit, and that only creates another set of problems. Financial shortfalls wear upon us, and as we sense the responsibility, especially when the disabled spouse cannot participate, the pressure mounts.

Constant need to adjust our lives highlights how much of life really forms from within the inner journey we travel as caregivers. I can only

113

imagine someone reading this and thinking through their own scenario, whether they are new to the caregiver's way of life, helping someone who is, or like myself, their tear ducts already have emptied on many occasions.

But might I offer here one thought that has served me well? It finds its roots in another man's inner journey, who, centuries ago faced a setting that left him adjusting his life to his complexities, though he never expressed it explicitly. Helpful for me, it has resonated time and time again through my heart, called me to slow down, and stabilized me as I have reached those points in my inner journey that I find difficult to address.

Psalm 13 is the passage and it contains only six verses of poetry. The first two verses unveil the problems that have overwhelmed the writer. He alludes to the apparent absence of God and the internal war this silence creates within him, as well as the sorrow that the circumstances leave that his enemy has triumphed.

However, by verses five and six, the psalm writer breaks into a declaration of confidence and triumphant praise as he basks in the truth of God's unfailing love. Now his heart sings like the morning bird freed from the night's darkness. "You have dealt bountifully with me," he now sings. Naturally the question arises, what happened? What moved the writer from such dire problems to an exalted state of praise?

At the center of this individual lament, we hear an entrusting prayer being offered to the One whose presence was in doubt. Pleading for light to be shown to his weary eyes and admitting that he has failed, his thoughts rise to God, the very One to whom the caregivers today pour out their inner consternation in hope of finding a degree of peace when all seems so overwhelming. What did the psalmist teach us, which for years has braced caregivers such as I against the howling winds that would overpower us? I find the theme and conclusion to this psalm as follows. *"Problems pivot to praise when we find ourselves on our knees in prayer."*

In the middle of this little psalm, we find ourselves face to face with the reminders of just how much He does love and care for us. The reality of our earthly world does not take away the effects of evil, at least not yet, but the awareness of His presence with mere men and women like us instills a peace that calms and satisfies our souls. God has heard my prayer. He has welcomed me directly into His throne room where He today seats himself upon a throne of grace, where we will "receive mercy and find grace to help us in our time of need."[95]

As we contemplate the adverse effects and the strain of constantly adjusting to life as caregivers, let us dependently discipline ourselves to make haste to a place designed for us to pray. Let us approach, as He requests, with confidence, for the battle that transpires within our own minds will be won when we find ourselves in prayer. Please accept this little sermon from one who has traversed these trails for years and remember,

Problems to Praise Pivots on Prayer

Hope and prayer go hand in hand. The tears that so often bear the message of our souls, find themselves snatched out of the air upon the wings of a dove. The great encourager, Jesus referred to this dove as the Spirit of God Himself. It is He who intercedes on our behalf and delivers these fuzzy requests to the same Jesus who is seated upon that throne of Grace and to whom all the angels, authorities and powers are in submission.[96] These angels of kindness await His command and impart His supply that often finds its way to us to meet our needs. So once again I conclude with the psalmist, problems to praise pivots on prayer. Hope waits for such moments.

Chapter 9
Angels of Kindness

The caregiver's script necessitates our commitment to be encouragers. Yet, often we cry out for someone to help replenish what our now empty souls seek. The silent scream, or lonely sigh, betrays a hidden tiredness that yearns for any form of genuine encouragement and comfort, not for any other reason than to help instill the strength we need to carry on.

Regardless of how we arrived at being caregivers, the adversity and adjustments needed in this situation present real obstacles to our happiness. Our energy, as well as our resources keep diminishing under the relentless demands of caregiving. Then, just in time, very welcomed helpers arrive, who can only be described as angels of kindness. Regardless of their stations in life, the appearance of them brings the sense that God, Himself, has directly sent them on a mission to provide the comfort, encouragement and advocacy that our troubled heart needs.

An Invitation to Involvement

It was 1971 when his wife Glenna, a school teacher and an accomplished vocalist, began displaying signs of multiple sclerosis (MS). At 41 years of age, this mother of four children between the ages of six and fourteen was informed of her need for rest and a stress-free environment. Looking back, Pastor Brunner recognized the challenge that they would face as a couple. "The problem," he stated, "is that preachers don't have the privilege to be free of stress."[97]

Nevertheless, one of the most touching examples of the kind of church in which he served came at the very onset. He tells the story of those early months following her diagnosis:

"After the first diagnosis and on the next to the last night before Glenna got out of the hospital, I came home and noticed 30-40 cars in the church parking lot. I whipped out my calendar to determine what meeting I had overlooked. Seeing an empty calendar, I went into the church, and there were 40-60 people praying just for us. That would prove to be one of the most indelible memories in my life when the church congregation bound together for us."[98]

Prayer changes things, because it draws into action the mercy and grace that marks God Himself. When one finds himself as the object of a group's petitions before God, words fail. It is a humbling experience and one that evokes in us a spirit of gratitude. Yet, it is even more so when the prayers of others request for us God's great kindness. When the angels of kindness arrive as answers to those prayers, we are astonished at the sense of value these human-looking angels communicate with their every move.

On one occasion, matters in caring for our home had gotten away from me. They were just too much. Sitting at the kitchen table with Dawn early one Saturday morning, trying to formulate a plan as to how to do it all, a knock occurred at the door. There stood in plain clothes and gloves a state patrolman whom we knew. "I was at a men's breakfast and some of us overheard that you need some help."

Then another patrolman drove up, followed by five women who pulled out every kind of cleaning tool that you could think of. Getting a layout of the plans and what was needed, they all went about their merry way, laughing, talking and accomplishing in a few hours what would have taken me days. Pictures grace my screen saver with their smiles, and even today, the thought of their kindness brings tears to my eyes. Uniquely, the same gesture opened up conversations among the whole neighborhood.

Pastor Brunner recalls learning a lesson that he would attribute as key to facing the stresses that mount as a caregiver and I wholeheartedly concur with his wisdom. When angels come, accept their help! They might do it a little differently than you, but what does that matter? The pressing question of "How do I handle it?" finds a partial answer in your willingness to accept help.

A disability to a neighbor heralds an invitation to a community for their involvement. Even for myself as a pastor, whether I knew it or not, because of our place in the community, especially the church community, our situation heralded a call just as soon as the news hit of my wife's disability. Since this was happening to the pastor's wife, it meant that the whole church was now involved, by virtue of the fact of their connection to their pastor. This is understood in any community. When it happens, the community is invited to step in and offer help.

First Responders

The initial wave of what I call, "First responders," springs into action out of the relationships that are already intact. Community and church relationships, business associates, longstanding friends and extended family, plus our immediate family, all qualify as relationships affected by the mention of both our names. Emotions and concerns run high when a tragedy hits. Due to the nature of pain's influence on learning, the ability of community members to recall their own personal events means that others will empathize with our painful experiences. With empathy comes involvement, for empathy cannot stand still, and with them comes the enrichments that they have learned to pass on with all whom they interact. Typically, they come out of the woodwork to be of assistance. The reason is simple: they understand.

Nevertheless, by means of association, the community knows that all are welcome in sharing in this crisis. Some will recognize the importance of the moment, and their concern will find expression in mobilizing people to prayer and in assisting.

However, the impact of the disability alone extends beyond those immediately affected. A whole different world comes to life. People, whom one would never have known nor perhaps even noticed, will appear. Those, who have been affected by a physical disability, arrive to offer hope. A person's prior experience with the disabled world allows them to have an easier transition into the lives of those facing the crisis. In our experience alone, just over 50% of those who responded to assist us had prior experience in working with or knowing someone who was disabled. Even medical personnel, whom we would have never known, stepped into the moment to apply their skills. Yet, those first responders whom the disabled may not have known, find a way to come in alongside to provide encouragement.

Again, when I refer to first responders, I speak of those people outside of the acute care team. There is no doubt the acute care people are front-line first responders, who deserve our utmost thanks for the commitment they bring to their profession. Yet for the caregiver, with the weight of all that will be needed riding on him or her, it becomes those first responders who nestle in beside him to voluntarily lift the load, if only just a little. These responders are those who will impact the caregiver's heart and mind.

The Gift of Calm

True first responders bring a gift which becomes subtly sensed: the gift of calm. They carry a calming effect amidst all the turmoil and adversity. They just seem to jump in. By doing so, they bring a sense of order which in turn calms everyone. Burdened to be of help, these angels of kindness arrive and quietly go about their business or offer an ear to hear. For the disabled they become a friend. For the caregiver they offer an encouragement of fresh air that just seems to allow the caregiver a chance to catch his breath. In turn the caregiver begins to realize that each gesture is big. There are no small acts of kindness just gestures that offer help and a momentary calm in the action.

Angels, 2nd Class; No Wings Just Love

During the Christmas holidays, an old classic, "It's a Wonderful Life," will at some time hit the air waves of our household, gripping all of us to sit down with some hot cocoa or coffee and take it in, as we travel back to Bedford Falls. The value of just how important one life is and what impact one life has on a community rings home loud and clear by the time everyone is rushing over to rescue George and the old savings and loan at the movies' end. Tears of appreciation grip anyone who gives thought to the movie's plot; but then a little bell rings, as George happens to read a note found on the inside of a book left behind by his guardian angel, Clarence.

In the movie, it is Clarence who grants George the wish of seeing life if he had not been born. He then walks through with George each of the key relationships, and shows him how they would have ended up, had he not been there. Clarence, though, in the movie was referred to as an Angel, 2nd Class. He had not won his "wings" yet, but he told George that if a bell was heard, it meant that an angel had received his wings, which is what happens at the end of movie just as George reads the inside cover to the book.

Second-class angels might be stretching things a little far theologically, but the association of such visitors, comes a little closer to the truth, as on so many occasions I have watched those so-called 2nd Class angels of kindness arrive to do what they do well. There are no wings that will ever be gained, but the admiration and appreciation for such wonderful people create a mood very much likened to the impact that Clarence had on George. Truthfully, love awakens love, and their gestures leave an imprint of kindness that continually refreshes the memories of one's heart.

The Imprint of Kindness

The lasting effect of angels in disguise brings encouragement to the whole family. One pastor, Dr. Keith Korstjens, had the ability to hire a live-in nurse to care for his wife in his absence during the day. Not all have that ability, though it would be nice. In our case, we had a rotation system that required each child to care for a certain area of the home. As the older children left, more of my help was needed to complete the cleaning tasks. Then, one couple, Ron and Carolyn, sent an angel in the form of a cleaning lady every other week to just clean our house from stem to stern. My wife greatly appreciated this, especially since we had so many guests coming into our home. Yet, the truth be known, though the cleaning angel brightened my wife's eyes she was an angel in disguise to me, personally.

On another occasion, a home-school mother approached my wife and asked if her daughter could be of help, as part of her service work for school. Since Dawn had led 4-H clubs for over 15 years, she asked Dawn to assist in helping her younger daughter gain familiarity in the kitchen and with the chores and skills of house cleaning. In this case, everyone was the winner. My wife looked forward to the time with this young lady; received a break from one more task, and our teenage daughter at the time was given the freedom to be involved with friends in school functions that otherwise would have been missed in order to take care of a need at home.

This was a real eye opener for me, as I realized that sometimes we feel that if there is someone capable at the home to do the work then we do not need to ask for or receive help. That thought may need some revision, as this young girl's assistance became a tremendous blessing to our youngest daughter, my wife and me. I was capable, just as my daughter was of doing the work; and did so on many occasions. Yet, as I watched the freedom the extra help gave my daughter, I learned to offer the same gestures of doing chores she would normally do, just to free her up to be involved in an activity that she could freely enjoy.

Fly-By Angels

Another lasting imprint, especially in the lives of our children, came in what I refer to as the Fly-By Angels. One in particular was Liz. She was always on the go, but in her busyness seemed to find time to leave an imprint that would last. On one occasion that was memorable to our children, she flew in and dropped off a box full of fresh rolls filled with meat slices all individually wrapped to be put in the freezer. Then instead of the customary peanut butter and jelly sandwiches their father lovingly prepared, they got to have a little different flavor for their lunch boxes. As well, the lunches were topped off with items from a second box that she left, which was filled with individually-wrapped cupcakes topped with candy sprinkles.

This was a small gesture, but a lasting impression of what a little act of kindness can do in the mind of a child. I also remember, when coming home from the hospital, families brought over dinner, which was a big help. Then there was the night that our dear friend, John, brought over a meal that for our children was a home run. What it entailed was a bag of fresh McDonald's Big-Macs, fries and pop. The smiles from those little ones brightened up the room.

These were all what I refer to as Fly-Bys—quick stops with items that I know took time to prepare and time to go purchase. Yet they were items that brightened the days of our children, and as parents who watched them smile, it offered a lift. What parent ever grows tired of seeing their children smile? In each case, as with many others, the fly by angels were present for only a few moments; but their imprint left a lasting impression upon the lives of us all.

The Extra-Special Friends

Probably one of the more meaningful times for caregivers comes when the one we love and care for finds a friend who willingly comes on their own to spend time doing things with them that they both enjoy. This occurred for me with-Mary Ann, Lisa, Bobbie, Carol, Linda and Marilyn, all of whom had an extra special place in Dawn's and my life. They enjoyed spending time with Dawn usually over lunch, where they just chatted then often prayed about matters that pertained to them. Often, they stepped in to take her to appointments, cleaned our home or accomplished a matter needed by Dawn.

As for me, I knew that on the days that these ladies showed up, Dawn would be well taken care of. She looked forward to it, and most often when their time ended, I knew she had enjoyed her day. During that time, I could take a breather and relax. If I wanted, I could accomplish a needed task or stop for a cup of coffee with someone. It provided refreshment to Dawn and a respite for me. Again, the simple smile on her face upon my arrival home spoke volumes, just because of a gesture of kindness arrived in a friend.

This does not just have to happen among adults. As our home was a habitat for fun and activity, community events were often held there. We had a basketball court, a ball field in the back yard, and places for the volleyball net to be set up. We had outdoor and indoor seating areas that accommodated all ages. Porches and swings provided safe haven for conversations, while balls were flying around. Outdoor grills were trucked in from neighbors, and soon barbequing meant the festivities had begun. The fire pit became a hangout that often lasted into the late hours of the evening, and these types of events made for some wonderful annual traditions that we neighbors did together.

The beauty of our community was that it allowed Dawn the opportunity to be involved, yet have a place to go if problems arose where she could confidently handle the situation and then return to the activities. People understood, and to further help, they jumped into the preparations. Other kids from the neighborhood, especially those who looked forward to the annual older/younger baseball games showed up to help mow the lawns. They did not have to, but they did. The kitchen was busy with activity, and everyone knew whatever they did was welcomed. Each guest and each gesture communicated for Dawn and me, just how much they all cared for us.

The Gift of Caring

Where first responders brought a gift of calm, the long term angels of kindness found in friends, family and community brought another gift that invariably is shared by everyone. The gift was that of caring, simple caring that spoke its own language by the act it brought. Any act of caring communicated one simple message, "I care about you." A meal, a visit for coffee, a time to pray, a trip for Dawn to the store, a fly-by meal all reflect some of the many ways these angels lifted our spirits. Even the public school where I coached left the back door open, just so Dawn could attend events and position herself so that she could be safely involved with people. Statement upon statement by one person after another communicated an accumulated message that typifies the Lynden, Ferndale, and Bellingham community where we lived: We care about each other.

It was quite revealing to ask this group what advice they would offer a community where someone has become disabled. A member of the medical community offered this insight:

"I think the disabled wish to be considered as much normal as anyone else. Let them think it. Yet, let's understand that compassion and patience are keys to doing this. When working with the disabled, caregivers and their families, it behooves us to make reasonable adaptations for the level of disability in terms of time and energy required, accommodating the disability and, if appropriate, to provide respite."[99]

Others responded with the simple thoughts or gestures that communicated the same sense of caring. "Find out and help with their emotional and physical support: Meals, clean house, laundry or extra financial burdens."[100] "Treat them as another person and always remember them in your prayers."[101] "If you know people with similar situations, arrange to get them together. If you encounter people who are new to being disabled or caregivers, get them in touch with someone more experienced and mature."[102]

Here is where the need for developing a support network for caregivers becomes a very worthwhile project to undertake. Do not be afraid to ask for specific ways of helping the caregiver and the family. Then, form a core group from within the community who just keep tabs on the situation, so it never gets out of control.

♥♥♥♥♥♥♥

If Christianity is anything it is involvement. If community means anything, it means being willing to lift a hand to help someone in need. Love initiates action, which then opens the doorway for loving neighbors to move toward those who find themselves encountering pain and suffering. Maybe for some, the act will be an initial sacrifice on their part, but they will soon learn that love engulfs the sacrificial mentality to the point that when one acts, the thought of it being a sacrifice is non-existent. With time, every act becomes more of a statement that spells out loudly and clearly, I care about you. It is this spirit that makes a community, and this spirit that joins communities around a moral fiber that ultimately makes within a nation a strength that cannot be broken. It is this spirit that God established into the fabric of His world, and they find something that truthfully awakens them to the ways of God Himself. Love awakens love, and the return gratitude awakens one's commitment to that community. As a caregiver and witness to such events and the angels of kindness that perform them, all I can do, is bow my head and say, "Thank you Lord." Then I ask in return, "How can I help?"

The thrust of this chapter has been to bring to light those individuals who, without knowing it, become angels of kindness. Their impact is profound, but most often their angelic ways seem minor to them. At the same time, caring for caregivers means that when the community grapevine offers information that a member of one's community is down, it carries an attached message that invites anyone to get involved in helping. Gestures of kindness are just that-acts of kindness. Each one, little as it may be, works together with other gestures that compile into a message for the caregiver and his family. "You are not alone. We care about you; we are here, and we are not going away."

So, whether you become involved as a first responder, a 2nd-Class angel, or a fly-by angel, or a friend, know that you are part of a whole that together becomes what God would have us become: a help in time of trouble. We carry the ability to calm the atmosphere and extend a message of caring that helps to lighten the load of caregivers, and allow them enough time to catch their breath.

Chapter 10
Best Friends by God's Design

Another relational dynamic that furthers the strain for life in the shadows begins at an altar when life is often normal. Young couples learn the safety found in a spouse was designed by God to provide a haven where the soul can find refreshment, while at the same time empty its pain. In trauma's face, eyes meet and the tears well up, only to stream down one's cheeks-the unspoken agony that the heart can no longer contain. Yet, as those same eyes meet, souls connect, and in that moment a true friend's comfort and relief is gained. The same person who has shared in multiplying joys now strategically enters to divide one's sorrows. Difficult, maybe the experience, but consoling the encounter, especially when by God's grace their memory banks solidify a shared image that forever marks their lives and love together. There is something special in those moments that draw us together, if we are willing to allow it.

When agony emanates from this trusted confidant, who with a mere glance can see through to your soul, a caregiver's pain multiplies. First the hurt derived from helplessly watching a beloved spouse suffer, rakes one's soul; while a second hurt hits from the fact that the one to whom you turn in crisis is now decommissioned. Potentially brutal, yes, but it does not have to be crushing. It can be perplexing, but it does not have to be despairing. It can be destabilizing, but it does not have to destroy our lives and marriage.

So, how do we handle the torment that arises, as we helplessly encounter a precious loved one's anguish? What do we do when the cause of our own personal agony flows from our own ineptness to resolve the hurts that afflict our precious loved one? How do we make the house a home filled with an atmosphere that brings fulfillment and draws family, friends and visitors to feel welcomed?

The Caregiver's Marriage from an Insiders Point of View

Life in the shadows brings a painful side to one's marriage; there is no doubt. Yet, I found that the adjustment phase as a spouse presented the opportunity to move us towards each other. It is here that I offer an inside look at the sustaining concepts that have stabilized our household, refreshed our relationship and energized us through what I would conclude have been tumultuous times. It is here that in hearing the voice of God resident in the precepts He has given for life in this world, we found the help that anchored our relationship.

My intent is to focus upon caregivers, though what follows has ended up in many hands because my situation and profession constantly find me face to face with those who want to know my answer to, "What holds our marriage together?" In their minds, if it can stand the most excruciating of circumstances, it can surely benefit those who are fortunate enough to not have to endure such obstacles.

The last 20-plus years have provided a brutal testing ground for our marriage. Test upon test, trial upon trial, we held on to what we understood as precepts given by God in the Bible, because, in truth, that is all we had.

I cannot escape the fact that we had 20 years prior in which our house was made into a home where we loved to be. Then the trial by fire began its refining process, which we have utilized and offered on scores of occasions to assist couples in their growth with each other and with God, just as we found. I begin, therefore, by presenting two major premises or themes that run concurrently through the Scriptures that to this day comprise our lives. Over and over again, these concepts provided direction and brought stability, when I wondered how in the world I would make it through another episode. These two concepts are:

1. **God designed the marriage relationship as a best friend relationship.**
2. **Marriage as God designed involves the husband and wife both individually and together in harmony with God.**

Marriage: A Consultation with the Master Designer

It was in our junior years of college that Dawn and I met. Enthralled in the classes that focused heavily on our majors, our relationship was more of an acquaintance until half way through the year. It was a cold Palouse evening on the Washington State University - Pullman campus, as students returned for the spring semester. I asked her to take a walk that found us sitting on a university steam tunnel in deep conversation that would expand to include our thoughts about God, family, our upbringing and our personal dreams. Over the next months a friendship developed, until we found ourselves anticipating our interactions and time together.

Call it what you want, we look back and recognize that we were on a course to become best friends, which then led two and a half years later to an altar. Different in many ways, but completely committed to the same purposes, the friendship characterized our relationship. We had grown to be each other's most trusted confidant and today, it is not even a question. We do almost everything together, and we still enjoy it. For our household and our marriage, this simple fact has permeated all that we are about. In fact, the central truth that governs our model for marriage and family fixes itself on our being best friends. It is the number one answer that I offer, set and reset for couples in all our marriage counseling. It is magnetic and generates in the household atmosphere a sense of stability, security and the ability to enjoy the moment.

Families need it, and friends and guests detect it. Children sense the energy derived from this one bond, and it carried over to all parts of the household, even amidst our adversity. Simply put, this fact permeated every decision, every challenge and every adjustment. Even as the crises continually pounded us, we found ourselves cleaving all the more together with an unselfish concern, respect and tenderness for each other. This drew us closer to each other and to God, in whom we had learned real meaning was found. It was our saving grace.

We had no role models from our own upbringing with whom we could interact. Plus, the church seemed void of models that both exemplified and could articulate what their reasons were for their success. We heard about how we were to fit certain roles as husbands and wives, but we also realized that approach did not fare well with many we knew, as it created a tendency to individualize couples rather than to draw them together.

As I matured in my profession, I found myself challenged with understanding more precisely what God had to say about the issue. And why not? Why not consult with the Master Designer? Marriage, after all, was His dream. He created it. If there was something more that I did not know, I wanted to know. If what we had learned was in harmony with His design, then maybe then we could rest confidently and carry on, building upon what we had and refining it: Being best friends in honor to God.

So let me take us back for a moment to the opening chapters of the Bible and the Garden of Eden. Many may question its validity, but I do not. Many may want to lock wits over the scientific debates that have been hammering out for decades, but I would prefer to focus upon the original intent of the writing.

The Garden of Dreams: Not Ours, but God's - Genesis 1

Though the story of creation had probably been handed down via stories to Moses, the actual penning of the words was a necessity for what lay ahead for him and the people of Israel, as they approached the Promised Land that God Almighty had promised to Abraham centuries before. It was approximately 1450 BC, and the movement by Moses with the Hebrew people across the Sinai Dessert served as a great opportunity to remind the people of their roots and place in history. They needed to understand their place in God's plan. They had all witnessed the unique escape from Egypt with the plagues, the rise of Moses as their deliverer, and then the parting of the Red Sea.

Now they were being prepared to occupy a land that God had set apart for His story to unfold. It was a land where the surrounding tribes were serving other gods and in need of the very truths the Israelites as a nation were bringing. Coming as a nation of priests, displaying before those who observed from a distance their love for the one true God, they were to be God's spokesmen to mankind.

It, therefore, rested upon Moses as he was moved by God Himself to write down the truths and stories which had brought the people of Israel to this point in their history. As Moses' pen moved across the pages, his words unveiled the highlights to the story of God's beginning relationship to man. It revealed the quest of God for a restored relationship with mankind that would come through one of their descendants. It then passed to Moses' present situation, in which God led him to etch out a covenant that would serve as the constitution for the Hebrew nation in this new land. These writings, including the books of Genesis through Deuteronomy, became known as the Law and served as the foundation for the establishment of their nation, and, might I say, even our nation.

The thrust of the opening chapters in Genesis brings to the reader an inside view of God and His place in bringing man and woman into a relationship with Himself. Here His heart for man comes to life just as mankind came into existence. What highlighted the words that flowed from his pen had much more to do with the events of those six days of creation that would culminate in the creation of God's masterpiece, man and woman in harmony with each other and God. For indeed, Eden was the garden of dreams: not ours but God's. Marriage was His dream and still is His dream, not in the sense of a whimsical wish or fantasy, but an anticipated vision and predetermined plan that would actually take place. He was and is the designer of marriage. Because of this, there is reason to be optimistic; because He is alive and present.

I can only imagine, along with Moses and all the heavenly hosts, the full impact of those moments within God Himself. The first five days saw earth come into existence and then come to life with the vegetation and the creation of the fish and fowl. "It was good," summarized God's activity, as did the opening to the sixth day with the creation of creatures that would roam the land (Genesis 1:10, 12, 18, 21, 25). But the sixth day would end differently, bringing God's creative orchestration to a great crescendo. Now, before His very eyes came His masterpiece: the very creation of man together with woman in harmony with God, and His closing response, "It is very good."[103]

God's Master plan – Genesis 2

Where Genesis 1 speaks of the creation of man, Chapter 2 of Genesis finds God pushing the rewind button and offering the slower, more detailed version of those moments on the sixth day with the creation of man and woman. Genesis 1 speaks with a broad brush of truth pertaining to God's creation of man, but chapter two provides a closer look at this same creation account, but repaints the picture of the 6th day in more detail as well as unfolds God's Master plan for mankind.

The setting finds that God has created man out of the dust of the earth (Gen. 2:7). He then planted a garden (park) to be known as Eden and placed man in it (Gen. 2:8). All we know about the garden is that it was full of trees, pleasing to the eye and full of fruit. It was a forest and an orchard in one (Gen. 2:8-9). In the middle of that garden two trees stood that would later challenge the volitional free-will of man: The tree of life and the tree of the knowledge of good and evil, to which God gave specific instructions:"You are free to eat from any tree in the garden, but you must not eat from the tree of the knowledge of good and evil, for when you eat of it you will surely die."[104]

There was a river that watered the garden and served as the headwaters to four other rivers (Gen. 2:10-14). Man was given the job of being the first "park ranger," to work and care for the park (Gen. 2:15). The skies above and all that man saw, had to have produced in man awe and splendor as he walked with God in the garden.

God's Evaluation: Alone and Incomplete - Genesis 2:18

The completion of man and his placement into the garden then triggered God's evaluation of His own creation. Now, in the midst of His work and in His walk with man, He gives insight into His own heart, which in turn reveals His Master plan. No doubt, He is still clapping His hands with excitement, for it is His dream. Yet, before even the introduction of any kind of evil, we hear His evaluation of all that He has done, and we are somewhat surprised: "It is not good for the man to be alone" (Gen. 2:18).

This observation of man's aloneness is by no means an indication of God's inability to form a flawless creation. It is, however, evidence that God had not yet finished His creation. The term, "alone," means "in a state of aloneness by itself, isolated," or maybe better yet in this context, "incomplete." Keep in mind that it was God who had just created man. He did so and then evaluated man's condition with Himself still present and in relationship with man. The implications are profound in that God was literally stating that even with Himself present and in relationship with man, man was still incomplete. So, what can we conclude? Man was created to need another of his own kind as well. Socially, physically, mentally and relationally, man was created for a relationship, not only with God, but with someone other than himself.

Although man's relationship with God is sufficient to meet his deepest inner longings, God viewed the condition of incompleteness amidst the rest of creation as a legitimate need. God had designed man to need another of his own kind, and there was nothing immoral or wrong with that need. He made man with a longing that God Himself did not intend to meet, except through another of man's own kind.

I would like to suggest that what we are reading is a descriptive sense to the tri-part nature of man, and its distinction between the soul and spirit of man. The first part of man's nature is that of his physical body or material part of man. The soul speaks to the inner part of man that utilizes the capacities of the heart with its longings for security and significance, plus the mind, the will and emotions in relationship to another of its own kind. The spirit speaks more to using the same four capacities in terms of a relationship to God. The passage, therefore, revealed man's need for relationship with both God and others of his own kind.

What God was doing in this scene was exposing man's inner soul as being incomplete. In Adam's case, his spirit was full, because God had already met the deep longings of Adam's spirit. However, the longings in his soul were unmet.

Though the text does not address Adam's unmet need as painful (more a state of incompleteness), it does offer an explanation as to why we experience a sense of emptiness and even pain. Even with God present, the legitimate needs of the heart (soul) can go unmet, and when that aloneness becomes recognizable, it surfaces in one's emotional side as legitimate pain. The pain levels then rise to the degree of value that had been placed on the object lost. This is why having the marriage rocked by loss due to disability can be so devastating. Grief or legitimate loss, even for a person in harmony with God, reflects an unmet, legitimate need.

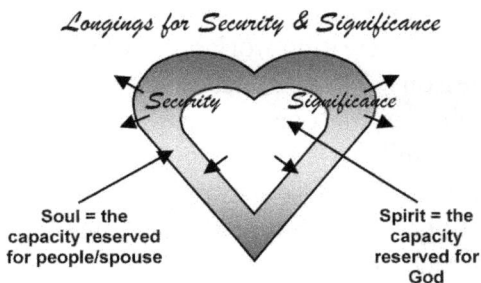

Longings for Security & Significance

Security   Significance

Soul = the
capacity reserved
for people/spouse

Spirit = the
capacity
reserved for
God

The story's beauty ends with the introduction by God of woman to man. With the appearance of the woman, man would be set back on his heels in awe of God's creation. He would sense the completeness relationally, not sexually. "…bone of my bones, and flesh of my flesh; she shall be called 'woman,' because she was taken out of man."[105] With a full spirit, completely trusting in God's character and God's plan for himself, Adam gazed upon the woman whom God had created and then brought to him. Soul to soul, he experienced completeness with one of his own kind, and yet he was definitely different than she. Adam's response to Eve displayed a fulfillment that he had not yet experienced, even while he had enjoyed an unbroken fellowship with the Almighty.

In naming "woman" (Gen. 2:23), Adam expressed that he saw her as a distinct reflection of himself, and his poetic words of praise for her echoed to the Lord that he knew she was part of the Master plan of the Sovereign Creator. It was not her appearance, performance or background that gave her worth. It was the fact that she was a gift from God, made like Adam in God's image, that established her value in Adam's eyes. The marriage was complete, and the aloneness remedied. Adam and Eve, with their souls filled with excitement for each other, began their tenure in the Garden of Dreams. Indeed it was "very good."

Four Timeless Qualities - Genesis 2:24-25

In the closing lines to Chapter Two, Moses provides a commentary that further explains God's vision of His master plan. It is likely that these words entered the Garden story via Moses, rather than being part of the original creation story. The opening words to these last lines, state, "For this reason..."[106] and refers to the completeness experienced by Adam and Eve while in the presence and harmony with God. Then, for the generations that followed, Moses offered four timeless qualities that when set in place, provide the foundation which was meant to guide a couple in bringing about the fulfillment God intended. In fact, it would be these words which years later Christ would refer to for his teaching on the sanctity and importance of marriage, as would the Apostle Paul (Matthew 19 & Ephesians 5).

*"For this reason a man will **leave** his father and mother and **be united (cleave)** to his wife, and they will **become one flesh**. And the man and his wife were both **naked, and they felt no shame**."*
Genesis 2:24-25

The four timeless qualities can be summarized as **first** bringing each couple to sever their interdependent ties to their parents and establish a commitment that transfers their interdependence to each other. The **second** includes the continued long-term cleaving as a couple, reflected in being each other's best friend. **Third** is the oneness, or unity, that comes from being best friends, and **fourth** is the shared intimacy that gives genuineness to God's wonderful dream. As these four qualities become woven into the fabric of the marriage relationship, a fragrance emits that draws one to desire the company of the other.

As all four qualities add a wholesome dimension to marriage, it is the second quality that sets the atmosphere for the marriage and home and marks the marriage as God intended it. "[Cleave] to your wife," said Moses. Just as the first directive moved man toward his wife, the second directive established the atmosphere for his home. In setting up his household, the man was to cleave to his wife. Literally it meant that he was to cling, stick, paste or be glued to her permanently. This was more than just a contract.

In a relational context, cleaving to someone carries the idea of clinging with affection and loyalty, graphically pictured as one holding on to the other with both hands. How appropriate, when one considers that this action serves to bring completeness to one's mate. In fact, genuine cleaving emits an ambiance that permeates the atmosphere with a lasting security. It produces a state of permanence in the relationship, and why not? Who wouldn't want this kind of atmosphere for their home?

Yet, "to cleave," picks up even more of a meaning when one recognizes that the term depicts the activity of a genuine friendship. It describes the strong bond that occurs between two people who are true, loyal friends as expressed in Proverbs 18:24 – "A man of many companions may come to ruin, but there is a friend who sticks closer (cleaves) than a brother."

Friends cling, stick, or are found in each other's presence. They are inseparable. The power resident in cleaving only underscores the uniqueness of that word's choice in setting the atmosphere of the home and relationship between the husband and wife in Genesis 2. It highlights the activity between a husband and wife. It is no wonder why in the same context, the writer has highlighted the precious favor and relationship that a man receives from God, he finds in his wife (Prov.18:22).

Cleaving to one another highlights the activity of friends of which the husband-wife relationship stands out as primary. Each couple must recognize that this directive suggests that by their actions, they leave an imprint on each other of being best friends. They are side by side and hand in hand, holding onto each other tightly by their actions and in their manner toward each other. Within the walls of their home, they cling to each other with utmost affection and loyalty befitting those who are best friends. How appropriate to have chosen a word that highlights permanence, for the one true expression that depicts a friend is caught in the statement, "I will be there." Here lies the explanation behind the power of those words, "I do," which gives to one's spouse a power that makes or breaks one's day.

Though the meaning captured by these words is strategic to a marriage, there is more that comes out as to its importance, when we realize this is the core idea to Moses' words. As we read the text, we find that a man leaves his father and mother, which is an act or in some cases a process, that is eventually accomplished. Once accomplished, the man finds Moses' words follow-up with a key directive to cleave to his wife. This is then followed by a futuristic declaration or result that gives us the third and fourth qualities of unity and intimacy. Essentially, these last two are by-products of the lifelong development and enjoyment of the couple, brought about by working toward and being best friends.

One cannot miss the profound importance placed on this concept of cleaving to each other. Being best friends in harmony with each other and with God, stands as the major focus God gives for marriage. Regardless of age, or how many years a marriage has been shared, or how many difficulties they have together endured, it is the friendship quality that gives the real stamp of genuineness to the marriage. It is this dynamic that yields as its outcome what I refer to as a "hallmark marriage."

It is the kind of relationship in which two completely different individuals with different upbringings, temperaments, talents, scars and dreams come together in spirit, soul and body. The man in becoming one with his wife touches the deep longing of her heart for security, while she satisfies his legitimate need for significance and worth. Show me a couple who handles these cries from the heart of their spouse, and we will witness the unity and oneness of them both. How profound that when God's final act of creation ended, it was with the establishment of man and woman, joined together with Him. It does not include children, affluence or success.

It is at this point that the detailed account of creation recorded in Chapter Two folds back into Chapter One and we find those words, "it is very good," being an appropriate ending for the creation story. For God it had to have been a moment where even that was an understatement. His creation dream was complete, and His desire for a long-term relationship with a free-willed being was in place.

Can I Say It Again? - Conclusive Precepts

No matter how many times I have studied this passage or asked colleagues to critique our work, I find the evidence experienced in couple after couple, disabled and not, has only served to validate these conclusions.

1. God designed the marriage relationship as a best-friend relationship.

For our household this relational model of marriage with the focal point of being best friends, we found through the years set the atmosphere for our relationship, home and ministry with people, even amidst the crises. The very fragrance of our home derived its wholesomeness from the friendship that we shared together with the Lord. It has been this concept of being

> Friendship is a trust relationship between two people who are mutually drawn to each other. Their unselfish concern, respect, and tenderness influence them to draw closer to each other and to God, in whom real meaning is found.

best friends or true *trusted confidants* that has carried us through everything. This trust relationship drew us together and drew us to God in whom we learned real meaning was found. This was God's intent and dream, and, as we would experience, the glue that held us together. As the friendship grew in expression, a fragrance filled the home atmosphere. As we joined that friendship around our growth in the Lord, as well as in our joint activity serving Christ and our community, we found our friendship to only be enriched.

2. Marriage as God designed involves the husband and wife both individually and together in harmony with God.

It would be easy to miss the importance of God in the Garden, if we did not realize He was giving an account of His dream for creating mankind. He sought a relationship with a free-will, volitional being whom He would not only create, but who would have the ability to choose to relate to Him. Did He need it? No! Did He desire and plan for it, and then bring it to be out of the pure desire to share Himself and all that He has? Yes! Then on that sixth day He brought man into existence, and Adam found Himself in a harmonious relationship with God Himself, while he toured and enjoyed his opening moments with God in the Garden. What Adam did not know was his own incompleteness or aloneness (Gen. 2:18). God made the observation to Himself (Gen.2:18), but God also had a plan that involved the introduction of woman in what would become marriage and the priority social relationship that would mark every culture.

Yet, let's look closely to realize that for Adam and Eve, marriage as God designed involved the husband and wife to be in harmony with each other, but as well, individually and collectively, with God. It was a triangular relationship that fulfilled what God dreamed, having a creation that could individually relate to Him, while at the same time enjoy each other. What an amazing idea!!

Best Friends: Not a Sometimes Love

Peter Kilborn, in an article in the New York Times, notes that, "As modern medicine extends the lives of people with chronic diseases, the rate of divorce among them is increasing, leaving a growing number without income, health insurance or support at home."[107]

He goes on to quote John Edwards, a professor of sociology at Virginia Tech, who says that "declines in health have an adverse influence on marital quality. Tensions develop because the disabled spouse carries less weight in the household, shares in fewer activities and withdraws or becomes moody, angry or critical."[108]

Further in his article, he notes that lawyers say that "divorce among the disabled is also influenced by factors that have been driving up the overall rate of divorce, like more casual public mores (cultural norms and ways that embody a group and are accepted without question), less stigma attached to divorce and more wives who work outside the home. Therefore, it is no longer considered necessary to hang in there with the disabled spouse."[109]

Increased personal stresses between a couple and heightened threats of divorce as being an acceptable course of action lend to destabilizing the home atmosphere. Simultaneously, the music of our day rings of a love for one's spouse in the tough times, but this love is not a "sometimes" love. Dr. Keith Korstjens says, "Great marriages are not built on a 'sometimes' love. Ours is a love that sticks. It's a love that takes the unexpected, the distasteful, even the hurtful, and turns it into steel-like fiber for endurance. It's a love that stubbornly refuses to die."[110]

Dr. Korstjens penned these words, not only as a pastor, but after serving for over 40 years his wife, who was physically disabled early in their marriage by polio. How gripping a statement and standard for life is captured by these words, "not a sometimes love." It is not up and down with the selfish fulfillments that our hearts have become so disillusioned to think they rightfully deserve. There resides in this type of enduring love an unfailing commitment that surrounds the relationship, sustains them, strengthens them and surfaces with patience and kindness that "is not easily provoked" or "acts unbecomingly" to get its own way. It knows how to bear all things, believe all things, find hope in all things and endure all things. This sounds like Paul's description of the love of Christ which was recorded in I Corinthians 13:4-7.

The reality of such a commitment takes on more than an ideal, when the truth of the setting becomes clearer in the minds of the family who faces these adjustments every day. In so doing it gives further credence to the meaning of "not a sometimes love." So, what holds us together is that by God's design and our choice, our relationship is a best-friend relationship-that involves both of us in harmony with each other and God; and I thank God daily that it is. In short, be best friends. It is amazing how embracing these simple concepts have kept us through the years giving for us what we refer to as a "hallmark marriage."

♥♥♥♥♥♥♥

Couch Time

God's design for marriage sets the husband/wife relationship as the priority social relationship in which friendship should permeate its atmosphere. To keep it as the priority relationship means just that: keep it as priority. To help you, we suggest that each couple establish what we call, "Couch Time."[111] This interactive time together involves spending 15 minutes a day sitting together in a special spot, reserved for just the two of you at a favorite couch or table. (Favorite dessert is highly recommended.) For those with children, instruct them that they are not to interrupt Dad and Mom during this time. If you must, prepare an activity for them to do to allow you to privately talk.

In establishing this time, the conversation is not to involve anything concerning work, family or money, but rather, it should focus entirely upon the two of you. Going longer than 15 minutes is allowed, but not shorter than this allotted time. If you find this habit difficult, do your best to set a realistic goal of sitting down together at least three times a week.

Since God is central to the making of marriage, do not hesitate to ask each other how God has showed up in your day's activity. If this is a new thought, then start looking. He is there. Remember marriage is God's dream, and it was His original design to be involved as central to our lives. We all need Him. His delight is in being there with us.

- For beginners a good question to consider can involve writing down one's definition of friendship. Then discuss your answers together with an idea of developing a working definition that agrees with both of you. (Don't forget the dessert.)
- Then progress to a discussion about what qualities in your view make a best friend a best friend. How are you doing? What can you do to help each other improve?

Chapter 11
The Fingerprints of God

"God's fingerprints are all over adversity but probably not the way we would think."

As adversity takes up permanent residence in our homes, the challenges it brings necessitate the need to make adjustments. As the days give way to weeks, then months, and even years, we learn that adjusting is a process, a very time-consuming process, that requires our utmost attention.

The last two chapters were meant to breathe some fresh air into the caregiver's adjustment setting. Though adjusting to adversity for both the caregiver and the disabled may not be associated with the easy life, the angels of kindness and the all-important friendships, especially when the trial infringes upon a married couple, offer an immense sharing of adversity's load. "Two are better than one . . . If one falls down, his friend can help him up . . . A cord of three strands is not quickly broken."[112] Personally, the gratitude for these people in my life and the preciousness of a wife who is as near and dear to me has carried me through many bleak moments.

Adversity's Pity Party

Adversity has a way of hovering like a mist over one's thinking that clouds out the wonder and majesty of our friendships and even God. If the caregiver's private time becomes a pity party wallowing in the feelings of being robbed of the good life, then adversity's fog can reap its destructive ways. It is at this point that decisions are made that can ransack the soul and cloud the atmosphere of any home. Cynicism can set in along with another medical bill. Skepticism, pessimism and even frustration can seep into one's mental attitude and, if we are not careful, influence our ways. The smallest involvement can become an entanglement that leads even the most well-meaning caregiver to become totally disengaged, because the preparation for a simple task requires so much more too just participate.

"Wheel-chair? Check! Walker? Check! Warm wraps for Mom (even on a sunny day)? Check! Medications? Check! Complete change of clothes? Check!"

And, if it's an overnight excursion; "Foot board to keep the bed sheets from setting off the nerves? Check! Shower hose and shower chair? Check! Check! Gluten free food? Check! Further medications? Check!"

It may seem small, but when every activity, and I mean "every," involves so many potential challenges, our attitude to participate can be easily swayed to find the pity party as an alternative. The problem arises from the company we find at our own pity parties. The potential for slipping into adversity's pool of despondency, lends to recognizing that we as caregivers are called to a very important discipline to take our "every thought captive to the obedience of Christ"[113]. This brings each caregiver into the constant awareness that what confronts him is a battle that seldom ceases and happens right in his own mind.

Battle for the Caregiver's Mind

As the adjustment period settles down and a routine to life develops, the battle for the caregiver's heart and mind forge forward. Enticements play on our personal weaknesses, baiting (tempting) us with thoughts that clash with our value system. Tiredness causes us to let down our guards and yield to entertaining ideas that would normally be foreign to our ways of life. Now the, "Why God?" questions reappear, or at best, looms on the horizon, until they can engulf our thoughts in the darkness and silence that keeps us awake into the wee hours of the morning. Legitimate questions and spiritual questions that can challenge the deepest of thinkers now come to light.

Some fair-weathered thinkers, who acknowledge God's place in life, as long as life is good, are quickly overcome. In a similar fashion, others, who diligently search for reasons to their suffering, sometimes conclude that their seeming logic grants them the right to rant against God and any who whole heartedly accept His personal loving ways with man. It is interesting to note that throughout my years as a pastor and caregiver, I have found these skeptical types number far fewer in comparison to the God-fearing individuals who honestly just want to make sense of their faith and the God of their faith. Still, others seek to expel the guilt that torments their souls, by seeking forgiveness from a past wrong that they have stored until that moment; while the majority humbly and nobly make an all-out effort to steady their faith, which has been rocked by the adversity that seems to mock it.

In so many cases, life and death questions arise, especially if their experience has narrowly escaped the traversing over "the valley of the shadow of death."[114] These are real questions generated from the real world where good and evil, right and wrong, just and unjust are hammered out. Yet, it is here the battle finds us standing face to face with God. We may be demanding an audience with Him like Job, or lamenting our seeming injustice like the psalmist, or pleading for mercy for wayward friends like the prophets of old; but the ultimate clash with God cannot be avoided.

It is not my intent to get lost in theological debates; rather, it is my desire to encourage caregivers like me. It just so happens that I am a pastor. My world spins with people. People are my business, because people are His business. As a student of people, it has been my habit to stop and watch life. Issues about God, the complexities that we face and the joys that we share are all part of my work. Reading and studying the Scriptures constitute a major part of my life, not as some kind of theological exercise, but to better understand and relate to God.

My life's work has sought to identify with the Scripture's meaning for my own life, my household and all with whom I am blessed to relate. Prayer and my communion with God are regular activities for me, lending in one moment too much rejoicing, when again I see His handiwork in a person's life. Just as much, I cry with those I love whose paths find hurt, loss and grief tearing at their souls. Yet, it is in these moments that my perplexed heart battles, as I reflect upon the agony that people like my wife and I face daily.

Corner Piece #3: Adversity Transforms Us

As the battle rages within me, I find myself being drawn back once again to the image of my wife's smile, as she joyfully separates her puzzle pieces that she has amassed before me. In that momentary dream, a glimmer in her eye interrupts my search as she places in my hand what she knew I would treasure. Glancing down as her hand retreats there in my palm is the prized third corner piece to the puzzle. Immediately, the leading question that has focused my attention throughout our ordeal reappears. How are we to understand and handle adversity? What is at the heart of such difficult moments?

Reflecting again for a moment I refresh my memory of how answering that question has helped frame my thoughts and direct my energy. Adversity awakens us to the hidden and painful side of life. Adversity then forces us to define our struggles and calculate the challenges, which then necessitates the need to make adjustments. Now a further development to handling adversity appears, as the third corner piece to puzzling events drives home the truth that adversity ultimately transforms us. We will be transformed by this crisis.

A transformation, different than change, implies that something acts upon us. Yes, we still make the decisions, but at the same time a force often supernatural at its origin, lends an outside influence in shaping those decisions. What we can expect, as we hold this third corner piece, is to discover how God's fingerprints end up all over adversity and how this can turn the adversity into a meaningful venture.

It is here, wrapped up in people's lives, that we will find ourselves observing dynamics that are woven into the fabric of humanity. These dynamics enable a perseverance that makes that transformation possible. It does not just happen, and seldom is it even noticed or attributed to God. Yet, each dynamic puts an exclamation point as to God's gracious involvement, when adversity takes its toll. We seek to make sense of our ordeal, and we like meticulously investigators on a crime scene, spread our dust powder looking for any evidence we can find that substantiates our concepts of God. What we find are God's fingerprints all over our adversity, but probably not the way we would think.

I am constantly reminded that the same heat that melts the ore, hardens the clay. The same adversity that lends to growth can also hardened the hearts of caregivers and their loved ones. This is not a stone-throwing statement, but it is made to lure those who are finding their resources depleting or empty to stay the course and to press on.

Whether one is Christian or not, the fingerprints of God on humanity work a life-changing power that, over time, yields a profound impact. Yet, let's be honest enough to give credit to whom it is due, and recognize that God has a pathway through pain and suffering that leads toward our enrichment in life, especially with Him.

Strength of Human Spirit

It is January 21st, and, as Dawn begins her morning reading at the breakfast table, what she reads emerges from her soft voice:

"Tribulation is the door to triumph. The valley leads to the open highway, and tribulation's imprint is on every great accomplishment.

Crowns are cast in crucibles, and the chains of character found at the feet of God are forged in earthly flames. No one wins the greatest victory until he has walked the winepress of woe. With deep furrows of anguish on His brow, the 'man of sorrows,' namely Jesus, said, 'In this world you will have trouble" (John 16:33). But immediately comes the psalm of promise, 'Take heart! I have overcome the world'... Tribulation has always marked the trail of the true reformer."[115]

As I listened to my dearest friend read, I sensed the calm reassurance that she knew what this lady author had penned. A sip of coffee and pile of pills followed, all designed to help her cope with her day and rebuild depleted enzymes and other essentials within her body. Today the pain levels are more in check, her mental faculties clearer, her spirit encouraged and her smile energizing. Reflecting upon her reading, she says, "Oh the Lord is so good." In only moments, she looks up, turns her wheels and heads to prepare for her day.

Over the years as I interact and watch her, I marvel at the attitude and tenacity that marks this remarkable lady. Chronic, debilitating pain marks her bent-over body. For her to stand straight or even lie straight are impossibilities. Difficulties mark her every day, beginning with just trying to get prepared. Then the smile fills the atmosphere with a pleasantness that invites conversation. In her case, adversity transformed her, and her situation precipitated over time a change within many people who shared a prolonged association with her.

To recap her story, in 1966 she lay on an x-ray table in the very place where she was to be working, only to have her friends not even recognize her because her condition was so bad. Seven months followed on a Stryker bed, not knowing if she would be able to walk, mixed regularly with the fact that all her dreams had been shattered. Yet a strength from within surfaced in her being and she rose to the challenge.

Twenty-five years later, cysts in her spinal cord stopped her again, and again and again. Each time she found strength within to address her plight. A major surgery with five more months in a body cast, and then the second devastating tragic accident left her completely wheel-chair bound and in chronic pain. By 2001 a doctor confided with her that her state was grave, and he was not sure if she could pull out this time.

At that point, she prayed that God would grant her the privilege to hold just one of her children's children, which was quite a prayer, considering that none of our children were yet married! The tenacity and determination that erupted into action within her revealed a strength of spirit and desire for life. As the ravages of pain, weakness and the ways of old age engulfed her every dream, a greater and more compelling desire to live rose to the challenge. In each situation, her strength of human spirit and an inner determination kicked into gear. It was a miracle we could see and sense. At the same time, for me during the time allotted to adjust, the determination, self-discipline, and stamina to resolve matters reflected the same strength of human spirit. A power that we did not know we had enabled us to do our part.

Jill Krementz, in her work with disabled young people, speaks of that "strength of human spirit …and how it can overcome vast hurdles, but also how it needs to be loved and nourished."[116] Not that we have to overcome to become whole again, but the ability to address the issue and make the most of what one has calls for both something from within oneself and from sources other than oneself.

From the mouth of a 12 year old boy who was paralyzed at the age of two during a corrective heart surgery, Krementz' pen records his thoughts:

"My friends and family were very important to me, because they made me realize that I was really perfectly OK the way I was."[117] "I learned that I am not the only person with problems and that other people have gone through more serious difficulties than I have. I think that every handicapped person who has lived a tough life deserves a trophy, not just me."[118]

Realizing that his life involved adjusting to his life's situations, he understood what all of us need to recognize and opened wide his heart when he concluded with a statement that applies to us all. "All people with disabilities – and without – need friends who will treat them with respect, will not make them feel foolish, and will help them when they need it."[119] He then recognized the fact that, just as every human being, the disabled seek to be accepted and loved as much as they want to be accepting, loving friends.

An Innate Quest to Live

From within this young man's very soul, came an innate quest for life or strength to live and experience life. It is true within all of us, but for the disabled and caregivers who do not succumb to their own self-pity, this inner drive for life rises from the inner man to address daily their hearts' longing for life. They wear it on their sleeves every day. It is visible to everyone.

Author Alan Rucker reaches some general assumptions that again speak to this strength of spirit:

"Your capacity to deal with any kind of severe ailment is probably much greater than you think. You have more emotional grit, more resolve, and greater perseverance than you imagine. Let me be the first to tell you: you are not the weak sister you think you are… I don't know where so many people get the idea that they don't have what it takes to bear up under such stress. Maybe, as the pass-the-chip-dip Americans, many of us have had so little true stress in our lives that it looms as more unbearable than it often is. The catastrophizing, in other words, is worse than the catastrophe. Or maybe it's just human nature to fear the unknown."[120]

Life in the shadows reveals daily an inner resolve from both the disabled and caregivers alike that rises to meet the situation at hand. For the disabled, when they are nurtured by those around them, it offers reinforcement to their journey to rise up and make the adjustments to life's difficulties.

There is no doubt that when disability strikes, the disabled are just that – disabled. They will awaken to a disability that will require an internal strength to carry them through the day. The support network offers encouragement, but each battle still requires perseverance, as well as a determination for reinventing one's life. And though the outward signs are not as visible for the caregiver, the same inner determination, the same will to reinvent life, awaits his every morning.

Where does this inner drive to live come from? Why does this innate resolve surface especially in the face of adversity to empower a person to expend his all, when that life is in question? How is it that, even the great accuser before God in Job's story would summarize how, "Man will give all he has for his own life"? How is it that regardless of nationality, race or sex that man, woman and child seek in death's face to live and fight for life?

I believe that God's fingerprint on the human soul has provided every human being with an intrinsic quest for life. This innate drive to live stems from mankind's first breath, which was inbreathed by God himself. The Scriptures attest to the fact that in the creation account of man, regardless of how one wants to account for God's method of creating it all, "God formed the man from the dust of the ground and breathed into his nostrils the breath of life, and the man became a living being."[121]

Man was not an already-existing, animate being that appeared to develop in stages. He is from dust, and God fashioned him into man and then breathed into him, life. He gave to that first man and each human since the unique quality that comes inborn in us all to live, and that life was intended to be lived in harmony with God, the author of life, forever.

God, by being God, has always existed. He gave us life with the full intent of having us live life, and to do so in harmony with Him, forever. Though there is temptation to understand what happened and why death's entry befell the ways of mankind, the point here is that life and the desire to live need to be recognized as God–given, inborn in every human being, because that was God's way with man. That was God's fingerprint upon man, along with the dignity that marks man in being made in the image and likeness of God.

Therefore, when death's doorway or adversity's challenges encroach upon us, this life blood within us, the grit, perseverance, tenacity, and quest to live, rise to the occasion. They surface as the inner resolve or strength of human spirit, because God's fingerprint on the soul carries a DNA to live! God Himself breathed into man life and therefore the want to live. It reflects His very being.

Dawn's tenacity, as with all who contend with such issues, along with all the caregivers who rally to support their loved ones, provides us with evidence that God is present. The strength of human spirit implanted by God in the very heart of man leaves His fingerprint, and this could not be clearer than watching both the disabled and their caregivers. He is present. He has not left us in this world to our own.

Transforming Acceptance

As I mentioned, there are distinct but ever so powerful dynamics that have been imprinted into this world by the Almighty to surface in those dark moments when adversity strikes. Like gravity, these dynamics are part of the laws of this world that just work. Maybe we do not want to attribute these dynamics to God, but a thorough reading of Job's account in the Bible has a way of leading us to retract such a misunderstanding.

In the same vein, maybe we can understand a little better if we recognize that this world is filled with paradoxes. For example, why is it that when we give, we are the one who receives? Or why is it when we show honor, we receive honor; or why is it that love begets love? These are called paradoxes. Maybe just like laws and paradoxes that stem back to the Creator, accompanying adversities are imprinted dynamics pressed by God into the web of our existence that reflect the very ways of God Himself.

So just like nature's laws that God has planted into this world, or like life's paradoxes which He has woven into this world's fabric, adversity finds dynamics that surface over time and can be traced back as evidence to God's personal presence and concern. Though any association with God may be in question, such denial does not nullify God's dynamic power and grace being placed into operation.

The first dynamic we observed was the strength of human spirit and the innate quest for life. It surfaces quickly in the scheme of adversity as we have seen. The second dynamic, transforming acceptance, and the closely related third dynamic, power of the powerless, come to light only after the adjustments have been settled upon.

Acceptance Surrenders Total Control

For the caregiver, holding the third corner piece often begins in a pool of tears. Following the second car accident in 97 found Dawn in surgery in early 98 to assess the damage. As Dr. Grady approached, his countenance carried the message. His opening words registered, "I am so sorry," and those words echoed around in what I would later recall as an empty chamber in my heart. Hopes had been so high following that massive corrective surgery a few months prior. But this time, any hope had all but disappeared. Any anticipation that maybe we would be able to truly enjoy life again had momentarily vanished.

Then his words, "Please do not lose hope; we are developing so many new avenues of help for people in her condition." As if someone slid the floor back under my feet, I found myself at least stabilized enough to realize that her condition, though grave, was not the end. Though at the moment the full effects were yet to be felt, I still had her, and I would be taking her home to love her, regardless.

The following days would be difficult, but with each day I found more of an acceptance of her condition. Her condition was absolutely worse, her pain levels extreme and constant care necessary. Her condition undoubtedly was outside my control other than one point: she was going home to our home. I would have my best friend at home to love, as I would find in ways far beyond my capability.

Back in my study, the moment arose where I bowed again at my desk and surrendered to God. It was out of my control totally. I felt absolutely powerless, but I could accept it. Much like the alcoholic's first step toward recovery requires him to acknowledge his powerlessness and to surrender to a power higher than himself, so also the caregiver requires a similar acknowledgement.

Opportunity Knocks

In His kindness, God gave me a wonderful teacher-my wife. Her pathway had brought her to a place of surrender on more than one occasion and with lessons that transferred easily into my world. Tenacity and determination had carried her through so many adversities, but she recalls how at one of her own self-proclaimed pity parties, she felt she was nothing more than a millstone around especially her family's neck. "Oh to just be able to contribute and help people again," Dawn shared with an older lady whose adversities included the loss of her husband on a return to help the Chinese people after WWII. Winnie turned to Dawn and said, "Adversities are nothing more than great opportunities for God to display Himself. Dawn, see your disability as an opportunity for the Lord. Be better not bitter."

Dawn's recollection of that moment with this dear China Inland Mission missionary blew the lights out on her party, even though to have a pity party crash is no big loss. To see her disability not as losing her ability, but as an opportunity for God, challenged her. Eventually this new thought established for her a confidence not in herself but God. Her disability meant for her an opportunity for God to display Himself. Uniquely, it was this same lesson that would filter into my own setting. Even though I may have been aware of it in other scenarios, I needed to see afresh that opportunity was knocking.

Whether we stand as the disabled opportunist or the opportunistic caregiver, the key to movement from just adjusting to adversity to finding a true transformation begins with acceptance of the circumstances. From within my soul came that acceptance, when I figuratively threw my hands into the air in an expression of absolute surrender to One greater than I. There was a reckoning that her condition would be permanent, and I realized that healing was not the way. I accepted her plight as mine to bear. Even though I cannot remember the exact moment, the acceptance I would later take actually initiated a transformation within my own life.

Genuine acceptance opens further the doorway for transformation to occur. Acceptance releases the need to control and overcome. In my case, acceptance consciously acknowledged that our well-being was outside our control. Opportunity then knocked with the gentle reminder that all there is of God is available to the man who is available to all there is of God.

God was not taken by surprise when the evil ways of our world unleashed a moving bomb down the road and wreaked havoc upon our household. Evidences of His presence though were there in our adversity, as we continually observed this strength of human spirit in us both making adjustments, and then gaining acceptance in the appropriate moment. Here the door opened to transforming our lives and looking for opportunities to arise. Whether one acknowledges it or not, this fingerprint of God on humanity works its life-changing power.

Acceptance: Pathway to Grace

Why shouldn't acceptance lead to grace? Think about it. Acceptance implies a complete honesty with the situation. Honesty is the core to humility. Here we reach a point of total honesty with life, what we can and cannot do, what we control and do not control. We see our own helplessness before Almighty God. The illusion that we are somehow in control stares us in the face, and we choose to either run from it or accept that it is an illusion. We recognize our own hopelessness, and either choose to reject Him or live as though He is not there, or we bend the knee and reach out to Him and find the transforming acceptance. This acceptance leads to opportunities to achieve matters that truthfully matter most to God. It is here that we once again find a throne noted for its dispensing of mercy and grace "to help in time of need."[122] And to whom does He express this? He offers it to all of us, because grace exudes from His very nature.

He gives grace to the humble (I Peter 5:5) or honest, while at the same time He fuels our endurance, not as some kind of power demonstration to beat the odds, but because it is fitting of God. Transforming acceptance opens the doorway to God's grace. God, being far beyond my thinking, calls from the midst of our pain and suffering, as He reaches for us to lean upon Him. It is here that we find the open door to the experience of God. Amazingly, this is where, when dealing with people who have faced adversity, one detects a peace that permeates their way of life. They have it, because it comes with the God of grace, whether its recipient chooses to acknowledge God's bestowment or not of that grace and peace or not. Surrender usually brings some form of peace and that peace is indeed priceless. Now gift-wrapped by the God of grace, another fingerprint, if one chooses to see it, graces the situation: transforming acceptance.

The Power of the Powerless

Closely connected to this transforming acceptance comes another noteworthy dynamic. Simply put, at the heart of adversity a power is released, a power from the powerless that induces a life-altering transformation upon those willing to participate with those contending with the adversity. This includes all the caregivers. This power is unique, because it does not explode, but draws out like a healing salve qualities within us caregivers that may never have found expression.

Even as we observe God, we know He is compassionate and ready to extend forgiveness to us all, even though we do not deserve such grace. If one stops long enough to contemplate this very simple thought, one can see that God's compassion and forgiveness to be expressed, required that evil and its ill effects be present in order for Him to display such qualities. These are qualities of God that would not have been seen or understood apart from evil co-existing with God in this world. All the hosts of Heaven must have stood amazed at what they were seeing.

Compassion: God's Undeniable Quality in a Perishing World

Once again we find ourselves standing on the third corner piece to life's puzzling events. Once acceptance of our plight as caregivers was knowingly or unknowingly understood as our cross to bear and our calling to express, a power began altering our lives by drawing out of us qualities that would forever mark our being. For some it is a refinement, while for others, it is an awakening of love and compassion that with time becomes part of our very nature.

Daily contact with the powerless undoubtedly alters the caregiver's activities, but even more so it alters his being and his character. Something happens in his association with the disabled that becomes a source of transformation. In turn, the caregiver not only changes, but he becomes an instrument of change among those with whom he associates.

This was beautifully illustrated in a work by Christopher de Vinck, entitled, "The Power of the Powerless: A Brother's Lesson." Appearing as an essay in the Wall Street Journal on April 10, 1985, the essay and later the book with the same title addressed how he was transformed by his invalid brother. Though he would never see his work with his brother as a sacrifice, he expresses how his daily contact would mold him to understand life and God, not just from what gets done, but from what truly lasts in moving people closer to each other and God, in Whom real meaning is found.

His story began with Christopher describing life growing up with his brother, Oliver, who had recently passed away and for whom he wanted to give a tribute for the impact he had on him.

For 32 years, he (Oliver) was on his back in bed, in the same corner of his room, under the same window, beside the same yellow walls. He was blind and mute. His legs were twisted. He didn't have the strength to lift his head or the intelligence to learn anything.[123]

Oliver was born with severe brain damage, which left him and his body in a permanent state of helplessness. "My family and I fed Oliver. We changed his diapers, hung his clothes and bed linens… We bathed Oliver, tickled his chest to make him laugh. Sometimes we left the radio on in his room. We pulled the shade down on the window over his bed in the morning to keep the sun from burning his tender skin. We listened to him laugh as we watched television downstairs. We listened to him rock his arms up and down to make the bed squeak. We listened to him cough in the middle of the night."[124]

"Feeding Oliver throughout his life was like feeding an eight-month-old child… Though we breathed the same night air, listened to the same wind, **slowly without our knowing, oliver created a certain power around us which changed all our lives.** I cannot explain Oliver's influence except to say that the powerless in our world do hold great power. The weak do confound the mighty."[125]

151

The outcome of that one essay brought an onslaught of responses from all over the country, including personal letters from then-President Ronald Reagan and Sargent Shriver, who requested permission to print the essay for members helping with the Special Olympics. The next day, the New York Post called requesting to reprint the essay, and with time came Reader's Digest, Catholic Digest, the Chicago Sun, Campus Life and a host of others.

In the introduction to the book, Henri Nouwen makes this observation:

"The Power of the Powerless breaks with all human logic, all intelligent predictions, all normal norms of success and satisfaction. It turns everything upside down. It speaks not only about the power of the powerless, but also about love offered by those who cannot speak words of love, joy by those who suffer grievously, hope given by those whose lives are complete failures, courage enkindled by those who cannot make the slightest move on their own. In a world that so much wants to control life and decides what is good, healthy, important, valuable and worthwhile, they will find that the hidden truths of life are hidden from the learned and clever and revealed to those who are mere children (Matt 11:25)."[126]

Christopher de Vinck adds these additional thoughts:

"If Oliver had not been born, I wouldn't have the same joys and fears and secrets I dream about today... There was a substance in the house beyond science and philosophy and theology, for these are man-made explanations. We always feel confident that we can make decisions in the present which will guarantee comfortable results in the future. Those guarantees never exist, unless the choices we make embrace the fire (the needy in life) in an act of love."[127]

Listening to what they have observed parallels what those who are caregivers learn, if they want to learn at all. Caregivers will be people marked by compassion and love. Even I cannot explain how just being around my wife day after day and month after month, emitted an unseen power that drew compassion and kindness from within me. Yes, she is my best friend, a fact which made it easier; but this unseen power refers not so much to what is in us, but the power through us that will accomplish its end in transforming people. For the weak, disabled and the caregiver, their power draws out of others a spirit of compassion, kindness and empathy that in time transforms those who are the dispensers of such qualities. As this

152

compassionate spirit works its ways, a fragrance emits from the setting that attracts its viewers and inspires its onlookers.

Why does God encourage us in so many places to be concerned for the weak and needy? Spend time with the disabled. Adjust as a caregiver adjusts, and sooner or later the truth of what de Vinck expressed appears in our own lives. When you hang around the disabled, needy or weak whose acceptance of their plight and sheer enjoyment with what they have is evident, life will transform. It changes. They express love without words; joy in the midst of suffering; hope from what seems to be failure.

I am drawn back to the Scriptures and the writings of Paul. After being affected by a thorn in his flesh that in his words "tormented me," Paul pleaded on three occasions for the Lord "to take it away."[128] Apparently, Paul's thoughts rang with such sound conclusion that he could do so much more for God, if He was freed from this debilitating thorn. Yet, the Lord's reply dealt with not only Paul's inept quest for self-sufficiency, but all who frame their thoughts around being self-sufficient and production-minded, which characterizes most of those in the western world.

When one stops to contemplate His answer, its truth cannot be denied and brings immense value even to those whose existence seems so meaningless. "But He said to me, 'My grace is sufficient for you, for power is made perfect (complete) in weakness.' Therefore I will boast all the more gladly about my weaknesses, so that Christ's power may rest on me. That is why, for Christ's sake, I delight in weaknesses, in insults, in hardships, in persecutions, in difficulties. For when I am weak, then I am strong."[129]

Weaknesses, even in the form of disabilities, have a way of demonstrating the power of the Almighty. Clearly, He shows up, and His power rests on the afflicted. In turn, He does His work of grace on all who come near by drawing out of others clear acts of compassion, kindness and love. More like a drawing salve, this power acts by quietly pulling these precious virtues from all who find themselves willing to lend a helping hand.

The transforming power of the powerless, I like to think of as witnessing one of the fingerprints of God on humanity that is still woven into the fabric of humanity. Witness Christopher de Vinck making all the adjustments to care for his brother. Unbeknownst to Christopher, his brother's weakness drew from him a spirit of compassion and kindness. With time, sensitivity developed not only for his brother, but for others. Acceptance initiates transformation which implies a willingness to change; and then exposure to the needy draws from us a spirit of empathy and compassion. Love that we did not know we had finds expression, and the joy of one mired in pain and suffering has a way to warm our souls.

Devotion, wisdom, perseverance, patience, kindness and faithfulness become byproducts of being the disabled. We caregivers learn that the importance of our service is not exclusively in doing for others, but also in allowing them to do for us, but for certain they are more than a foil in our story.

In fact, in my life my wife remains the heart of the story, and she like many, is God's messenger. They each act as divine instruments of God's healing presence. They are the ones who bring truth to a society full of lies, light into the darkness and life into a death-oriented world. It may seem contrary to common sense, but how can those who cannot see, walk, talk, feed themselves, or, like some, not even communicate in any way, be the most life-giving presence in their families?

The disabled ignite a transformation that can only be understood by acknowledging His fingerprints are all over adversity. The power of the powerless enacts a transformation that works its magic in developing compassion and love, reflecting the very nature of God. For the caregivers, these very qualities become their trademark, and such transformation leaves them numbered among the ones Jesus spoke of when he said, "Blessed are the pure in heart for they shall see God."[130]

Keeping Perspective on Suffering

I am not an advocate for seeking pain and suffering. Being a masochist and being a Christian are completely different things. If suffering were good, then we would think that the Scriptures would have exhorted us to pursue suffering. Joining in Christ's work will lend to suffering, but it is not a pursuit. Christ Himself warned us of these facts.

"If the world hates you, keep in mind that it hated me first. If you belonged to the world, it would love you as its own. As it is, you do not belong to the world, but I have chosen you out of the world. That is why the world hates you. Remember the words I spoke to you: 'No servant is greater than his master.' If they persecuted me, they will persecute you also…They will treat you this way because of my name, for they do not know the One who sent me."[131]

Personally, I cannot see any good in suffering alone, and this is only reinforced by the fact that the few glimpses of heaven that God gave in the Scriptures, such as in Revelation 21:4, leaves pain and suffering as only a memory. They are absent in heaven, where the sheer ecstasy of being in His presence finds such experiences non-existent.

Yet, in the midst of adversity within this perishing world that has been marred by sin and evil, God Himself beckons to us from the midst of our pain and suffering. His fingerprints are all over our painful misfortunes and act to draw our attention to Him. There may be situations that require remedial correction, refinement of one's faith, or maturing of our ways so that we can identify or better serve others, but God's involvement within the framework of pain and suffering appears more as an expression of love and help.

Strength of human spirit, a transforming acceptance that exposes us to His grace and then the power of the powerless that draws from and forms such virtues as compassion, kindness, forgiveness and love into our very being in ways we would never imagine all are outcomes of adversity.

The third corner piece acts as a transitional piece to understanding adversity, and rightfully so. For so many of us, our vision of life becomes blurred, until we see the little glimpses of His presence in our pain. The danger is that we want to blame Him for our misfortunes. We equate at times any blow to our pursuit of freedom and happiness as an injustice that demands God's immediate resolution.

Please keep in mind we now only have three puzzle pieces of a very large puzzle. Don't think for a moment we have the where-with-all to dogmatically think we have this life and the woes of evil all figured out. For those of us who would like to blame God for our misfortunes, I would like to end here with a story that has helped our household in refraining from lifting any blame toward God throughout our whole ordeal. His love, as we have learned, never fails. His love is present tense, as we have observed in our finding His fingerprints all over our adversity.

When Life Stings

There was an occasion many years ago, prior to wheelchairs and daily pains, when Dawn and I tended our little vegetable garden while three of our children played around us. Dawn was pregnant with our last child, and our nearly two-year old son frolicked in the grass next to the garden. Our enjoyment and peace was broken with a scream from that toddler. Gazing in his direction, I saw that he had fallen into what I thought was nettles. "Oh Lord!" I cried, but as I rose to tend to him, I was overcome with a horrific sight. There before me with his mouth wide open was our son covered with hornets from a nest that lay hidden in the tall grass. "Run, get out of here!" I yelled to my wife.

As Dawn and the other two children fled for the house, I ran directly at our toddler, grabbed him up, and threw him in the air, as I began running in the opposite direction as my wife. Having worked in the woods, I knew this type of bee would chase us down, so at full speed, I set out across the yard throwing our son up and catching him, while swatting the bees as they tried to sting his little body. One in his ear stung him, only to find my hand swat it. Another appeared on his cheek, bringing another swat. Then in his shirt collar, on his leg, near his mouth and in his hair, bees appeared. Though we were still on the run, each of them found my hand knocking them away. His tears were many and rightfully so, and when we had covered enough distance, I turned and realized we were ok. I could see my pregnant wife waddling across the yard and hear her encouraging the other two into our little house. So, I headed in their direction with one very hurt child. Reaching the house and entering, I found Dawn had been stung in the leg, and she was already swelling; so we quickly got her taken care of, only to find our toddler longing for the comfort of his momma.

Having removed his clothes to make sure the intruders were not hiding, I placed him in his mother's arms and slowly he settled down. As they rocked in the chair, I sat down to catch my breath on the couch. Silence filled the room, then the arm of our young son lifted, and pointing at me and addressing his mother, he cried out, "Oweee! Oweee, Daddy! Oweee Daddy!"

Finally, his accusing eyes pierced mine, and I broke into tears. I realized that from his perspective, every sting equated to my hand hitting him to remove the culprits. Every swat I administered to kill the enemy, he saw and felt me hitting him. Every pain that he had was being blamed on me, and my heart was overwhelmed. (To this day, tears still appear when I think about it.) My wife's eyes caught mine. Words could not be said that in any way could be understood by our child, but in that moment, I realized my son honestly felt that all his pain was because of me.

Time passed, but the lesson stayed, and with each slap of anguish and hardship created by the crises of Dawn's disability, we were reminded that, when pains come and I want to point my finger at God, maybe I had better rethink this. Evil stings! Often God in His love and compassion finds our hands lifting with a pointed finger to offer our blame for our pain. Some day we may know all the circumstances surrounding our pain, but until then, I know that the pains, if they are from God, come only from His love in driving the evil from our midst. His love never fails.

Adversity is guaranteed in a sin-filled and perishing world. The evidence for such a statement comes in the truth that death will come to everyone. Yes, it will come, just as adversity will pound upon you in the most unsuspecting of ways and times, yet rest in the facts that the fingerprints of God are all over adversity and remember God will be there swatting away the bees.

♥♥♥♥♥♥♥

A note of interest to Dawn's prayer that she prayed about holding a grandchild is that on June 3, 2005, Dawn was graced with her answer to prayer. She held her first grandchild-a granddaughter, Katiree. The next day I held a prayer session with the Lord seeking a renegotiation that she be able to hold a second grandchild. On Jan 20, 2006, a second grand-daughter, LilliAnne was born and adopted by our oldest son and his wife. Dawn was able to be there. The next day another prayer session sought another renegotiation as have all the rest which now includes ten grandchildren. They keep me on my knees.

Chapter 12
Where Noble Dreams Are Born

In the opening chapter we acknowledged how the caregiver leads a life in the shadows of the one whom people can often see is disabled. It comes with the turf, just as do the expectations for the caregiver. Caregivers reach a point in which their place is just appearing to care for the one in need. They are just there. The world sees them much like a mother to her children. They have the amazing ability to know when to be there. They cannot get sick. It is against the rules. "Rain, snow, sleet or hail," the caregivers outdo even the postal service, as their requirements extend to 24/7, forever, and ever and ever.

The Need to Stay Healthy

Such an undertaking implies that the caregiver needs to stay healthy. Truthfully, it is not an option, but a necessity, as someone else relies upon our ability to be there. In my own setting, I had learned the importance of such a task. Mind you, there were far too many periods of time when exhaustion had overcome me. After all, the caregiving usually accompanied a full day of work, and as a pastor, that work seldom was for only 40 hours per week. Still, my personal commitment recognized the importance of my own healthiness.

As an old, college baseball player and a pitching coach at the local high school until just a few years ago, I knew that the disciplines to be prepared for what happened every spring made it necessary that I exercise regularly. Cutting wood and caring for five acres of property offered ample opportunity for what little time I had to keep me moving. Even after moving to Ridgefield, Washington, where I set up shop while I finished my doctoral work required that I map out an active path for getting exercise. Walking three to six miles a day and making the last mile a healthy cardio-vascular run against my own time schedule enabled me to stay in shape. I often made many of my phone calls along the walk or spent time praying about matters that weighed upon my heart. Then when grandkids came to visit, the walk to town with them required that I hoist them to my shoulders to carry them back up especially the half mile long hill that led back to our house. All I knew was that I had to exercise daily.

Just as important was the dietary workout especially since, like many caregivers, I was the chief cook and bottle washer. It was easiest to adjust to my wife's diet, as it was very lean and healthy. That I did, except for the ice cream. I had accepted the advice of an old monk who when asked what he would do differently now that age had crept up on him, responded with a simple, "Less beans and more ice cream," and that sounded real good to me, in fact almost godly! Still good exercise that included a cardio-vascular work out and a healthy diet left my cholesterol and triglycerides all in good shape. My blood pressure was a little high, but living without any stress or pressure was not likely.

By April of 2010 my first draft to my doctoral thesis was returned, and the renovation of this project was under way. A home modification had been approved by the bank for our home and office by early June, and the matters that seemed so insurmountable were within reach.

When the Caregiver Goes Down

On Father's Day weekend, 2010, I awoke on Saturday morning to see my daughter, Marjie, off for the camp she was to direct for the next week. She turned and said, Dad, you don't look good. Are you all right?"

"Well, as a matter of fact I don't feel good."

I had awoken early and felt pressure in my throat area and my heart racing which for me was totally abnormal. Dawn, not being overly alarmed, thought I needed an antacid pill and a little time for it to work. Following her advice, I then retreated to my favorite place in the office to talk with the Lord. Oddly, the pressure never left, and after a few more hours Dawn found me still not on top of the day.

Quickly, she called our son-in-law, Travis, who was a cardiac-rehab specialist at a hospital in a neighboring town. Listening to Dawn, he quickly sent his wife, Beth, our oldest daughter, to transport me to the hospital that was noted for their cardiac unit, as he felt that what Dawn was describing was a heart condition. Within minutes Beth was there, and shortly thereafter, we were waiting in the SW Washington Medical Center ER.

Initial tests revealed no heart attack, but the cardiologist on call, Dr. Shaw, was not satisfied. They gave me some nitroglycerin to settle down the pressure I felt on my chest and reduce the blood pressure. My blood pressure dropped from 165/110 to 55/40 within two minutes!

Bells and whistles went off, and when it was finally over, Dr. Shaw had made accommodations for me for the evening. A stress test followed the next morning, which happened to be Father's Day, and all went well, until shortly afterward when, as I sat down, the EKG went irregular. Not satisfied, he then requested an angiogram, which I have no recollection of, and to add to my surprise, neither would I recall the next five days.

I woke up hearing my younger son, Josh, and son-in-law, Travis, talking. It sounded so odd to me that they were there, especially since my younger son lived in Arizona. "What is going on?" I wondered. The only reason they would be here is if something serious was going on, and being an experienced pastor, I knew that the cause had to be someone in that room. It did not take but a minute to conclude that the object of concern would be yours truly, although I definitely could not get a handle on it.

I do remember colorful explosions that had graced my room, flowers of all different color lighting up my life. I also remember the wall looking like a giant set of pork ribs and wondering where I was; but the truth was I had no idea where I was or what had gone on. All I knew was I heard voices and sensed the tubes that were all around me as well as coming out of me. Again my experience enlightened my waking brain with the fact something must have happened to me.

It was Thursday and where the other days went, truthfully, was of little concern to me. At that moment, all I wondered was what was going on and what it would take to find the exit. Yet, that was not in the day's plan, as I found that it took one good-sized therapist to help get me to accomplish my exercise for the day, which was sitting in a chair for 10 minutes. Excitement filled the room with each moment of improvement, and come Saturday I had passed the exam that got me released from the intensive care unit to a private care unit, where therapy would begin and I would be reintroduced to food.

Late Tuesday afternoon had brought the release for which I had waited. Though the next few days would be rough, they were at home where at least I could rest. With almost two weeks passed, questions began hounding my mind. Serious heart surgery had occurred, I was very aware, as all I had to do was cough without my special heart shaped pillow to recall just how serious. But I would not understand fully what had happened until the next Friday afternoon.

Dawn had been sent to take an afternoon nap, totally exhausted. Josh, his wife Karen, and Beth were sitting with me, so I figured now was the time. Looking at them I asked, "Would someone here like to tell me where the last two weeks of my life have gone? I have no recollection and no idea about what really has taken place." Sure I had heard bits and pieces but comprehend it all, that was another story.

The Rest of the Story

My brother and sister-in-law, Tim and Jackie, had arrived at the hospital that Sunday afternoon in lieu of our planned rendezvous at Canon Beach, Oregon. Dr. Shaw had finished his angiogram, but instead of quick news of stints to put in or an easy procedure, no news came to Dawn, Tim, Jackie or Beth for the longest time. Instead, Dr. Robert DuBose, an experienced heart surgeon, from Portland, Oregon, had been called for help. The on-call surgeons were all in surgery, but Dr. Shaw realized that my condition on the table in the exam room was to remain until the surgeons and needed doctors were present before they would even move my body.

Dr. DuBose, after his briefing, then approached the family with the news. "Tom has three arteries on the left side of his heart 99% plugged, and two on the right are 95% plugged. The reason he is still alive is because his heart is in excellent condition, making it therefore worth the risk for a five-way arterial bypass surgery."

Everyone was shocked. Others, including our sons Matt and Josh with their families, had all been informed and were travelling at the moment to Vancouver, except Marjie, whom everyone felt needed to stay and direct the camp for which she was responsible, until more could be determined.

"It's called the 'widow-maker' and very serious, but I have been involved in a thousand heart surgeries," explained a very sure Dr. DuBose. We would later learn that even post-op, he had gone back to Portland only to arrive at his home and have his phone ring that my blood pressure was not coming up. Back to Vancouver he would drive to meet Dr. Shaw. They would spend the next two hours sitting by my bedside trying to figure out what to do.

Typical heart surgery would have the patient awake within eight hours and hopefully all the tubes out, but in my case, the Sunday evening surgery found no wake period on Monday. Questions grew as the time

161

frame increased, until they thought that perhaps I had a low tolerance to pain medication. Reducing it again and again finally led to the Thursday morning wake time and a whole hospital wing of happy faces. Typically, this surgery ended with getting up and out of bed, exercise, and cautiously and carefully being introduced back to life. However, this was not to be in my case, as the extended down time meant an extended recovery time. Weakness had set in and just to get out of a chair was an exercise.

It would not be until my eight-week checkup that I had the privilege of personally meeting Dr. DuBose, though I had written him and his staff a personal letter of thanks that included asking him to ask his wife to give him one big hug from me for giving up her husband on Father's Day, and I am sure he would appreciate it more from her than from me. In our meeting the question arose, "What happened? What do I tell my family?"

The response was simple. "Tom, you have a heart disease. Do you know of people who just drop and they are gone?" My mind quickly recalled friends to whom this had happened. In my case there were no indicators, just the event. In fact, if my son-in-law had not made the decision to get me immediately to a hospital equipped to handle cardiac issues, I never would have made it. If Dr. Shaw had not been so persistent in his diagnostics to keep pressing as he did, I would not be here. And if Dr. DuBose had not been so wonderfully skilled to perform this surgery, there would be no way that these words would appear in this book. I am grateful to God for them all and for the medical teams that diligently gave of themselves to work together. What do I tell my family? It is simple. "Life is a gift from God. Cherish it!!"

A Heart of Thankfulness

Tears and thoughts of appreciation flow from my eyes even as these words find expression. Imagine the countless hours and years it took for each of these individuals to have gained the skills they had. Imagine their selfless actions and devotion to help someone they had never met and how, on a Father's Day, each of them would rush to a hospital and join hands under the watchful hand of Almighty God, who had been flooded with requests from those who had bowed to pray on my behalf.

As the information from my family continued to penetrate my bewildered mind of friends from around the country who stopped to pray, send notes of encouragement and called to talk with family members, I found myself becoming overwhelmed. Then to hear of a brother and sister-in-law who stayed until I was out of hot water, only to have him return a week later to join the recovery team, I found to be the type of gesture that caused my heart to grow two sizes that day. There was the family jumping in to take shifts of time to be at my bedside, as well as undertaking financial responsibilities that had arose during my absence. A heart issue, there is no doubt, I had overcome. Yet a new "heart issue" had become apparent. My heart was enlarging and overflowing with gratitude for what I knew so many had expressed through their acts and thoughts of kindness.

Quietly, in the midst of it all sat a little lady to whom everyone looked. Only a few days before, she had watched with glee as her husband had a grandchild on his shoulders and others at his side laughing and playing in the creek that flowed through the back-yard. Now, another major crisis engulfed her, but this time, it was not her, but the one on whom she had come to depend upon who now lay unconscious in an adjoining room waiting for a miracle. Needing strength beyond anything she had had to face, she found herself surrounded by loved ones, as well as an inner strength that offered an assurance that the Lord who had carried her for years was the One she could rely upon now from a completely different perspective. An anchor of strength when needed, she herself would later express how she had to reach a point of holding me with open hands, for in truth I belonged to Him.

The Value of Family, Friends and the Church

The caregiver was down--an unexpected and total surprise to neighbors, friends and family. Yet, the recovery had now begun; but in this situation the recovery involved not just a heart patient who was down, but a spouse who was already in need of a caregiver daily. Absolutely no driving was possible for me for six weeks, as it would be a minimal amount of time for chest recovery. I had been opened from top to bottom. Another week would pass with the Fourth of July and then the parting of a son and his wife back to Arizona. Quite a void entered at their departure.

But in came a daughter, Marjie, and a brother, Tim, who, having had a heart stint himself was up to date on further dietary changes and exercises that I would need. The help he gave me was profound, as was his care for his extended family. By now a walk meant going to the mail box just three houses away. From there it was short excursions adding a little more each day, but his support helped establish a pattern that would be carried on after his departure a week later. By the time of his departure, a complete menu had been refined to become a mainstay for our household. I could walk with help about a quarter mile on the flat, but Travis and Beth who had already expended hours of help, would then come to coach me the rest of the way.

As the family support was beyond what one could expect, the support from friends and neighbors was not far behind. A recliner chair, which was much needed, was supplied by Lisa and the neighborhood church where she served. Another church group brought a second chair for use in the family room, while still another group showed up to take care of our entire yard.

"My God!" was our cry, and He bent over to hear. Yet more than just hearing, He put into action His Church, the very people He has gathered to be there for each other, and who then together visibly demonstrated to the world that they were followers of Christ.

The Priceless Gift of Time

"Priceless," we hear marketers tell us, as they appeal to customers, marketing items of interest to others. However, when crises hits, what is truly priceless, jumps into action: family, friends, neighbors, devoted professionals and even strangers. And what do they offer? The most priceless commodity they can give: themselves and their time. No need for asking what was needed. It was obvious and they just responded by doing. They responded by being there, giving their time, resources and beseeching the Almighty to intervene. Again the angels of kindness appeared and the fly-by angels were in and out; but all together they left a note that filled the atmosphere with a realization that the Lord had once again drawn upon His resources and sent them to our aid. They together were all expressions of His love.

Tears and smiles mingle in crises, but even as the tears dissipated down our cheeks, the outstretched arms of an angel pulled us close, as if it were the Lord himself. Strength to persevere and the consolation that God was not taken by surprise by this perishing world began the recovery for the family, when I went down. The seeming impossible situation found people rising to help as visible expressions again of the power of the powerless. Crisis has a way of bringing out the best in people, and when that entails a family and church which are already indebted to Christ for His amazing display of love, the outworking generally will leave all amazed. Personally, this could not have been more evident than what I witnessed the Lord do in four grown children and their families.

Personal Endurance and Good Coaches

The following months focused entirely on my personal adherence to all that was necessary for my recovery. Evidence of the Lord's presence and strength surrounded our home. My energy was limited but utilized for pushing myself, especially physically, as my body was in need of being rebuilt. The quarter mile soon stretched to a half mile, and with Travis walking by my side, I eventually tackled walking a portion of the hill that traversed our back yard. It was actually a road that was one of the main avenues into town a half mile away, but it was all downhill and up if I wanted to come back.

Six weeks would pass before I would even be allowed behind a wheel of a vehicle. Mowing the postage stamp lawn was forbidden, as was about everything else I enjoyed doing or knew to be my responsibility. Time reading was limited, as retention of what I read was slow. My 61st birthday would pass, and my gaunt reflection in a mirror and in pictures wore on my soul. Gratitude for being alive and able to share life with Dawn and my family filled my days. Looking at our memorial wall in our living room, where so many family pictures refreshed our hearts with thanks for loved ones and great memories of the Lord at work, brought about the fact that I could so easily be numbered among one of those who are now just memories.

Even as time passed week after week, the physical struggle and mental strain were noticeable. I thought that I would at least be able to write and finish the second draft of my doctoral thesis, as well as meet with people, as these were things that were completely within what the doctors implied were within reason.

Yet, all the best laid plans came to naught, as I found that my ability to concentrate had been immensely affected. As I wrote, I would think of an idea, get to the end of a paragraph, go back to my thought and find a complete blank in my mind. Once, twice and then I realized it was a consistent problem. Frustration set in, as well as trying to find ways to stay focused. Even though my awareness to His presence was not in question, the ineptness at writing and conversations became a personal battle zone. "Lord, how can I be of any help and value if I can't write or communicate?" I asked.

In a conversation with a dear friend and counselor, he gently but encouragingly acknowledged what I needed to hear. "Tom, for heaven's sake, you may have a shortened memory span, but you were in a coma for five days. Your heart was traumatized, and the fact that you are even alive is a miracle in itself. Give yourself some slack and allow your body the time it needs to heal, including your brain."

Thinking we are in control truthfully becomes an illusion when we find our faculties slipping, yet I would find my time with the Lord to be my ultimate time of refreshment. The discipline of reading and studying on my own every day lent to as much a discipline for my brain as it did for my heart and soul. Today, it has been regained.

Renewed Hope: Encouraging Words from God and Loved Ones

The post-crisis time brought many more challenges for this downed caregiver, as one might think. After all, my spouse was disabled. As my recovery brought improvements, the caregiving responsibilities that had gone by the wayside waited for me. The household chores, cooking and the care for my disabled wife were all part of the recovery. It was not until November that I was finally able to reopen my counseling work and reconnect with church and community leaders who had offered to help us in our work with caregivers and their families. Then there was the added stress that I knew our situation placed on our grown children. It was not just one of us who needed help, it was both of us. When I was healthy, I was able to handle the hardship, but now the realization that our situation was taxing them weighed upon us.

Again, being in control ultimately shows itself as an illusion. Recognizing such a truth and making the proper adjustments do not come easy, as our inner man wrestles with having to give up such control. Even though there were overwhelming displays of His guiding hand, the mounting pressures and losses were almost overwhelming, again. Crushed in a way, but not out, I learned the importance again of taking bite-sized chunks in my recovery and setting small goals that were necessary steps to just get the known objectives accomplished. Yet, the battle raged as I wondered if He had left me. Was this some kind of joke, just so the world can laugh at this old preacher who should be thinking of a rocking chair and reading the Bible to his grandkids, while he and his beloved waited for the next chariot to heaven?

Where my mind wrestled, it did so against a backdrop that slowly overcame those crushing questions. On one occasion that autumn my youngest daughter, Marjie, asked to share what God had done with her when I was in the hospital. "If you recall," she said, "it was June 20th when all broke loose. As is your habit, I opened the Scriptures to Psalm 20 and read what would have been your habit for that day. Listen to what it said, and hear how the Lord undertook in my life to console me as I found myself waiting for the outcome."

> May the Lord answer you when you are in distress;
> May the name of the God of Jacob protect you.
> May he send you help from the sanctuary and grant you support from Zion.
> May he give you the desire of your heart and make all your paths succeed.
> We will shout for joy when you are victorious and will lift up our banners in the name of our God. May the Lord grant you all your requests.
> Now I know the Lord saves his anointed; He answers him from his holy heaven with the saving power of His right hand.
> Some trust in chariots and some in horses but we trust in the name of the Lord our God. They are brought to their knees and fall, but we rise up and stand firm.
> O Lord, save the King (my father). Answer us when we call.

"I knew, Dad, there was no losing hope. God wasn't done yet. There was way too much that needed to get done. So please get it done."

Accepting that God has Granted an Extension of Days for a Reason

The mere fact that I breathe means that I am part of His plans for the day. In my case, God had granted an extension of days which in my mind meant I was aware of the fact that He had His reasons. Yet, before revealing His full plan, a personal lesson in practicing what I was learning necessitated a willingness on my part to reconstruct my own life. This led to the healthy plan of setting small, achievable goals, not only physically, but in terms of our ministry. A crucible of personal pain and suffering has a way of grinding out of us what is unnecessary, while at the same time establishes new passions that could not have been gained in any other way. This became even more real when sitting with my daughter Beth who expressed her thoughts. Beth had her teaching credentials and a master's degree in education. She had written a book, and her qualification provided the opportunity for her to be one of my readers for my doctoral work. Yet her words were more as a loving friend, as well as a daughter.

"Dad, God has granted you an extension of days. Please do us all a favor and get your writing done. That begins with getting your doctorate done and then the writing, so that others can have what you have spent years learning. It is for you alone to finish. No one else can do it; but we all need it."

An Emotional Milestone

It was not until January of 2011 before the second draft of my doctorate was submitted, but when it was, we rejoiced. My physical strength was being regained, and a spiritual freshness had been breathed into my spirit; but, unbeknownst to me, another storm was brewing.

The second draft being finished by January made it possible for it to be returned, corrected and submitted for publication. It also gave me enough time for my oral presentation to be made to graduate, though it meant that I would have to travel to where my primary adviser lived and where I could get an audience to attend the presentation. Thoughts arose about going back to Bellingham, which would be the first trip out of town since that fateful day in June. Our oldest daughter was expecting her fourth child, but the only weekend available for all the above was that of March 19th.

Work began for the return for the presentation and the final draft. Phone calls were made and with my former secretary and dear friend, Sherryl Hazenberg, all was set up, and the party was being planned (without my knowing) to follow. I knew that just seeing many of these people would be emotional. They had only the opportunity to have prayed and all of them did, so I knew what lay in store when that day in March would arrive.

And Did I Say, "Personal Endurance"

Yet, as February blew in with the snows, so did some further complications which carried all the potential to shipwreck the entire party. Dawn's pain levels began to mount again. The need for oxycodone to curb the pain in her back grew, and the necessity to return to her neuro-surgeon at O.H.S.U. lent to a series of scans and tests. The outcome would arrive by the end of February, and her pain levels had reached a point where providing for her care was essential.

Meeting with Dr. Birschel led to the devastating news that a new cyst was forming in her spinal cord, the first since the major surgery in 1997. This time, though, the ability to remedy it was clearly shown to be impossible. Tears filled his eyes and ours, but again we were thrown back to our trust in the Lord. Another pain-relieving narcotic was added to her pump to help calm her situation, but a solution was not to be found. The outcome was inevitable, as it grew, it would shut off all her function from the break down, which already was becoming a problem.

Then a second difficulty raised its ugly head. Dawn had another escalating pain that was running throughout her body. Every joint was swelling and pain rising daily. Rheumatoid Arthritis had become full blown, and now every move or long spell of sitting was affecting her. At this point the March winds and the cold damp Northwest were our enemies. It reached a point where I finally looked her in the eye and said, "It is not worth it. Let me back off this high-pressured deadline and reset the schedule to graduate in the summer and walk the aisle next year."

Once again, we faced a transforming moment in our lives. What was eternally valuable and worthwhile faced us. We found ourselves again asking, "What, Lord, do you really want of us? We have trusted You and are utterly dependent upon You for everything."

At this moment, Dawn rolled in and from her chair with as serious a look as she could display, she said, "You will finish, now! I can endure it, if you can; but you need to finish now, so we can get on with life, whatever that looks like."

Commencement Day

We had arrived in Bellingham and were staying out at Ron and Carolyn Vekved's summer home in Birch Bay. When March 19th arrived, at 6:00 a.m. a text woke me up: "Kezia is here and we are doing well."

What a way to start the day! Our seventh grandchild had arrived to start our day. Needless to say, we were excited! As the day continued, so did the anticipation. The party began late that afternoon, and following the oral presentation, the cake was served and a big weight was off our shoulders. Tears filled our eyes later, as we rehearsed the magnificent gifts granted by the Lord on that day and for the amazing number of smiles that filled our memories from people who had become so dear to us over the years.

Graduation day on April 29th came quickly, and the festivities began with family arriving to our Ridgefield home for a big rehearsal dinner. Morning came early, but the excitement for us all was pounding through our veins as the day finally arrived when we would graduate. I say "we" because both Dawn and I had worked an amazing number of hours to get it all done. She just happened to be my chief editor for all my writing, so she was celebrating with me, and I with her. As the festivities finished and books and articles were packed away, a great sense of accomplishment was enjoyed by all.

Smiles filled our faces as we recognized again another commencement had ended and, in its true meaning, a new venture had just begun. For us our eyes and hearts opened all the more to how the Lord would have us to utilize what He had given us over the years. Though we thought we knew in a general way, we would find the next few months would again rock our lives.

It's a No-Brainer

It began within weeks when the news came that Matt's wife, Laura Jane, was having difficulty in carrying the twins that had surprised them after all these years. Taken to a larger hospital in the city of Everett, Washington, she would spend a few weeks before returning home to Bellingham, only to have another rush to a local hospital end in her giving birth to Wesley and Talitha on June 27th. Having adopted LilliAnne at birth, they now, with a little heavenly humor, were parents of three.

July brought our first visit with the twins, and how heartwarming it was! Yet while the wonders of birth and new infants were exciting, a quiet visit with Dr. Wessels to address the pain issues in Dawn presented a crushing blow to everything I was thinking. This same doctor was part of that team that 10 years earlier had saved her life. Now with the Rheumatoid Arthritis (R.A.) creating such discomfort, he simply put it this way: "Tom, it is a no-brainer. You have to get her out of the Northwest, or you will lose her. With her high pain levels, any more will be too much for her to handle."

I asked if he could say it in a more gentle way or offer me some alternative, because if I heard him right, it meant we would have to move from the Northwest to a drier climate. Once again he said it. "You won't believe me until you see it, but it is a no-brainer."

I prayed, "God, what does this mean and how in the world do I pull this off? All my resources and connections are throughout the Northwest. Sixty years for the both of us, and now we just pick up and move? Lord, what is going on?"

The outcome lent itself to calling upon our son and daughter-in-law who live in Arizona to see if they could allow us to come down for a period of time to just see what the weather would do for Dawn, if we were there for a month. I could keep writing and test the waters by connecting with churches and groups while there, but we needed to know if it was for real.

The trip came and went and just two days (October 1st) after returning home from a month in AZ, I found Dawn's eyes were filled with tears. "What is wrong?" I asked.

She responded by just lifting up her swollen hands. "I am back on the oxycodone, and it has only been two days. Every joint is swollen and all that had been gained in Arizona is gone. I will not make it through another winter. I just can't do it."

Tears now filled my eyes for her and for what it meant. I had never heard her say, "I can't," so I knew it was serious.

"That's it. You are much too valuable to ask of you to even try." And with this, I turned around with the decision made. "We are moving to Arizona now, and I mean, now!"

As the decisions unfolded, the full impact of what it all meant was crushing. For we were leaving family, friends, work, associations, and everything we had been dreaming, to go to the desert. "Lord, I can only say that I trust that You know what You are doing, but I am ready for whatever You have in mind."

171

Where Noble Dreams are Born & Passions Conceived

In a crisis, inevitably, we meet face to face with God. Disability and being the caregiver makes that an everyday experience. Having an emergency bi-pass surgery from which I woke up five days later made for a transforming moment in life. Months passed and the endurance to recover called for me to seek the Lord daily, while I again refocused life. Then, I experienced that perseverance paying off with the final doctoral project that had become an insatiable passion. Reaching a pinnacle at graduation, only to find that I was not at my destination again led me to the mercy seat of God.

To be told, "You need to get out of the Northwest to provide the proper care your wife needs," meant simply, transplant everything. Pull up and out from all your connections and go start all over again, but this time, it would be a little more difficult. The limitations included medical indebtedness and the fact that I was 62 years of age. By the way, this would be permanent, so this would entail a complete redefining of life, again. How much more could I handle?

If ever life had been reduced to time in a crucible, this was it. The pestle was once again grinding down on what little I felt was left. Once again the suffering brought about by this sin-wracked world found me quietly opening was being read.

All I had left was the truth that I had found myself clinging to as the grinding continued. **God has a future and I know I am part of it; therefore, I have hope.** As long as God has a future, I have hope that will ultimately end with my eyes opening as Isaiah, to see Him.

"Christian leadership involves drinking a bitter cup and experiencing a painful baptism of suffering,"[132] wrote Oswald Sanders. And now, as the page had again been turned, the new chapter carried a whole new dream and corresponding passions that only God could write upon our hearts. Trials consciously awaken us to God who continually offers that invitation to "come to Me, all who are weary and burdened."[133] Trials are a blessing, in that they double my energy and drive me in directions I would never have taken on my own. Heaven will wait, and my eyes will open, for I know that God is at work. "God causes all things to work together for good to those who love God, to those who are called according to His purpose."[134]

Whintley Phipps, in the preface to his singing the song, "It is Well with My Soul" made an inspiring remark, which I find *so rhymes with the psalmist's thoughts in Psalm 90:14-15.* , Taken as my own during this period and doctored a little for my life, I offer Mr. Phipps inspired words for all of us who find ourselves overwhelmed by another transforming moment that confronts us as caregivers. As the sense of being totally powerless to accomplish the given task and a redefining of life has only allowed us to go forward, our faith in God finds us reciting over and over again:

**"It is in the crucible of personal pain and suffering
that the noblest dreams are born,
And God given passions are conceived
in compensation for what one has patiently endured."**

Chapter 13
Let's Make Music

New Year's Day found us standing on Arizona soil. Three months had passed since the day we chose to lift our northwest roots, pack our belongings and transplant to Arizona. Being residents of Arizona for only two months, we were still overwhelmed by the situation facing us. Yet, the reflections of our Lord's goodness that filled our minds actually posited a confidence to our faith. We knew God had something in mind. His grace and His unmerited involvement in the lives of one disabled couple loomed in our thoughts, as we pondered what we had personally witnessed throughout our lives and especially in the past months.

We had a rental home to cover our heads in Arizona, thanks in part to our son, Josh, who is a realtor, and his wife. As important, especially to a father, was the fact that our daughter, Marjie, who had lived with us, had a place of her own. Also, the property manager, who our son had arranged for us to meet, had leased our Washington home, a challenge that initially seemed insurmountable. Amazingly, the house ended up being empty for only nine days. Add to this the move itself, which was greatly aided by my brother, Tim, who once again made himself available to come and help us and also make the long, arduous drive to Arizona. What a godsend he and so many others were in making the transition possible for us. Angels of kindness arrived one more time.

Of greater significance was the fact that in the two months we had been in Arizona, Dawn's pain had been reduced to the degree that she was outside puttering with her flowers that now graced the entries to our home. What to Dr. Wessels was a "no-brainer" was now a living reality. As another doctor friend expressed, "Tom, the mere fact of Dawn's condition being so improved should be evidence enough for you to know that you made the right choice."

I could not deny that this was the right choice. Our weakness draws His grace and strength into action. Yet, even with much rejoicing, there still lingered one unanswered prayer. "Lord, what more lies underneath this move at this time to this place?"

Phrasing it another way, "How does all that we have experienced and learned now find expression, and where?" What did He have in mind?

How do the skills, gifts and God-given passions which He had developed within us over the years fit into this traumatic change of events which could only have been directed by Him?

As each day found this prayer flowing from my lips, there should be no wonder then, as to why I should be surprised that each morning I found this prayer overtaken by a nagging voice that laughed at our condition. Still, I knew that God's answers to prayers embolden our faith, while at the same time reinforcing us, as we await His response to those unanswered requests. This happens to be the theme of Psalm 138, where David in response to God answering His prayer, states how it, in turn, made him bold and stouthearted. Even though further trouble reared its head, David's confidence while waiting rested in the truth that, "The Lord will fulfill his purpose for me." Therefore the same dependence upon the Lord that accompanied my every effort, led me to make acquaintances with hospital chaplains, pastors, churches and counselors, as well as reopening my counseling work.

Nevertheless, I prayed the same prayer to see the Lord daily, while the nagging voice contended for prominence so as to rob my trust in God. Job applications became a common experience, as well as interviews, while our financial needs all found answers. Where the pressures did mount, so did the sensitivity to Our Lord, and while Dawn's R.A. came under control, her disability still complicated matters. Like those early days when we first ventured into the ministry, our present adventure in a whole new world seemed so familiar, especially those precious interactions that daily made our home a place we enjoyed.

I must admit there were times I felt like I was racing against the sunset, and the darkness would overtake us, but His calm and the confidence that He had heard my prayer enabled me to lay my head down at night and rest. Still with the rising sun each day, my voice sounded within the throne room of the Almighty. "Lord, it's me again. I know that in addition to my wife's health, You have us here for more than just us. Please Lord, help us to understand. Open my eyes to see and ears to hear, and open an avenue where we can be of help to others. "

January, February and March all passed, but still all I could say was that I was writing and meeting people continually. Yet with each contact, each interview and each speaking opportunity, I found our focus being sharpened for families contending with the pressing needs of disability and caregiving. Churches wanted to hear, and the more I became aware of the Arizona culture with its high number of disabled people and caregivers, the more I began to understand the reason for our change of address.

Corner Piece #4 - Crises Culminate in Mobilizing Us to Action

As the agony of my own unanswered prayer called to mind the chronic pain that I remember enduring when solutions to my wife's problems seemed insurmountable, I once again found the Lord to place His fingerprint upon my soul. This time a passion for the many caregivers, disabled and suffering people, as well as their families, stirred within me. The Scriptures say that at the heart of God's own desires lies His delight in displaying righteousness on earth, for in these I delight."[135]

Some translators use the idea of mercy for lovingkindness, (... do justice, love mercy[136]) while still others find the Old Testament word, (חסד – "chesed") better expressed by the words, "unfailing love." Whichever the choice, one truth cannot be missed in that this word captures the very nature of God. He delights in exercising His unfailing love – loving kindness – His mercy for those in need.

How fitting to have this impassioned desire churning within my soul to help those whom many would see as societal challenges. The awakened passion and then finding opportunities to address such issues, now had even my own feelers looking in areas that I would have not considered before. The needy, the wounded, the families who contend with overwhelming complexities brought on by disability, dominated my thoughts. What I realized was that I now discovered the fourth corner piece to puzzling events that was handed to me.

Remember the questions? How are we to understand and handle adversity? What is at the heart of such difficult moments in life? When a crisis (disability) hits, what do I need to know? This is what we have been seeking to answer, knowing that in our pursuit, we will gain stability by at least finding the four corner pieces that frame our understanding of complexities. Yet, like the Scriptures, we will not in any way have the complete picture, any more than we think we can fully understand everything God is doing. Reviewing for a moment where we have come from to get to this point, we have come to see that at the very outset of any adversity all the participants find themselves awakened to certain immediate and adverse effects that accompany the painful sides of life. They in turn alert us to these unwanted effects that become somewhat overwhelming, when they begin to pile up one on another. The compounding nature of such effects and the degree the severity of the problems that arise, then present a series of challenges that call us to adjust, even before the long-term effects are firmly established. Adjustments are not change, but they ultimately lead us to an acceptance that bring a personal transformation and causes change to occur, leading to a meaningful mobilization toward God and others in need.

How are we to understand and handle adversity? What is at the heart of such difficult moments in life? When a crisis (disability) hits, it...

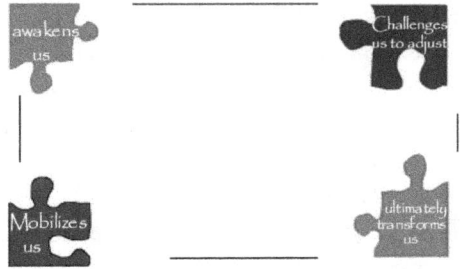

awakens us

Challenges us to adjust

Mobilizes us

ultimately transforms us

Crises and their corresponding sufferings have a way of redirecting our thinking, our priorities, our values, goals, dreams, and our source of strength in our relationships with God and people. They have a way of making the spiritual look beyond our immediate circumstances and our human egos, and when in harmony with the Lord to ask, "Lord, how can we join You and be of service to You this day?" "How can we take this adversity and turn it to be of help to others? How can we take what we have learned from Your comforting ways with us to comfort others?"

It is at this moment that adversity begins its transforming ways, while the fingerprints of God, whether we recognize them or not, begin their life-altering changes to our character. The strength of human spirit, the transforming acceptance and the power from the powerless that draws out of us a spirit of compassion, mercy and kindness, bear evidence that the God whose delight finds expression with His mercy, further births passions that mobilize us to action.

The Attitude of Gratitude

The word for grace, in Greek, is charis (χάρις), which means the unmerited favor of one to another. For the Christian, God's grace is the unmerited bestowment of His love, which brings reconciliation and restoration between God and sinful man. It continues and goes beyond the redemptive work of Christ that changes man's destination from hell to heaven and restores one's relationship with God. Now begins the regenerative work of God that brings new life to us. This part of grace brings God out of heaven to dwell in man in the person of the Holy Spirit, who empowers each of us grow to be like Christ and live as God intended man to live, like Christ.

In turn, we become the embodiment of this grace that the world seeks. It is a divine work of God in man. As one unknown source so wonderfully expressed:

The grace of God cost everything for the giver and nothing for the recipient.
It is love that stooped to bring the best to man, free of charge.
Grace means that there is nothing more that we can do to make God love
us more, and there is nothing more that we can do to make God love us less.
Grace already loves as much as any infinite God can possibly love.

When we realize grace is a gift, we understand why the Romans used the word, *grata*, to translate the word, *charis*. It is from the word, *grata*, that we get our word, "gratitude." Inherent in the understanding of grace is the intrinsic or inner sense of gratitude that is awakened. Therefore, when grace is understood, it awakens gratitude and gratitude awakens commitment. This is the primary and most unstoppable form of motivation, for it is intrinsic and focused completely and solely upon one's relationship with Christ. It is also why Paul could say what he did: "But by the grace of God I am what I am, and his grace to me was not without effect. No, I worked harder than all of them – yet not I, but the grace of God that was with me."[137]

Paul was who he was because of God's unmerited love. He labored all the more, but not because he was trying to earn points with God. It was the overwhelming sense of gratitude awakened by his awareness of God's gift that empowered his commitments to serve Christ. Try and stop a man like that! As in Paul's case, this gratitude empowered him to accomplish so much more for the sake of Christ.

Grace, like a triangle, carries three distinct but essential parts. The first is the unmerited act of love as a gift from God that brought Christ to us. The second is the enablement that accompanies His presence in our life. The third is the internal, intrinsic motivation called gratitude that is awakened to empower the heartbeat of man for God.

Unmerited act of love as a gift

Divine enablement

Internal, intrinsic, motivation of gratitude

It is this attitude of gratitude, derived from an awakened sense of appreciation for what Christ had done, that spurred Paul in his journeys and writings. Reflecting upon his words again to the Corinthian Church, he reveals how it was in a personal crisis that the Father of compassion and God of all comfort came to his rescue and comforted him. Where did this lead? As with so many others who would find it true, it led to preparing him to comfort others.

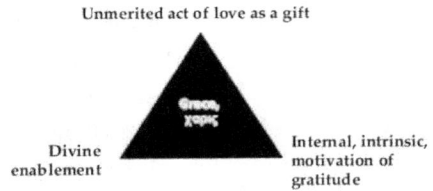

Motivated by Grace and Compelled by Love

For those who become conscious of His unfailing love and unending grace, an unstoppable gratitude awaits the opportunity to find expression. Helped people, help people, and when they do, it shows up with gestures of compassion, comfort and kindness. True heroes appear, and for these angels of kindness there is almost an anticipation of seeing God at work in and through them. For us puzzle makers, the realization now sings within our soul. We hold the fourth corner piece to adversity's puzzle, namely that crises culminate by mobilizing us to action.

A city under attack, another buried in debris, while another recalls being covered by water. Still, another lies crumbled, as its foundations gave way, bringing death and destruction that leave all gasping in disbelief. What follows in these crises? What surfaces out of this muck and mire are the true heroes of life! They do not arise for the sake of a medal or an honor, but to extend their hands and hearts to assist those in need.

After Christopher de Vinck's disabled brother's death, he found himself wanting to use his skills as an English teacher to express his brother's story. He wanted to tell how the power of his powerless brother had transformed his life. Motivated by his gratefulness for what his brother gave him, and compelled by a love for his brother to keep his story and influence alive, de Vinck wrote *The Power of the Powerless*.

The Bible finds the Apostle Paul expressing how he was compelled by God's love to extend his hands and heart to assist people in need.[138] His encounters with pain, which he later recorded,[139] would make any

179

psychologist wonder about his masochistic tendencies, unless there was something more in him that drove his very being. Yet, his explanation of what mobilized him to action[140] would unveil a compelling love and overwhelming sense of gratitude that had combined to awaken his commitment to give all for the sake of Christ.

Paul said it this way: "For Christ's love compels us, because we are convinced that one died for all, and therefore all died. And he died for all, that those who live should no longer live for themselves but for him who died for them and was raised again...All this is from God, who reconciled us to himself through Christ and gave us the ministry of reconciliation: that God was reconciling the world to himself in Christ, not counting men's sins against them. And he has committed to us the message of reconciliation. We are therefore Christ's ambassadors, as though God were making his appeal through us...As God's fellow workers we urge you not to receive God's grace in vain."[141]

In this passage Paul speaks of the ministry of reconciliation granted to all who are in Christ, because of His matchless love. It is this love that compels us into action, because we are convinced of the immense and extensive sacrifice Christ paid for removing the curse and consequence of all our sins, namely our separation from God and death. As well, it is this great love that changes our outlook toward people and life, for again we are gripped by the underlying truth that love awakens love, which now the Lord will work into every fiber of our thoughts. We are new creatures in Christ, because we are in union with Christ. Therefore, we have the privilege of an audience with the Father. All of this is because of God, Who reconciled us to Himself through Christ and then commissioned us as His ambassadors of compassion, kindness, mercy and love to bring this same opportunity to people everywhere.

Paul's overriding summary is expressed with these words, "...we urge you not to receive God's grace in vain."[142] All of God's love that is reflected in the person and work of Christ was described as an act of grace and was not to be taken lightly. As Christ's love for us awakened a love in us for others, so grace awakens our commitment to dispense His love and reconcile others to God. In short, gratitude awakens commitment.

At a later moment in his letter, Paul exposed how this great truth pertaining to God's grace was revealed by God Himself as the driving source of his sufficiency. "My grace is sufficient for you, for power is made perfect (complete) in weakness."[143] In fact, it was in the overwhelming situations in which Paul found himself weak that he then found he was strong.

Truthfully "God has chosen the weak things of the world to confound the things which are mighty."[144] Even reading the responses to de Vinck's writing some 25 years later brings tears to my eyes. A mere expression of love and gratefulness for a weakened brother opened the flood gates that touched millions and brought responses from sources far beyond what he could have known. First, love awakens love. Then grace, when it is truly understood, awakens gratitude, and there is no halting a grateful heart.

Gratitude Awakens Commitment

There is no life void of value even among those who are recognized as the weak among us. They are not a burden that we stoically bear. For in them, we see who we really are. Pastor Brunner, Pastor Malmin, Pastor Korstjens and I can all attest to the difficulties we faced. Yet, we can also sing songs of thanksgiving to God and join with de Vinck to acknowledge the inner transformation and compelling love that surfaced in our own journeys as caregivers. It continues its daily work in us and through us even now. We can all attest to how caring for our most cherished friends, whose lives knew immobility, pain and weakness to be the daily norm, yielded a power that transformed our lives. Weak in body, they might be, but their strength in spirit exceeded their expectations.

I still have my wife and our shared love looks for ways to give to others, regardless of their limitations. It makes no difference to us. Abused, broken people, people disabled from a personal crisis or struck by a mental disorder—all seem to find a pathway to our door. We are amazed and yet extremely grateful to the Lord, whose love has awakened in us an understanding of His love, which He has for us all. Sure, people take advantage of us, but we will let the Lord settle those scores.

Motivated to Work together

I have one last thought pertaining to the ability of crises to mobilize us to action. It comes, with a knock on the door, followed by hugs and tears that are unspoken words in themselves. Crises have a way of helping us see the need that we have for each other. "If one member suffers, all the members suffer with it; if one member is honored, all the members rejoice with it."[145]

We are not creatures designed to be independent. God made us as interdependent, needing Him and each other. Anyone who has faced a crisis surely would offer a hardy "Amen," as they reflect on those warm faces that helped divide their sorrow.

Crises can paralyze us and zap our strength, just as every American witnessed on September 11, 2001. When our strength is knocked out, just like a power outage in a storm, we learn to lean on others for help. The Apostle Paul gave counsel to the Galatian Church, "Carry each other's burdens, and in this way you will fulfill the law of Christ,"[146] which we know is to love one another. Inasmuch as we are united together in service to each other, we are united together. Crises mobilize us to action by bringing us to work together for those with needs.

I Couldn't Have Written the Script

Between the New Year and spring of our first year here in Arizona, I was invited to join a group of pastors in their prayer time. Collectively, they took it upon themselves to pray that the Lord would make a way for our passions to be fulfilled. In April of 2012, the position of Care Pastor opened up at a community church in Gilbert, Arizona. The position entailed overseeing some of the ministries within the Mercy Department, such as counseling. However, it also entailed the oversight of ministries on the cutting edge of providing care for those crying out for mercy and hope that crises bring.

A few weeks later my interview for the position of Care Pastor at the church concluded with the questions, "Why would you want to invest your skills and training in a ministry that takes you into such difficult settings continually? Why not retire?"

My answer was simple: "I couldn't have written a script that better fit my personality and passions. I couldn't have landed in a more wonderful place, if I had planned it all myself."

Amazingly, it is unbelievable that I found myself living in a world where thousands of weakened and disabled come to live, especially during the colder winter months up north. In turn, I found myself writing in my Bible, "He answered." For months the vision and passions that God had stirred finally found a way to be expressed, resulting in an overwhelming joy.

Even more observant was a former seminary professor who concluded that "with all you have learned and utilized in the fields of counseling, family work, as well as among the world of the disabled and caregivers, plus all your education and experiences, it appears that the Lord has created a convergence of it all into one ministry, which allows you a privilege that many your age never attain."

I had to agree, and I write this today as a note of hope for all who find their worlds turned inside-out due to crisis. Our confidence and hope find substance in the One who holds the future, and His existence brings with Him a plan whereby when we join Him, we have hope.147

What did it all mean for me? Well the irony began when my immediate boss and now dear friend, who leads the Mercy Ministry, happened to be named, Randall Thomas. (Tell me if God doesn't have a sense of humor!) We are already having fun and have been daily humbled that God still allows us the privilege to join Him in service to hurting people. Indeed it is not easy, but the word, joyful, is an understatement. All I can say is, "What a privilege!"

What a privilege to be given the opportunity to be the helping hand to someone as Christ has been to us. What a privilege to offer to others the truth that has sustained us when everything we had was taken. What a privilege to be able to join with others in this wonderful place called the church, bringing the good news of the Lord's mercy and grace to help others in time of need and then to see the answers to those prayers. Truthfully, what a privilege to have walked so strenuous a path, yet find Him faithful in restoring "the years the locusts have eaten!"[148] What a privilege to witness a dream fulfilled in compensation for what we had had to painfully endure.

A Touch of Hope Ministries

Crises culminate in mobilizing us to action. Undoubtedly, my place in being a caregiver has seen a transformation within my being that has mobilized my lifestyle in the particular care of one lady. The outcome of becoming that caregiver, though, has marked all my relationships, as well as provided ample opportunity for me to meet many others. The sensitivity

I learned now extends a hand to many whose personal worlds have been rocked by adversity.

Over the years, passions and then ideas have surfaced, which mobilized our household with others to spur a work among caregivers. Give me the caregivers, and I have access to their entire households. Help the caregiver and I help another family. Now my "pastor" button took over, igniting a brainstorm as to how to reach families who are confined or burdened physically and spiritually, yet who need help. Prayers for wisdom were sounded out and the result was a mobilized effort that saw **a touch of hope Ministries** being conceived.

Arising from the crucible of personal pain and suffering, the dream and passion to extend a hand to caregivers and their families via community support networks, both online and within communities of faith, has now begun. At the heart of those involved with **a touch of hope Ministries** is a group of understanding Christian professionals and caregivers who found themselves mobilized to join in the action by nothing more than the acceptance of their own situations, as well as the Lord's calling upon them to offer a caring hand to the weak and their families.

As one gentleman said, "Helped people help people," and in our case the seedling ministry now exists. I could not in any way have written such a script, and all those who join with us find themselves personally responding with a joyous, "Amen." The dream was born and the passions conceived in the crucible of personal pain and suffering, but remember again, God delights in expressing His unfailing love and He delights in using us as His instruments in doing so.

Let's Make Music with What We Have Left

It was November of 1995 when violinist Itzhak Perlman walked onstage at the Lincoln Center to give a concert. He was stricken with polio as a child, so he used leg braces and walked with the help of two canes. The audience waited respectfully as he slowly made his way across the stage, then sat down, lowered his canes, released the clasps on his braces, and finally picked up his violin and prepared to play. Just a few bars into the piece, however, and one of the strings on his violin broke. Everyone heard it snap. And everyone wondered what he would do.

Perlman sat for a moment with his eyes closed, then signaled the conductor to begin again. The audience could see him sweating through the piece, modulating, changing, recomposing in his head and retuning strings on the fly to pull new sounds out of them.

Asked after this astonishing performance how he pulled it off, Pearlman said, "You know, sometimes it is the artist's task to find out how much music you can still make with what you have left."[149]

Although his point appears to speak of the music made with his violin, his words and life spoke of his ability to make music as one who was handicapped. Robert Molsberry, the disabled pastor whom I earlier mentioned, tells the story of Perlman, then echoes his refrain that the true artist makes music with what he has left, which he then concludes, "... is everyone's task."[150]

Though his words are meant for the disabled, they sing to not only the disabled, but to their caregivers and anyone associated with them, as well as to those who have been granted skills and talents without limitations.

So, let's listen to His music. Let's open our eyes to His plan, like the prophet Daniel says, "be strong and take action,"[151] or Habakkuk, "the just shall live by his faith."[152] Let's step up with what we have and join Him in His movement of His story toward its ultimate conclusion, to bring a divine judgment on evil and the restoration of His kingdom, with God Almighty Himself dwelling in our midst, as He said He would. Let's hold tightly to the truth that His future offers us hope and confidence. Let's recognize that the end of the story is what gives the whole story meaning. In fact, says Ronald Allen, professor of Old Testament at Dallas Seminary:

> "It is only with a divinely given hope for the final victory of right over wrong, that we, and those who have lived before us in the continuity of the faithful community, may relieve our sense of frustration at the ambiguity, uncertainty and enigma of our own existence. Unexpected, unexplained evils that come into our own lives, be they locusts or *disability*, disease, war or disaster, are placed in a divine perspective when we have some knowledge of God and God's future dealings with evil itself. Further the demands of righteousness in the lives of believers are magnified with a proper sense of final judgment."[153]

Therefore, disabled or not, let's not get lost in our why's and forget that by our mere breathing, we are part of God's plan for that day. Let's put the puzzle of life together. Let's paint the picture that finds its beauty by being in relationship with Almighty God. Let's make the music with whatever we have left and make it count for God. May our lives sing with the lesson learned by Job, who in facing his trauma, loss and demands on God for answers, found his clarity in his vision of God[154] being the very tool that cleansed His soul,[155] enriched his inner man and restored anew and afresh his vision, understanding and walk with the Lord!

My journey as a caregiver, both in my home and among people, will never end. I do not think the Lord would allow it. Frankly, I do not think I want to veer from it either, since it mirrors so much of how Christ has dealt with us. Periods have arisen in which even Dawn in her despair has confessed that she feels that she is nothing but an anchor around my neck, holding me back from so many things that God could do. Such nonsense needs a gentle correction, whether that be directed at her or in myself, when I throw my own little pity party.

God has granted an extension of days and for certain the script He has allowed to be written involves a path that I on my own would never have chosen. Yet, we are here and our heads are lifted up. Our eyes can still peer into each other's and for me, having my best friend still at my side means much, regardless of how slowly we literally roll along. I can only foresee that for us, we will spend many more mornings sharing coffee and interacting about the Lord, as well as the situations He has brought our way. We know each day is a gift from God and the heightened complexities that have re-entered her situation makes each day precious. Trials, including the complete extraction from our home to the desert of Arizona, await us every morning; but still, "This is the day which the Lord has made,"[156] and again the mere fact that we breathe means we are part of His plan for the day. Therefore, they that "know their God will be strong and take action."[157] So, let's make music together with what we have left.

Chapter 14
A Touch of Hope: Communion with God

"…If anyone is thirsty, let him come to Me, and drink." John 7:37

Holding the four corner pieces to any of my wife's massive puzzles, just as with a crisis helps build a hope that a framework exists to dealing with adversities that encroach upon our lives. These crises have served their part to awaken us to our world as it is. As they release their ill effects, these same crises call us to adjust. Then for those who choose to accept their new norms even with God, these crises do their job to bring a transformation that then mobilizes us in service together for God and man.

Sadly, there are many cases where the complexities tragically ignite bitterness or present an overwhelming set of circumstances that inflicts its ill and ruin upon its victims. Hearing of such stories or even recalling my own similar sensations, especially following the crises years after the second accident, is heartbreaking. I found my sustaining strength in my relationship with the One who offered to us in our dry times to come to Him.158 There, alone in communion with the Master Comforter and Teacher, came the quenching comfort and the touch of hope that would rescue me from myself and my inability to work through my dilemma. Without the calm that only He can provide, I do not know where I would be today. My heart still finds its strength from the amazing hope that He offers each day.

The Great Mystery

Throughout the years, the Christian faith has persistently expressed one great mystery, namely that God seeks man through Christ to grant him the privilege of communion with Him. God Almighty seeks an intimate, personal relationship with each and every human being. Grasp this fact of life before we go on. God seeks to interact with us continually. It was Jesus who said, "…If anyone is thirsty, let him come to Me, and drink."[159] On another occasion He would again offer His invitation to "Come to me… and you will find rest for your souls."[160]

Mysterious as it may sound, this communion has been underscored by men and women alike in their reflections of the fullness, comfort, encouragement and joy that filled each of their souls in times of adversity and prosperity. Hudson Taylor, founder and director of the China Inland Mission (now the Overseas Missionary Fellowship International), called it, "the exchanged life," which provided, "instead of bondage, liberty; instead of failure, quiet victories within; instead of fear and weakness, a restful sense of sufficiency in another."[161]

Writing to his sister, Taylor would exclaim, "The sweetest part is the rest which full identification with Christ brings. I am no longer anxious about anything, as I realize this; for I know that He is able to carry out His will and His will is mine. It makes no matter where He places me or how. That is rather for Him to consider; for in the easiest position He must give me His grace, and in the most difficult His grace is sufficient."[162]

Communion with God

With God, all men and women, stand on level ground at the foot of the cross. For those who enter into a union with Christ, the way for a lifetime privilege, "to experience God . . . to worship God . . . to fellowship with God, where He speaks about Himself, His will and His working in our lives."[163] It is a communion that grants us an audience with God, where concerns are expressed, as well as dependence acknowledged and which is granted from the Lord on the basis of His grace alone, a grace that comes through Christ.[164] As insignificant as we may think we are before God, the psalmist calms our fears by recognizing God's involvement in our lives comes from His delight in us. "He rescued me because He delighted in me.[165]

The honored position of being a pastor has created no immunity to the pain and suffering which has accompanied mankind since the introduction of evil. Yet, time and time again that sweet communion with the Lord dried my tears or calmed my embattled mind by just experiencing His presence. On more than one occasion this quiet moment and the peace it brought, revived a confidence that left me knowing that we would make it. It was here that the Bible and a meditative time of prayer around those very Scriptures produced the solace that my heart longed to sense. Even when the outcomes were extremely difficult, I gained a peace, as well as a steadfast fortitude, in the assurances that He was leading me.

Therefore, to not at least address this part of my story as a caregiver, as well as the communion that opens the relationship with God Himself, would be like leaving a story half told, especially for this older pastor and caregiver. Even without the corner pieces in place, the underlying truth is that our spirits yearn and search for what we absolutely sense is essential: peace with God. As a result, I, just like the many caregivers and disabled with whom I have met, find myself seeking to catch a simple glimpse of Him, the One who reaches toward us. Here lies His touch of hope for us; communion with God, Himself.

The Heart of Adversity

Earlier in this work we recognized that our inner spirit longs for the consoling comfort which can only be met by an interchange with God, Himself. The reason is because there is a spot reserved in the deepest part of our being, which apart from His

Longings for Security & Significance

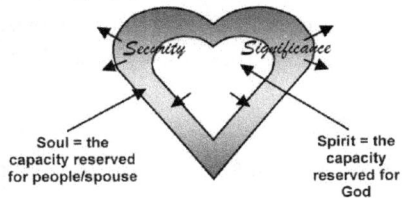

Soul = the capacity reserved for people/spouse

Spirit = the capacity reserved for God

presence leaves us sensing an inner emptiness. Over the years I have come to recognize that spot as the spirit of man. Tucked away within the heart's legitimate longings lies a vacuum of need searching for the security and significance that only God Himself can give. Just as my wife's love, as well as my family and friends' love, legitimately satisfy the longing in my soul for others, a deeper longing for peace with God finds that the love of Christ satisfies that longing in my spirit. In fact, it is reserved for only Him, and He allows nothing to fill that part of our hearts but Him.

Putting these ideas together finds us again pressed with our leading questions. How are we to understand and handle adversity? What is at the heart of such difficult moments in life? When a crisis hits, it invariably presses any person into a place where the illusion that we are in control is erased. In turn, we are brought face to face with our own heart's longing for answers from God Himself. What is at the heart of man is simple. Listen to your

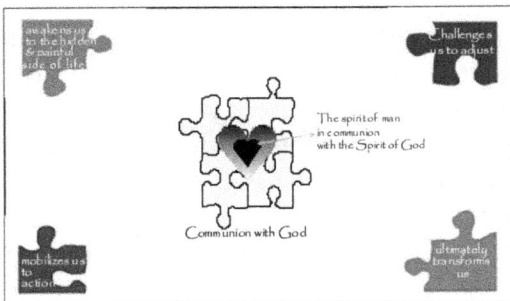

How are we to understand and handle adversity? What is at the heart of such difficult moments in life? When a crisis (disability) hits, it...

awakens us to the hidden & painful side of life

Challenges us to adjust

The spirit of man in communion with the Spirit of God

Communion with God

mobilizes us to action

ultimately transforms us

189

heart's cries for answers. The answer you seek can only be found in one's communion with God. Whether one understands all that crashes into them or not, the heart's cry for good news from God becomes central to life.

Communion with God – Becoming a Lifelong Learner

Over the years, making time to read, study and interact with the Lord has become a primary daily practice for me. Most often I find myself arising early, usually much earlier than my wife, whose general pattern involves addressing the pain issues that stir her through the night. Letting her rest in the morning has been necessary, while at the same time, it has become a precious time for me to savor the moments with the Lord. Tucked away in my home office or cozied up on the living room couch, with my coffee and Bible in hand, the familiar atmosphere is set for my thoughts for the day. Much is involved in those precious moments, but for certain they begin the same way each day.

Focusing on his Majesty and Love

"Our Father, who art in Heaven, hallowed be your name,"[166] are the opening words Jesus modeled for his followers in opening their time of prayer with His Father. From the master himself, our communion with God opens with a prayer that focuses each participant upon the majesty of our God. For me, these opening moments I find to be a privilege, in that I am able to have an audience with the Almighty. This fact brings with it an immediate awareness of His majesty. As the pages of my Bible open, I often go to select passages that have become endeared to me and which stir my consciousness of the Almighty.

Picture, as I have done on many occasions, being in the shoes of Isaiah when he found himself being taken into the presence of Almighty God. Overwhelmed were his senses as his eyes and ears filled with the wonder of God's throne room and the reverberation of the angelic hosts, singing a praise song that extended beyond his understanding. With a perfect pitch unlike any other, their words captured only one phrase of a song that totally humbled Isaiah, as it had the angels whose voices filled the room. "Holy, holy, holy, is the Lord of hosts; The whole earth is full of His glory."[167] Imagine the absolute awareness of His majesty that flowed through the air and Isaiah's corresponding sense of humility that engulfed him, as he stood in the very presence of Almighty God.

Then listen to the psalmist who pictured a similar but relatable experience when he found himself standing underneath a clear sky, as the heavens poured out their speech, and the moment evoked words of splendor from his mouth. "When I consider Your heavens, the work of Your fingers, the moon and the stars which You have ordained; what is man, that You take thought of him...?"[168]

Is there any wonder why the psalmist began this same psalm with an ecstatic claim to the Lord Himself? "O Lord, our Lord, How majestic is Your name in all the earth."[169]

Yet while His majesty leaves me in total awe each morning, it is His unfailing love, His eternal, everlasting, relentless love that welcomes me personally into His presence through Jesus Christ, leaving me again absolutely humbled, yet full in my inner being. As I focus upon His love, I realize a conscious awareness to His ever-present choice to commune with one so unworthy. Picture the transcendent God of the universe in all His majesty, extending an invitation for me to enjoy Him and to call upon Him in our time together. His open arms of grace and mercy ready to receive us,[170] is an expression of His personal love for us.

Our union to His son, Jesus Christ, roots us and grounds us in His love so that we "may be able to comprehend with all the saints what is the breadth and length and height and depth, and to know the love of Christ which surpasses knowledge, so that we may be filled up to all the fullness of God."[171] Is it any wonder why the sense of peace and security fill my spirit, even when the questions remain unanswered?

Facing Up to our Own Real Selves

In the context of His majesty and love, my thoughts then turn to my own inner man. Here I face up to my own sinfulness. My thoughts now shift to the recent day or days where I ask of God to help evaluate me. In Psalm 139 David pens such an encounter when he has recognized and reflected upon God Almighty. The outcome immediately surfaced in a request by David for God to search his soul and reveal his obvious shortcomings. "Search me, O God, and know my heart; test me and know my anxious thoughts. See if there is any offensive way in me and lead me in the way everlasting."[172] This is what happens when one spends time with the Lord. The point though is not to step back from the encounter, but to anticipate it. We come to God as sinners. We come in the spirit of the tax-collector, "God, be merciful to me, the sinner!"[173]

As Christians, the truth is that our sins are forgiven and the eternal consequences are canceled, because of Christ. Nevertheless, this does not mean that we never address the sin issue again in our daily lives, for we still sin daily. It is this interaction which leads to the changes needed in our character and the awakened desire to serve.

When we honestly face up to our sinfulness daily, it is only a matter of time before our accumulated wrongs reveal that our indebtedness to God was and is enormous. Jesus implied a truth that, "he who is forgiven much, loves much."[174] Therefore, as the truth of how much we are forgiven becomes real, we develop a greater love and appreciation for the Lord. If I felt that my indebtedness to Christ for His forgiveness and love was great at the beginning of my awareness of my sin, imagine what it means now, some forty-plus years later, when I have a more realistic picture of what that gesture meant on His part. The fact stands--we are forgiven. Yet, recognizing daily the full extent of what that forgiveness entails has only enlarged my love and gratitude.

For some people, spending time reflecting on their sinfulness can create despair and a sense of hopelessness. Some will even prefer to avoid this exercise and adhere with the many that see it as harmful for the development of a healthy self-worth. Yet, the exercise of facing up to the facts of our sinfulness leaves us humbly bending our knee before God, as well as to a host of others whom we may have wronged.

Nevertheless, as we review the nature of sin which operates within us, there are times that we cannot help but scream, "Enough!" It can be so discouraging. And lest we get overwhelmed, let us remember that we are in good company. It is the godly who seek improvement. Men like David and the Apostle Paul sought from God correction to their courses in life. They opened themselves to be keenly aware of their own sinfulness, yet used it as a platform for improvement to their own lives and then to teach others to do the same.

Preaching the Gospel to Yourself, Daily

"...I have the desire to do what is good, but I cannot carry it out. For what I do is not the good I want to do; no, the evil I do not want to do—this I keep on doing... For in my inner being I delight in God's law; but I see another law at work in the members of my body, waging war against the law of my mind and making me a prisoner of the law of sin at work within my members. What a wretched man I am..."[175]

Yes, even the Apostle Paul had moments in which he knew he came up short before the Lord. "What a wretched man I am," he would utter as he found himself rehearsing his own sinful ways. How familiar to so many of us who find ourselves frustrated by our continued failures. Yet, while reflecting on his sinful condition, notice Paul grasping hold of Christ and rehearsing again the simple gospel[176] to calm his soul and address his heart's scream.

"Who will rescue me from this body of death? Thanks be to God – through Jesus Christ our Lord! ...Therefore, there is now no condemnation for those who are in Christ Jesus..."[177]

What he is doing is preaching the gospel to himself. The Good News, the gospel of Jesus Christ, which is a revelation from God that encapsulates the truth that Jesus died for our sins and opened to mankind a pathway to restore our relationship with God, becomes the focal point of Paul. He reminds us of forgiveness and that no condemnation befalls a follower of Christ, resulting in a peace with God. For the next 20 centuries, it is this precious truth that would calm many hearts stirred by their own shortcomings. "Thanks be to God – through Jesus Christ our Lord!"[178] to which he then adds the great anthem that rings throughout our communion with God. **"Therefore, there is now no condemnation for those who are in Christ Jesus."**[179]

It is here that the gospel extends beyond the vantage point of our introduction to Christ, with a relevant message that applies itself daily for the believer in Christ. There is no condemnation from God toward us for our present shortcomings, sin and failures. We may experience consequences or have to take remedial action, but the gospel resounds with one astonishing word that changes our destiny from hell to heaven: Forgiven. We were forgiven, once for all, on that day when we first acknowledged Christ as Lord and Savior. Yet, the daily awareness of the full extent of what Christ forgave in us is new and enlarged upon. Thus, our gratitude for the Lord continues to grow from day to day.

The Finishing Touch - Rehearsing our Forgiveness and Reflecting on His Grace

Daily, I reminded myself that the gospel culminates with the joyous proclamation that "There is now no condemnation for those who are in Christ Jesus."[180] This promise connected to His unfailing love answered the pressing questions that plagued my mind.

The first was, "How do I gain acceptance or know that I am acceptable in His sight?" The second, with multiple expressions, such as, "What is the remedy to the consequences brought upon myself by my own sinfulness? How can I satisfy His justice for my wrong?" And if those were not enough, "What was necessary to remove the curse of separation from God and restore my relationship with a Holy God?"

These questions that had plagued me found answers in that one statement of Paul, "Thanks be to God—through Jesus Christ our Lord!"[181]

God's mercy and grace, acting as the two arms of His love, reach toward us daily through Christ's death. Rather than getting depressed or overcome by my own sinfulness, I rehearsed the words that are new each day with the truth that we can stand acceptable before God Almighty because of One, Jesus the Christ, in whom there is no condemnation.

Gratitude once again awakens in me, and I find myself thanking Him for His matchless grace and the sweet communion that daily brings it to life. It is here that I find myself remembering how He would have me to begin my day. "Be to her (Dawn) as I am to both of you. Put a smile on her face and watch what I can do through the two of you."

So, in the words of Thomas Wilcox, "Let sin break your heart, but not your hope in the gospel."[182]

This is what the practice of **preaching the gospel to yourself** accomplishes. Here stands the heart of our communion with God, where we are reminded of the full extent to which Christ displayed His love for us, and I find my inner resource for living each day with my best friend. Whatever her state, her story is mine, and we live today serving the same Lord with the same spirit of gratitude.

It is this practice that begins my day, and I look forward to each and every day. It sets the atmosphere that sustains me as only a time with God can. It is here that my thoughts and reflections, as well as my reading from and intense study in the Scriptures, expand that sweet communion with understanding that guides me when another trial mounts. These truths become essential for my life, especially when crises inflict blows that are palliative in nature. As a caregiver, my needs that are more often unmet than met and the anguish that accompanies each setback that Dawn faces, find the personal refreshment that God supplies as an imperative.

So, even if circumstances have arisen with further ill effects and their demanding cry for further adjustments keep life in disarray, I offer here what I find has been true within both Dawn and me. We want to know God, not just about Him. We seek a genuine communion with the Living God, who not only created us, but created us to relate to Him. I do not want to guess what would have happened, had I not had a relationship with God when I was suffering such pain and confusion over my dear wife's physical condition. But God was there, and I am very thankful.

♥♥♥♥♥♥♥

As one who had to learn the value of my private time with God, I now look back with thankfulness. I can say that it will serve any person well to find a time to commune with the Lord. So, find a place or make one where a time with the Lord and His Scriptures can become a place of refuge and strength. Nothing elaborate is needed--just a corner in the living room or quiet spot in an office study. If needed, play some sacred music to set a serene atmosphere; but grab your Bible, a cup of coffee, pen and paper and bring your heart's longings to the Master, who is so willing to respond to those of us who sincerely need His presence.

Chapter 15
The Power of Caregiving

Opening the door to our empty home, I was exhausted. Kicking off my shoes, I nestled up in the corner of our couch and contemplated once again all that had happened. It was Mother's Day, 2013, yet the pictures repeatedly filled my mind were of a precious lady who was encountering intense pain. I was comforted in the fact that I had left her in a calm, safe place with a wonderful, experienced nurse who promised to take good care of her.

Yet, it was only hours before that I had tried to gently hold her as her body shook in pain, thrashing from side to side in my arms and then across her hospital bed. Her pain, like on so many prior occasions in these last two months, erupted in only minutes, then reached extreme levels. Cuddling her as close as I could dare, she thrashed about trying to find any position that might offer relief. Her digestive track was aflame, her back was throbbing, and her leg muscles were in uncontrollable spasms. The torturous, pin-poking sensations she felt through her lower extremities caused her to let out a shriek that left us all in tears.

"Dawn, I am right here!" "I am right here!" Yet, as the words gently slipped out into her ears, the glassy-eyed look that appeared communicated well that she was unaware of my presence. All she sought was relief from the anguish that could only be explained moments later when our eyes finally connected. "This is as close to hell as I ever want to get."

Hellacious can be the only word to describe the savage intensity that caused her body to thrash uncontrollably, looking for a way to find relief from its persecutor. The source to her pain had eluded teams of doctors. In addition, lingering in the battlefield of her own mind, it seemed as if God was absent, which only multiplied exponentially the internal anguish that rocked her soul, as the uncontrollable spasms and excruciating pain continued.

As I was holding her, she finally screamed for God to release her. Tears flowed from our eyes, as my mind flooded with the thought that she would be going into shock in just a matter of minutes. How much more could this lovely lady handle, I did not know; but in those moments a seasoned nurse of 40 years tearfully rushed for help.

In another moment Dawn's agony again escalated, yielding once again the tears and cries for relief. This time though, her cry echoed within my own soul, even as it filled our room. "How long? How long, O God?" Then looking into the pains from her body.

Looking around the empty room all I saw was its emptiness. Then, as I began to speak, my words found her momentarily listening, "Listen to me sweetheart. You need to trust and lean upon my faith at the moment. Pain cannot win here, because as odd as it may seem, God is here also. Christ has not left us. He has promised to never leave or forsake us."[183]

I have learned over the years that God and pain co-exist in this broken world. We cannot let the horror that accompanies pain rob us of the calming presence of Almighty God who often goes unnoticed, though the truth be known, He is there.

Having stated my thoughts, I then placed one hand upon her head, as I held her small, exhausted frame in my other arm, and then I began to pray.

"Lord, I know You are here. I sense and know that even amidst this ugliest of scenes, as pain seems to occupy every ounce of this room, You are here. The great privilege that You have granted us by our union to Jesus Christ is to have an audience with You. Lord, I recall how at one time Jesus expressed that He was the resurrection and the life, at which time he then called Lazarus from the dead. So, I ask that as He brought back life to Lazarus, once again, in His name, You would extend a finger and touch this precious, dear lady and cause her pain to subside and a calm come over her weary body. One more time I ask of You to restore her desire to live, because I know there is much that awaits us in service to you. No praise comes from the grave, though I admit I hold her life with an open hand. She is yours, and I can freely release her to the One who is the Author of life and death--but only to You. You knew the number of her days when there was not as of yet one. You knew each element of her painful life and have stepped in to touch her with that strength of human spirit and will to live, at each solemn and difficult time when it was needed. Please Lord, hear my prayer, for my spirit senses this is not the time for her home-going. It is the time for You, to one more time touch her and calm her ailing body with Your peace. Lord, we have come so far to not finish together, and I know You well enough to know that I believe she just needs your intervening hand at this moment, as nothing else is available. I ask this in the Name of the One, who said to ask in His Name, Jesus the Christ."

Holding her and watching her quivering body slowly come to a place of rest over the next hour, I once again realized the preciousness of Our Lord to hear our prayers. Exiting from her room that night had now brought me to our living room couch, depleted of any energy, yet wide awake, as the adrenaline still stimulated my whole being.

After I finished a small dish of ice cream, my mind raced with merciless thoughts about what tomorrow would bring. "Stop it," I finally said to myself. "You know better. Take tomorrow, tomorrow and no sooner."

Looking at the clock, I realized that tomorrow was now today, since it was after 1:30 a.m. "Thank you, Lord, for hearing my prayer, plus not only mine, but the many who have joined to intercede on her behalf."

The next day we left the hospital for the fourth time during this perplexing period, now in route to a specialist in pain management. The pause in the extreme pain was a welcome relief for both of us, although we knew nothing was solved. The specialist at the clinic would offer a brief hope, with an adjustment being made to her morphine pump that gave a temporary false solution. In the days after, we were to find the rising tides of pain to again have broken over her ability to handle the pain with any former pain medication.

Another week passed leaving us no closer to an answer than in the weeks prior. Pain still had its way, with the pain meds offering little help. Prayers continued for her along with the many questions.

Caregivers: The Real Angels of Kindness

Trying to explain to people just how our life together continually changes, due to Dawn's disability and pain threshold, often finds me grasping for words. Even trying to explain what a moment is like tests my communication skills to the hilt, oftentimes leaving me at a loss for words that could do justice to the tangled emotions that occupy such abominable times. Who could understand what is really happening when it seems in only minutes, the demand for my time and resources pulls me away to another obligation?

During this time, I ran back and forth to the office when momentary periods of calm allowed Dawn rest. Yet what I encountered meant dealing with people in their own plights. With my mind momentarily off our own set of circumstances, I found the Lord granting me the ability to provide the appropriate counsel to help others. I could do that! Yet, as I returned home and saw the resurgence of pain in my dearest friend, I often found myself back on our living room couch after each episode, looking again for some sense of consolation. Care for her? Yes! But, solve her issues? For some reason, that had mysteriously remained hidden from us all.

"Lord, it seems like I am all alone in this, yet I know I am not." Upon reflection, I could not count all the "angels of kindness" who were asking to help, but how could they help? Solutions to my wife's pain were outside the grasp of us all. Again the ravenous wolf of pain would bite, and her body would be engulfed by its attacker. Helpless, I would cry out once more to God, as her tormentor of pain came out of hiding and attacked her body over and over again.

It was Sunday afternoon, after only one week of being released from the hospital, and I finally cried out, "Please send us an angel of kindness." This time though, the response came almost audibly, "The angel is already present. It is you."

As His words echoed in my mind I finally understood what they meant. Quickly, I threw an overnight bag together, wrapped her up and drove her the three miles for the fifth and what would be her last visit to the ER room. As I entered, I stated up front that we were again in trouble. This time I laid out all the medical steps, using terminology that medical people understood.

"Look, I know you don't know me, but this time you need to understand that I am a doctor, not in medicine, but theology. Crises I understand, since I am not only a pastor but the crisis and care pastor for a church of 4000 people. I have worked with difficulties of all kinds. I understand pain levels. This lady has an endurance and pain threshold that far exceeds anyone I know. Mind you, I know her. We need help, and I can tell you what is needed to carry us through the moment. We have no solution to the cause of the pain as of yet, but it is not because we are not looking." Eye to eye, I then asked the admitting nurse, "Please help us."

In minutes, Dawn was rushed to the back room in the ER unit. A nurse was taking notes and administering the needed meds to begin the process for getting the pain under control. My cell phone rang, and it was our daughter, Marjie, from Washington. As I heard her voice, all I could do was put my hand on the wall to hold myself upright and cry between the moments of trying to catch my breath. After a minute, I finally found an extra measure of strength to respond to her plea, as I stood now leaning against the hospital wall.

After a short interaction with Marj, I went back to Dawn in the ER. "God, there has to be a reason for her whole neurological system to respond like someone is ramming a hot rod through her whole body and the convulsing and spasming of the muscles from her waist to her toes."

Again, the doctors would test her, but leave us with no answers. Our son arrived to offer help and to stay with me until we left the hospital that night. Once again the hospital kept her, allowing me nothing more than a chance to lay my head down before the early Arizona sun broke through the windows. Before my morning coffee could be poured and enjoyed, I was in communication with the pain clinic for further testing on Dawn.

The Caregiver: Pushed to the Limits

This time another trip north to Scottsdale brought us to Dr. Stearns, the head surgeon, stepping in to oversee the proceedings. Her communication with the hospital the night before had stirred her beautiful mind into action.

After only a short period, Dr. Stearns called me into the evaluation room where they had just tested Dawn. "We think we have found the problem," to everyone's surprise and relief. "The morphine pump that has been such a vital part in extending her days, has finally failed and is releasing the pay load designed for her spinal cord and all her neurological difficulties directly into her intestinal area of her body, disguising the problem and causing a whole other series of problems."

Surgery to replace this unique device was thrown into the schedule but the earliest opening was nine days away. At least the awareness of the monster's source gave us some hope. "Thank you Lord that these gifted individuals, who have spent their lives developing their skills for moments just like these, were there at a time when they were so needed," uttered from my heart. "But, nine days Lord?"

One night at home, even with all the pain meds available to help, found the sunrise greeting two sleepless beings, who had endured another hellacious night. As soon as Dr. Stearns' office was open the next morning, I was making a phone call and employing my doctor button.

"I know you don't know what I actually do, but I am a doctor/pastor who has been at the scene of many going through tumultuous times in their lives. I have seen excruciating pain. I have witnessed death with scores of people dying in my arms. I am telling you that I have seen people in pain with that glassy-eyed look and inability to comprehend or understand, just a step from going into shock. My wife will not make it eight more days and in truth, I don't know if I can."

Sleep had fled from us during those days but when the return phone call came that afternoon, it carried the hoped-for message, "We have Dawn's surgery planned for tomorrow morning. Can you make it?" Overwhelmed, I found myself releasing tears of thankfulness, to which I then responded with those precious words, "Thank you."

After getting control of myself, I gently approached Dawn whose spirit was wrecked and spent with the whole situation. "Sweetheart, everything has changed. We are 16 hours from surgery, not eight days.

"Oh Tom," she cried. "Is there any momentary help to relieve this pain?" Sensing the intensity of the moment I explained through my tears that there cannot be, as it would interfere with the surgery. "Trust me, we will take one hour at a time," as I knew that much of her anxiety came from the uncertainty of those extreme moments when hell's gate grabbed hold of her.

The Caregiver's Call for Reinforcements

Upon leaving her momentarily, I made a phone call, and before I could finish my request Colleen, from the office, was on her way to step into help. A change of faces has a way of encouraging people, especially if they are dear friends who know how to help. I knew her appearance could help break the hours into doable steps. As the evening approached, another phone call to a professional caregiver brought one who was more than willing to step into our situation. Cara showed up and I knew she was, as Colleen had been, the answer to the earlier prayer for an angel of kindness to arrive. At midnight, I gratefully went to sleep,

The next thing I knew, the sun was lighting up the room. It was past six and I could hear voices talking and praying in the bedroom. I knew we were going to make it. Cara confessed that Dawn had experienced two episodes of extreme pain that they battled during the night, but now the surgery time was in sight. We had packed and now the trip up the

201

freeway to Scottsdale and the renowned Shea Hospital with Dr. Stearns present, had pumped enough adrenaline throughout my body to keep me going. A few cups of coffee probably didn't hurt either, but because of Dr. Stearns' adjustment and the hospital staff 's willingness to adjust her surgery schedule, I found us sitting in the pre-op room thanking God that the surgery that had been so elusive was now waiting to be accomplished.

Crocus: The Sign of Harsh Times Being Over

One of Dawn's favorite past-times and exercises was caring for her flowers that would decorate our home's entryway. Each flower had its special place and was carefully placed to highlight the flower's beauty during its growing season. Also, each flower brought back precious memories, especially of her grandmother's flowers, as well as the uniqueness of our Lord in creating them. Yet none brought as much joy to her as her crocus. Winter's harshness and its cold had pushed her plants into dormancy. Even amidst the starkness of it all, it would happen at every winter's end that a burst of color would make its way, often through the snow or frozen ground, to usher in the first expression of spring, even with the lingering winter. "Crocus," our children used to announce to their mom, if they found these first, to which all came to see. A sign that the harsh times of winter were receding was always welcomed.

Only two days after the surgery, a little flower of a woman, a beautiful woman in her own right, made her way slowly up the side walk using her walker. I opened the front door to turn and see the smile on her face and the gleam in her eyes. I knew that there were still more healing ways to go, but my precious crocus caught my eyes tearfully connecting to hers. All I could do was pause and thank God that He had again granted her an extension of days. The harsh times of adversity appeared to have receded.

As I prepared her that night to really rest in her bed for the first time in months, I found myself drawn into my office. A needed letter followed on my computer screen in response to the many who had joined us in this journey.

Thankfulness fills the atmosphere of our home this evening as the door opened and Dawn walked into her own home. Her face carried that sweet smile that has been absent for too long. The twinkle in her eyes had replaced the overcast grimace that reflected so much of what her body had ruthlessly encountered. II Corinthians 1:8-9 records how Paul speaks of encountering an affliction which came to him and his team with such ferocity that, "...we were burdened excessively, beyond our strength, so that we despaired even of life." He goes on to say that, "...indeed we had the sentence of death within ourselves so that we would not trust in ourselves, but in God who raises the dead."

Dawn encountered five ER visits and two stays in the hospital over the last month and a half, just to try and get her pain under control, let alone meeting with doctors to find out what could be done. Moments of intense pain left us holding her with open hands, as her life has been a gift on loan from the Lord for so many years. Many tears were poured out only to be replenished daily, for the opportunities when we didn't think we could cry any more. Yet, as Paul underscores, this same God happened to "...deliver us from so great a peril of death, and will also deliver us, for He is the One on whom we have set our hope."

Time and time again during this last ordeal, we experienced extreme moments that we would wish upon no one. Our cries to our Lord turned to moments where no words could be found. Then time and time again, within the hour, a calm was present, even when medications could not be given. Our voices echoed our thoughts as we joined company with the Psalmist who unleashed his lament, "How long, O Lord? Will you forget me forever? How long will you hide your face from me? How long must I wrestle with my thoughts, and every day have sorrow in my heart? How long will my enemy..." (in this case the intense pain brought on through no fault of her own), "...triumph over me? Look on me and answer, O Lord my God. Give light to my eyes, or I will sleep in death," and my foes (pain) say, "I have overcome. But I trust in your unfailing love."184

Paul, like the Psalmist, found a truth that over the span of their anguish stands true, even today. "He will yet deliver us, *you also joining in helping us through your prayers*, so that thanks may be given by many persons on our behalf for the favor bestowed on us **through the prayers of many.**"185 There is no doubt in our home that the reason Dawn's eyes glow tonight stems from the many prayers of all of you throughout this ordeal. Extremely anguishing times found momentary relief. With each setting there was progress made in seeking to understand what might be the problem. Skilled professionals were called upon only to find what the problem was not. Your prayers continued with His continuous Presence. This last week God answered all of us as the psalmist pictures it. God arises to the occasion and "He parted the heavens and came down..." to deliver her, and He did so, because, "...He delighted in her."[186]

Why? I, like Paul, attribute and understand that our Lord heard you and your prayers on her behalf. Through your prayers she rests at home tonight. There is no moaning and no heavy medication, other than that which miraculously flows from a pump inside her body to the injury site in her spinal cord. This is an amount so small but accurately applied, because many dedicated people devoted their time and lives to develop and help those in need of such palliative care.

Thank you all, and tonight join us in giving thanks. We feel privileged that we get to serve alongside such a compassionate group. You are immensely endeared to us both.

"Problems turn to Praise when we find ourselves on our knees in prayer."

With thanks again,

Pastor Tom and Dawn

Caregiving: A Way of Life

A caregiver's responsibilities do not just end. Over the last months, the countless hours I spent in consoling this precious lady left us both sleep deprived and drained. Countless visits to doctors, new medications, momentary hopes that maybe the problem was found, were followed by more trips to another doctor's office or hospital.

All of the events were on top of my daily work schedule, which included phone calls and messages from other hurting people. Our family members wanted updates, of course, which often came coupled with a walk or a trip to the grocery store. And, yes, there were the household chores which piled up alongside the personal strains of consoling and encouraging one who knew her hands were full trying to get her body to cooperate.

No doubt, for any caregiver, life is full; and when extreme times inflict their loved ones, the stress levels rise accordingly. Fatigue and strain upon the caregiver's every fiber leaves them often just seeking a moment to stop or maybe rest.

In our case, another surgery confronted us; but this time it came with a welcomed sense of relief with the success of the surgery and seeing Dawn awaken from her nightmare. Even so, the new normal meant further appointments, adjustments and challenges that came with the surgery.

With the excruciating time behind us, I then found myself face to face with a different doctor. Dawn, now well enough to assess our situation, had arranged a visit with our family doctor; though this time the appointment was uniquely set for me. After listening for a short time, the doctor concluded that the recent events most likely had created what some call Post-Traumatic Stress Disorder (PTSD). I quickly retorted by asking if I needed to see a counselor, to which he laughed. He did say that I needed more than just some self-talk, to which I said I would talk with my dear friend and counselor, Randy Thomas. I would also make it a point to get some rest and reacquaint myself with some meaningful exercise. He offered to write me a doctor's excuse letter, but I assured him that such help wouldn't be necessary.

The Power of Caregiving

Through this last particular ordeal, I reflected upon what God had now built into my very make-up. Although much of what I wrote in these chapters was what I had learned, I found that this last two-month ordeal had taken me through a crisis that once again left its ill effects. With them came a reintroduction to the painful side of life, along with the challenges that accompanied them, but more noticeably a transformed way of life that over the years had become who I actually was. As I thought about it, I could not help but realize how my life has been so affected by my being a caregiver. I cannot explain when it all occurred. I only know it happened, and my life has been immensely affected by it all.

Piece by piece, event by event--or should I say ordeal by ordeal,--the cycle of adversity with its adverse effects, challenges necessitating my need to adjust, and the slow acceptance of each challenge has brought a character transformation that resembles much more the person and ways of Christ than I could have ever imagined possible. Not that I have arrived, for there are still short comings that need my attention; but what I realized was that I countered my pain with kindness. My limitations, I could acknowledge, and when help was needed, I asked. I found myself taking the time to cry, while I nurtured a source of inner refreshment especially with the only One who calms the spirit and soul.

I would tell myself, "It's not about me, but I must stay rested and healthy." I knew that acceptance of my losses came with the situation, but also, I was prepared to redefine the outcome into a new norm. Still, through it all, I found myself every morning rehearsing my many wonderful blessings that ignited within me a grateful spirit. Though I still cherished and even missed the meaningful relationships I had up north, the investment in new ones brought God's angels of kindness as before. Trusted confidants mixed among a wonderful support network that came alongside both Dawn and me. Still, this last episode brought to the surface talk about my future, eternity and my relationship with God, while again strengthening my values concerning God, family and relationships. In all of this, compassion and love marked every move, especially for Dawn.

I couldn't help but hear in one of my quiet times with God, His words to me. "Do you see it? Do you see it? If you look you can't miss it. It's the way of the caregiver who is honest with life and Almighty God. It's the way of Jesus Christ, the Master Caregiver that I have worked into you, because through the storm I never stopped being Lord of All. I love and care for you so much that in your weakest moments my power is perfected."

What I had become was due to His guiding hand drawing out of me that same compassion that He has shown to us all. It enabled me to see people as God sees them, all with flaws, but bearing His image and, in turn, to be to them that very present help in trouble, regardless of its cost. How did that happen? It is as the Apostle Paul said, "My grace is sufficient for you, for power (God's power) is perfected in weakness."[187] The mere sense of pain, suffering or difficulty now compels me into action.

Over the years, God drew compassion out of my inmost being so that I could help the helpless, especially my wife. Then, He gave me a mentality of "As you wish," and cultivated the compassion to maturity by constantly exemplifying it Himself. From the example that our Lord accomplished in His work upon the cross, where our relationship was restored and remedied, His very character drew me to Himself with His constant gestures of kindness. I was one so undeserving, yet I was one whom He encouraged and loved in spite of myself.

I could not miss it! It is Philippians 2 personified. The very attitude of Christ, "who did, nothing out of selfishness or empty conceit, but with humility of mind regarded others as more important than himself," should not be missed. He expressed it in the past and expresses it now by His love, fellowship, affection and compassion toward us, which in turn flows from each of us as caregivers with the opportunity to respond to others, as He has to us.

As I implied in an earlier chapter, caregivers own an ethic which willingly gives, not for what one receives in return, but because it is what is honorable and right before God and man. Once a caregiver accepts his place, his life transforms. Now this same ethic brings with it an atmosphere that communicates to others that life around them is safe. Genuine love, which one did not earn and from which one knows he cannot be lost, fills the air. In my case, when that caregiver directs his skills toward that person who also happens to be his dearest and closest friend, his trusted confidant and the bearer of his children, I wake with gratitude each day.

Such gratitude has me on a very special daily mission to stimulate her soul, entrust her with life's precious thoughts and concerns, as well as include her in as much as she can handle. It means that I accept my call as her husband and caregiver to encourage, comfort and stand alongside her in time of need, 'til death do us part. It means that I also sacrifice my ego, (not my soul), and be to her what any lady needs from her spouse: a best friend, a trusted confidant and one on whom she can depend, because she knows that he loves her dearly.

Yet, it does not end there. This friendship looks outside ourselves to those around us for whom the Lord seeks, as He did us. How can we help them and introduce them to the Person and ways that have given us a life of meaning and purpose, in spite of all the complexity? How can we together offer a touch of hope to the many who are bewildered by life's misfortunes? How can we help clean up the muddled thinking that leaves people in a state of perpetual doubt? Together, the power of what He has done within us awakens a spirit of gratitude that compels us to join hands and walk each day looking for ways to be to others what Christ has been to us.

The Caregiver's Secret

Caring! That is what caregivers do. Care! What a quality to be known for! What a characteristic to be displayed from your heart that even you wonder where it came from! How unique that in the crucible of pain and suffering, a powerful display of God shows forth a transforming power that draws out of its crushed objects a characteristic that could not be obtained, apart from a face-to-face confrontation with evil or the ugliness a fallen world throws upon its inhabitants. Yet, here the power of unfailing love gains the potential to be at its best. Here the power of God Himself, weaves in His compassionate hand and the mercy that draws each caregiver to action. Here lies the secret to the power of caregiving: *God at work in man, doing what only God does best-- transforming man to be like Him.*

Please, hear me. Sixty-seven years of life, 47 years as a diligent follower of Christ, 41 years as a pastor-counselor, with 26 years of practice as a caregiver provides a long time to develop and refine these aspects of life. It did not just happen immediately. Truthfully, I can only say, "Thank you, Lord, for the matchless compassion and kindness that He has manifest upon our household." As the quest throughout my adult years has been to know God and make myself available to be a vessel through which He could touch the lives of people, I have to admit that this pathway has allowed that to be done, plus more. His filling my very soul with compassion, mercy, kindness and love gives evidence of His willingness to transform us to be like Himself. To have a life that honors the Lord and to share that with my dearest and closest friend, my wife, has become an answered prayer for us both.

Amazingly, I still have her in my life, and I cannot explain that any more than I can articulate a satisfactory explanation to the theology of pain and suffering. I do not want anyone to be misled by the title to this work or the faith and steadfast endurance that such an undertaking demands. Caregiving is not easy. There is still no one whom I have met who would not have desired a path without the disability, and especially the chronic pain, as the wrenching us, and still for many the last step, which ends their palliative care will take place only when either the need for the care ends or the failure of the caregiver's body takes him down.

For decades I have carried in my heart a little poem that helps me lift my head and keep going. It rings as true for the caregiver.

> What care I who gets the credit,
> Only let the work be done,
> God Himself will handle credit,
> With the setting of the sun.
> People praise you, people blame you
> Rise above it every day,
> For soul, you will never win a battle,
> If you fear what men may say.

Most all of this writing flows from what I have encountered and learned along my own caregiver's journey. Yet no journey among mankind is identical to another, so what I have learned and expressed comes with a hope that the bits and pieces of information that have helped us can be of help to someone else on their own journey. Even writing this has taken years, and what lies ahead before we open our eyes in the presence of our Lord, Jesus, we anticipate only because we know that in the crucible of personal pain and suffering the noblest dreams are born and passions conceived, in compensation for what we have patiently endured. Expressing hope, as God has given it to us, is what we both seek, as we express our lives in honor of Him, who has given us an extension of days together.

It is my prayer that these words can touch the lives of those who are caregivers with a hope that instills the confidence to let God be God in their lives. If they have stumbled along like I have and can still smile, since they know what I have come to understand, I write this on their behalf.

May everyone who reads this recognize the true heroes that these caregivers are! May the caregivers, themselves, know that this pastor wants people everywhere to understand that they are part of a unique group that may look the same as everyone else, but whose way of life is drastically different.

At the same time I know the heartaches and difficulties that caregivers deal with daily. For those who are hurting and without support, this is a calling from one who is there to take the next step. Reach out your hand to accept the touch of hope that many of us want to give. Join or, if needed, start a support group in your church or community where a network of those who understand can be formed as a source of encouragement that can carry you through your hard times.

Where it has led us is simple! Today by the mere fact that we breathe, we know daily we have a gift of life from God. For Dawn, each day is a wondrous extension from that painful moment years ago when she was informed that she should be gone or, for that matter, 50+ years ago, when she found herself crushed face-first into a dashboard, unable to move and her back crushed.

Today we know by our breathing that all we encounter is part of His plan for us. We have come to understand that the total reason for pain lies hidden with God. As we face the pains, He stands true to His Word as our ever present and ever ready help in times of trouble. Communion with Him is our life blood. His grace is sufficient for each day, and to our astonishment, the power to change people for His honor is perfected in the powerless condition in which we live daily. The phenomena of our home is that our adversities and our handling of these adversities have now become platforms, about which this powerless couple has been allowed to be the Lord's mouthpiece to bring Him honor. Truthfully, we are humbled.

Precious Angels of Kindness Have Graced Our Lives

Where would we be without our grown children, the extended family and many friends who have graced our lives, along with those fresh new wonders that are known as grandchildren? It is not easy, especially in an independent, self-focused culture that applauds the over-comers, of which we are not.

I have learned that steadfast endurance and the call to care for someone weak carries more impact than any medal or trophy, since they place a smile on an appreciative, loved one, as well as the Lord, Himself. Truthfully, I can say that it is worth it all. It has been difficult, though I don't notice it much now, because I live in it every day. Yet, I can say with confidence that we have seen God use what we have encountered and learned to encourage others in their own situations. As the psalmist wrote, "They will still bear fruit in old age, they will stay fresh and green, proclaiming, 'The Lord is upright; He is my Rock...'"[188] We happen to be just simple enough to believe it.

Seven years have passed since God heard the prayers of my wife and family asking for a miracle by granting me an extension of days. Those days were granted by God and so was a promise from me to my grown children, who asked that I use my days to finish the writing He wanted me to do. As the day ends today, I can finally say, the writing is done and with its completion comes a smile on many faces.

Now I turn my sights to the pastorate at the church and A Touch of Hope Ministries©. There is much to be done. Our compassionate Lord has begun drawing families together that understand and want to be involved. We are set to make up for those years that the locusts have eaten and in compensation for what we have painfully endured, we anticipate the opportunities to share the love that He has so graced upon us.

A Final Adieu

I leave you with a story that offers a final word, to carry forth from this work as our mantra with each other. *Adieu* is the French word for goodbye. I have chosen this word carefully to end upon, as the word, adieu, actually is laced with meaning that extends beyond a parting farewell. The lesson of *adieu* came to me through the pen of Francis de Sales (1567-1622 AD) whose counseling ministry involved writing over 20,000 letters in response to requests for help.

In one case a young woman desired information about giving herself to God. His response opened with these precious words. "My dearest daughter, I say to you with all my heart, *Adieu*." From that point on, he framed his letter around a play on this French word which literally means, *for God*. It was his intent to allow this witty exchange to act as a masterful reminder to the sacredness of all life. In his response he would say,

"It is the great good of our souls to be adieu (for God), and the greatest good to be only adieu (for God)…He who is adieu (for God) only, seeks Him only; and because God is not less in adversity than prosperity, such a one remains at peace in adversity. Be completely adieu (for God), my dearest daughter, and be only His, only wishing to please Him, and His creatures in Him, according to Him and for Him. What greater blessing can I wish you?"[189]

As you stop and ponder what he wrote, you may begin to realize that his point focuses upon a thought that challenges our western mindset by asking these questions: What is there in this world that isn't for and about God? What activity or involvement is there that is not sacred? Not sacred, as in contrast to secular, but sacred, as being reverentially designed and devoted to honoring God. It is with this frame of mind that this inside look at being and caring for caregivers and their families has been composed and the place of the caregiver as an unsung hero brought to light.

It is my hope and prayer that it serves to that end and to exalt our Lord. Again I rejoice in Christ and that by His grace I still have my wife and she still has me. Until the day we find rest in His calling us home, I bid you, *Adieu*. Let all our work for Christ together be, adieu.

Adieu

*It is in the crucible of personal pain and suffering
that noble dreams are born and God given passions are conceived
in compensation for what one has patiently endured.*

Congratulations!!! You have finished reading the book!

What are Your Next Steps?

- **Step 1: Let the gratitude within you allow you to "dream a new dream!"**

- **Step 2: Envision yourself starting a Caregiver Support Group**
  How about utilizing what you have learned and letting the gratitude within you awaken your commitment to starting a support ministry to caregivers and their families in your church or community? Furthermore, in the age of online communication, think of including the ability to connect online with people locally, regionally, and even internationally through online support groups.

- **Step 3 – To get Started, Contact A Touch of Hope Ministries**

www.atouchofhopeministries.com

On this website, scroll down and click the "**Start a Group**" button and follow the guidelines.

A Touch of Hope Ministries was founded by Dr. Tom Randall, the author of this book. This non-profit organization provides training, hope, and support for caregivers and their families. If you would consider supporting this ministry through prayer or a monthly donation, it would help carry this dream forward to more people. If you or someone you know needs clarity or help, click on "**Contact Us**" at

www.atouchofhopeministries.com

We certainly will add you to our prayers. May our Lord open your pathways to many in order to offer support and hope.

Adieu – "for God"

Bibliography

Allen, Ronald. The Bible Study Commentary Joel. Grand Rapids, Michigan: Zondervan, 1988.

Ashok, Mala. "Unsung Heroes." The Hindu. Chennai. December 4, 2005. <http://www.thehindu.com/thehindu/mag/2005/12/04/stories/2005 120400090400.htm, November 28, 2007.

Banister, Katie Rodriguez. The Personal Care Attendant Guide: The Cost of Finding, Being and Keeping One. New York: Demos Medical Publishing, 2007.

Beach, Shelly. Precious Lord Take my Hand, Meditations for Caregivers. Grand Rapids: Discovery House Publishing, 2007.

Bridges, Jerry. The Discipline of Grace. Colorado Springs, Colorado: Navpress, 2006.

Bridges, Jerry. "Grace and Discipline: God's Discipline of His People" (quote taken from class notes presented at Western Seminary Doctorate of Ministry Class, Menucha Retreat Center), June 12, 2008.

Bridges, Jerry. Transforming Grace: Living Confidently in God's Unfailing Love. Colorado Springs, Colorado: Navpress, 1991.

Bridges, Jerry. Trusting God: Even When Life Hurts. Colorado Springs, Colorado: Navpress, 1988.

Brunner, Louie. Personal Interview. April 3, 2009.

Chinchen, Palmer. Waiting for Daylight: God's Hope for the Dark Night. Chandler, Arizona: Movement Publishing, 2007.

Coleman, Daniel. Primal Leadership. Boston, Massachusetts: Harvard Business

Cox-Gedmark, Jan. Coping with Physical Disability. Philadelphia: Westminster Press, 1980.

Cowman, L.B. Streams in the Desert. Grand Rapids, MI, Zondervan, 1997.

Crabb, Larry. The Marriage Builder. Grand Rapids MI, Zondervan, 1982,

Dawn, Marva J. Being Well When We're Ill. Minneapolis, Minnesota: Augsburg, 2008.

Dawn, Marva J. Joy in Our Weakness. Grand Rapids, Michigan: Wm. B. Eerdmann's Publishing, 2002.

de Vinck, Christopher. The Power of the Powerless. New York: Doubleday, 1988.

Eichrodt, Walther. Theology of the Old Testament, Volume II. Philadelphia, The Westminster Press, 1967.

Kilborn, Peter T. "Disabled Spouses Are Increasingly Forced to Go It Alone." New York Times 31 May 1999.

Korstjens, Keith. Not a Sometimes Love. Holiday, Florida: Green Key Books, 2002.

Krementz, Jill. How It Feels to Live with a Disability. New York: Simon and Schuster, 1992.

Lewis, C.S. The Problem of Pain. San Francisco: Harper Collins Publisher, 1996.

Lyons, Renee F. Relationships in Chronic Illness and Disability. Thousand Oaks, California: Sage Publications, 1995.

Malmin, Leif. Personal Interview. April 6, 2009.

Marshak, Laura E., Milton Seligman and Fran Prezant. Disability and the Family Life Cycle. New York: Basic Books, 1999.

McLeod, Beth Witrogen. And Thou Shalt Honor: The Caregiver's Companion. Emmaus, Pennsylvania: Rodale Press, 2002.

McLeod, Beth Witrogen. Caregiving, the Spiritual Journey of Love, Loss and Renewal. New York: John Wiley and Sons, 1999.

Molsberry, Robert F. Blindsided by Grace: Entering the World of Disability. Minneapolis, Minnesota: Augsburg Books, 2004.

Moore, Bobby. Your Personal Devotional Life. Southhaven, Mississippi: The King's Press, 2002.

National Family Caregivers Association. Caregiving Statistics. <http://www.nfcacares.org/who_are_family_caregives/care_giving_statistics.cfm (Dec.10, 2010).

Neal, Leslie Jean, Editor. Care of the Adult with a Chronic Illness or Disability. St. Louis, Missouri: Elsevier Mosby, 2004.

Peri, Camille. "Someone to Lean On." Reader's Digest, Dec. 2009.

Piper, John and Taylor, Justin. Suffering and the Sovereignty of God. Wheaton, Illinois: Crossway Books, 2006.

Randall, Dr. Thomas E. Physical Disability in the Pastor's Spouse, Doctoral Thesis, Western Seminary, Portland OR, 2011.

Rucker, Alan. The Best Seat in the House. New York: Harper Collins Publisher, 2007.

Sanders, J. Oswald. Spiritual Lessons. Chicago: Moody Press, 1944.

Schipper, Jeremy. Disability Studies and the Hebrew Bible: Figuring Mephibosheth in the David Story. New York: T & T Clark, 2006.

Sittser, Gerald L. A Grace Disguised. Grand Rapids, Michigan: Zondervan Publishing House, 1996.

Swindoll, Chuck. Hope Again, When Life Hurts and Dreams Fade. Nashville: Thomas Nelson Publishing, 1996.

Taylor, Howard and Taylor, Geraldine. Hudson Taylor's Spiritual Secret. Chicago: Moody Press, 1932.

US Census Bureau, 2006 American Community Survey. United States Disability Characteristics <factfinder.census.gov/servlet/STTable, (4/27/2010).

Waltke, Dr. Bruce. The Book of Proverbs: Chapters 15-31, The New International Commentary of the Old Testament.

Wilcox, Thomas. Honey Out of the Rock. (Pensacola, FL, Chapel Library, Tract).

Zacharias, Ravi. Cries of the Heart. Nashville: W. Publishing Group, 2002.

Endnotes

1   Robert F. Molsberry, *Blindsided by Grace: Entering the World of Disability* (Minneapolis, MN: Augsburg Books, 2004), 116.

2   Molsberry, 117.

3   Katie Rodriguez Banister, *The Personal Care Attendant Guide: The Cost of Finding, Being and Keeping One* (New York: Demos Medical Publishing, 2007), 2.

4   Banister, 2-3.

5   Renee F. Lyons, *Relationships in Chronic Illness and Disability* (Thousand Oaks, CA: Sage Publications, 1995), 5.

6   Beth Witrogen McLeod, *Caregiving, the Spiritual Journey of Love, Loss and Renewal* (New York: John Wiley and Sons, 1999), 13.

7   Molsberry, xii-xiii.

8   Banister, 2.

9   US Census Bureau, 2006 American Community Survey, United States Disability Characteristics <http://factfinder.census.gov/servlet/STTable (4/27/2010), 1-2.

10   Beth Witrogen McLeod, *And Thou Shalt Honor, the Caregiver's Companion* (Emmaus, PA.: Rodale Books, 2002), 5.

11   National Family Caregivers Association, Caregiving Statistics, < h t t p : / / www. nfcacares.org/who_are_family_ caregivers/care_giving_statistics.cfm (Dec.10, 2010), 1.

12   Lyons, 6.

13   Leslie Jean Neal, editor. *Care of the Adult with a Chronic Illness or Disability* (St. Louis, MO: Elsevier Mosby, 2004), 1.

14   Camille Peri, *"Someone to Lean On" Reader's Digest*, Dec. 2009, 130.

15   McLeod, *And Thou Shalt Honor*, 5.

16   Chuck Swindoll, *Hope Again, When Life Hurts and Dreams Fade* (Nashville: Thomas Nelson Publishing, 1996), 11-12.

17   Palmer Chinchen, *Waiting for Daylight, God's Hope for the Dark Night* (Chandler, AZ: Movement Publishing, 2007), 15.

18   Marva J. Dawn, *Being Well When We're Ill* (Minneapolis: Augsburg Books, 2008), 250.

19   Ronald Allen, *The Bible Study Commentary Joel* (Grand Rapids: Zondervan, 1988), 111.

20   Molsberry, 171.

21   Beth Witrogen McLeod, *Caregiving*, 14.

22   Beth Witrogen McLeod, *Caregiving*, 13-14.

23 Shelly Beach, *Precious Lord Take my Hand, Meditations for Caregivers*, (Grand Rapids: Discovery House Publishing, 2007), p.93.

24 Psalm 46:1 NASB

25 Mark 10:45

26 Philippians 2:3-7

27 Beech. 117.

28 Ashok, Mala. "*Unsung Heroes.*" The Hindu. Chennai. December 4, 2005, p 1.

29 Matthew 11:28 NASB

30 C.S. Lewis, *The Problem of Pain*, (San Francisco: Harper Collins, 1996), 5.

31 C.S. Lewis, 6.

32 C.S. Lewis, 11.

33 C.S. Lewis, 11-12.

34 Colossians 1:16

35 Marva J. Dawn, *Being Well*, 56.

36 Romans 8:20-22

37 Marva J. Dawn, *Being Well*, 54.

38 Marva J. Dawn, *Being Well*, 57.

39 Marva J. Dawn, *Being Well*, 55.

40 Marva J. Dawn, *Being Well*, 55.

41 Romans 3:23

42 Romans 5:12

43 Revelations 21:4

44 Molsberry, xii-xiii.

45 Jan Cox-Gedmark, *Coping with Physical Disability.* (Philadelphia: Westminster Press, 1980), 17.

46 Cox-Gedmark, 17.

47 Louie Brunner. Personal Interview, April 3, 2009.

48 Cox-Gedmark, 26.

49 Renee F. Lyons, Michael Williams and Paul Ritvo, *Relationships in Chronic Illness and Disability* (Thousand Oaks, CA: Sage Publications, 1995), 13.

50 McLeod, *Honor*, xv.

51 Ashok, 1.

52 Laura E. Marshak, Milton Seligman and Fran Prezant, *Disability and the Family Life Cycle* (New York: Basic Books, 1999), 1-2.

53 Cox-Gedmark, 88.

54 A8, Personal Questionnaire, October 2008.

55 A60, Personal Questionnaire, October 2008.

56 A57, Personal Questionnaire, October 2008.

57 A60, Personal Questionnaire, October 2008.

58 A59, Personal Questionnaire, October 2008.

59 A8, Personal Questionnaire, October 2008.

60 A8, Personal Questionnaire, October 2008.

61 A8, Personal Questionnaire, October 2008.

62 Proverbs 13:12

63 Larry Crabb, *The Marriage Builder*, Grand Rapids MI, Zondervan, 1982, p.29. Please note that the concepts of security and significance are being used here to merely capture ideas that we have expanded upon over the years. Also the whole theological concept of the sin nature of man would be essential to add to the mix but for the moment I chose not to expand upon such matters. This is not meant to be an elaborate detailing of the ideas but a mere description of man's nature, beginning with what is legitimate.

64 Ibid, p.29.

65 McLeod, *Caregiving*, 76-77.

66 Dr. Keith Korstjens, *Not a Sometimes Love* (Holiday, Fl: Green Key Books, 2002), 48-49.

67 Psalm 88:18

68 McLeod, *Honor*, xvi.

69 I Thessalonians 5:11 NASB

70 Hebrews 10:24 NASB

71 Romans 12:8; II Timothy 4:2

72 II Corinthians 1:3

73 I John 2:1 NASB

74 John 14:26 NASB

75 Alan Rucker, *The Best Seat in the House* (New York: Harper Collins, 2007), 227.

76 McLeod, *Honor*, xvi.

77 Personal quote from interview taken during doctoral research which was conducted with former ministry participants on physical disability in the pastor's spouse, 2008.

78 McLeod, *Honor*, xvi.

79 Psalm 142:4 NASB

80 Psalm 56:8

81 Hebrews 13:5 NASB

82 Psalm 46:1 NASB

83 McLeod, *Honor*, xvi.

84 Cox-Gedmark, 49.

85 II Corinthians 10:5 NASB

86 Cox-Gedmark, 93.

87 Jeremiah 29:11 NASB

88 Ecclesiastes 4:9-10
89 McLeod, *Caregiving*, 145.
90 McLeod, *Caregiving,* 147.
91 II Corinthians 1:4 NASB
92 Personal Interview from doctoral thesis with members of the ministry team, 2008.
93 Author unknown
94 Matthew 11:28 NASB
95 Hebrews 4:16
96 I Peter 3:22
97 Louie Brunner. Personal Interview, April 3, 2009.
98 Louie Brunner. Personal Interview, April 3, 2009.
99 A99, Personal Questionnaire, August 2008.
100 A27, Personal Questionnaire, August 2008.
101 A50, Personal Questionnaire, August 2008.
102 A102, Personal Questionnaire, August 2008.
103 Genesis 1:31
104 Genesis 2:16-17
105 Genesis 2:23
106 Genesis 2:24 NASB
107 Peter T. Kilborn, *"Disabled Spouses are Increasingly Forced to Go It Alone,"* *New York Times*, May 31, 1999.
108 ibid
109 ibid
110 Korstjens, 141-142.
111 This term "couch time" I picked up from Gary and Anne Marie Ezzo in their parenting works.
112 Ecclesiastes 4:9-12
113 II Corinthians 10:5 NASB
114 Psalm 23:4
115 Cowman, L.B. *Streams in the Dessert*, (Grand Rapids, MI, Zondervan, 1997), 42-43.
116 Krementz, 9.
117 Krementz, 18.
118 Krementz, 19.
119 Krementz, 20-21.
120 Alan Rucker, *The Best Seat in the House* (New York: Harper Collins, 2007), 226.
121 Genesis 2:7
122 Hebrews 4:16 NASB

123   Christopher de Vinck, *The Power of the Powerless* (New York: Doubleday, 1988), 8.
124   de Vinck, 9.
125   de Vinck, 13-14.
126   de Vinck, xvii.
127   de Vinck, 133.
128   II Corinthians 12:7-8
129   II Corinthians 12:9-10
130   Matthew 5:8 NASB
131   John 15:18-21
132   Sanders, Oswald, *Spiritual Leadership*, (Moody Press, Chicago, 1967) p.13
133   Matthew 11:28 NASB
134   Romans 8:28 NASB
135   Jeremiah 9:24
136   Micah 6:8
137   I Corinthians 15:10
138   II Corinthians 5
139   II Corinthians 11
140   Recorded back in II Corinthians 5
141   II Corinthians 5:14-6:1
142   II Corinthians 6:1
143   II Corinthians12:9
144   I Corinthians 1:27 KJV
145   I Corinthians 12:26 NASB
146   Galatians 6:2
147   Jeremiah 29:11-14
148   Joel 2:25
149   Molsberry, ix.
150   Molsberry, ix.
151   Daniel 11:32 CSB
152   Habakkuk 2:4 NKJV
153   Allen, 111.
154   Job 38-42
155   Job 42:5-6
156   Psalm 118:24 NASB
157   Daniel 11:32 CSB
158   John 7:37
159   John 7:37
160   Matthew 11:28-29

161 Taylor, Dr. & Mrs. Howard. *Hudson Taylor's Spiritual Secret*, (Chicago, Moody Press, 1932), p.157.

162 ibid, p.162-163.

163 Moore, Dr. Bobby. *Your Personal Devotional Life*, (Southhaven, MS, The King's Press, 2002), p.7.

164 Romans 5:2

165 Psalm 18:19

166 Matthew 6:9

167 Isaiah 6:3

168 Psalm 8:3-4 NASB

169 Psalm 8:1

170 Hebrews 4:15-16

171 Ephesians 3:18-19 NASB

172 Psalm 139:23-24

173 Luke 18:10-13 NASB

174 Luke 7:40-47 NASB

175 Romans 7:18-19, 22-24

176 I offer to everyone I meet the Bible tract, "*Steps to Peace with God*," by Billy Graham which gives a precise step process for helping people understand the gospel of Jesus Christ.

177 Romans 7:24-8:1

178 Romans 7:25

179 Rom 8:1

180 Romans 8:1

181 Romans 7:25

182 Wilcox, Thomas. *Honey Out of the Rock*, (Pensacola, FL, Chapel Library, Tract), p.11.

183 Hebrews 13:5

184 hesed = mercy Psalm.13:1-5

185 II Corinthians 1:10-11 NASB

186 Psalm 18:6, 9, 19

187 II Corinthians 12:9 NASB

188 Psalm 92:14

189 Francis de Sales, *Thy Will Be Done,* (Manchester N.H.: Sophia Institute Press, 1995), 243-44.